SEWING *FOR* 20th CENTURY DOLLS

100 Plus Projects

by Johana Gast Anderton

Published by Hobby House Press, Inc.
Grantsville, Maryland 21536

DEDICATION

To my sisters, Shirley and Carol for the many happy hours we spent together playing dolls and sewing for our doll families- to the three little girls we used to be.

ACKNOWLEDGMENTS

My sincere thanks to the many collectors, friends, and members of my own family who allowed their dolls' costumes to be examined and sketched.

Thanks also to my proof-reading friends and to my Mother who stitched up checking samples of the patterns whenever there was any doubt of fit or draftsmanship.

Special appreciation is extended to the H.D. Lee Company which so generously shared the original patterns for the Buddy Lee doll uniforms and Lee Riders.

And finally, thanks to all of you, the readers without whom this book would not have been possible.

WHAT THE COPYRIGHT MEANS

These patterns and the contents of this book are protected by United States and International copyright laws. The patterns are intended for use by hobbyist and doll dressmakers and may be traced for use by such persons in the creation of doll clothes for their own or customers' dolls.

At no time may the patterns herein be traced or otherwise reproduced by any method for purposes of selling the patterns or for giving the patterns as a gift. Neither may the patterns be reproduced in a magazine, newspaper, or other publication without the written consent of the copyright owner herein named.

When patterns are traced for purposes of sewing doll clothes, the following notation should be made on each pattern piece:

"From Anderton's *Sewing for 20th Century Dolls*, p. no."

Any misuse of the material contained in this book will be prosecuted under above mentioned copyright laws.

LIBRARY OF CONGRESS CATALOG
CARD NUMBER 72-77829

745.5922
Ande

Additional copies of this book may be purchased at $24.95 (plus postage and handling) from

Hobby House Press, Inc.
1 Corporate Drive
Grantsville, Maryland 21536
1-800-554-1447
or from your favorite bookstore or dealer.

©1972 Johana Gast Anderton

1st Printing – March, 1972; 2nd Printing – October, 1979; 3rd Printing – July, 1996

TABLE OF CONTENTS

INTRODUCTION

As work progressed in preparation of an earlier book, the seeds of this book began to germinate. Many of the dolls then being photographed for *TWENTIETH CENTURY DOLLS, From Bisque to Vinyl* were still wearing their original clothes, or were arrayed in home-sewn fashions made from original patterns. As I admired and mentally catalogued these old doll things, the thought recurred that other collectors might enjoy being able to reproduce authentic costumes for their dolls.

A companion to the *TWENTIETH CENTURY DOLLS* book was clearly the answer. As work on this earlier book neared completion, my new file was growing larger each day. This file was crammed with fashion notes from old catalogs, sketches, and actual drafts of patterns taken from the doll clothes found on the dolls as they were photographed.

Since many of the dolls appearing in the doll book *lived* in other cities, it was necessary to travel again to those places to examine the clothes and draft patterns. These were the dolls discovered early in the work on the doll book, prior to the *great idea* for this book. Revisiting the collectors and their dolls proved a delightful and rewarding experience, for in several cases *new* old dolls had been added to collections and more pictures were taken.

As the file grew, several things became clear. First, it seemed wise to divide the patterns chronologically wherever possible; therefore they have been arranged by decade. There will be, of course, some overlap since fashions do not automatically change as the pages of a calendar are turned. What was considered the latest thing in 1919 would still hold some merit in 1920 or perhaps 1921.

Moreover, gentle mutations may be seen in fashions, so that a detail introduced as revolutionary in one year becomes softened and refined in later seasons. Then, too, there are the classic fashions which change little. The cardigan, the blazer, the nautical costume, the shirt-waist dress, these are all examples of classics which are subjected to subtle changes in order that they may conform to the profile of current fashion.

Second, it seemed wise to give full-size patterns wherever possible, and for this reason we have used large-size pages. With a little manipulation of pattern parts, it has been possible to draw patterns full-size, even for the 28-inch K ★ R doll. In a few cases it has been necessary to break the lines and rearrange the pattern on a page, but careful study of Chapter 2 — Making Paper Patterns, will provide answers to most questions.

Last, it seemed probable that the whole project would benefit from a discussion of fabrics, accessories, and fashions of each period (decade). While there is a danger of taking oneself too seriously in such an undertaking, it seems worthwhile to provide a certain background or framework in which to set the dolls. One would not wish, for example, to costume a Bye-Lo

of the 1920s in nylon or dacron which was not available until the 1950s.

Since spare heads are sometimes available, it seemed a good idea to give a few body patterns. These have been provided in variety and should meet most needs. Old bodies may be ripped apart and additional patterns made. Notes are also included on making your own patterns, on making patterns fit your dolls, and on making shoes and stockings. The latter seemed of imminent importance since these bits of doll apparel are usually the first to be lost.

No one realizes more than this writer the shortcomings of this book, yet a real attempt has been made to be of assistance to doll collectors and costumers. Many of the patterns appearing here have not been previously attempted. Yet it seems good to record the vagaries of even this latest decade.

We live in a swiftly moving civilization. Paper dresses and disposable fashions are a reality. Tomorrow may see us walking through a dressing room each morning where a film of dressing material is automatically wrapped about us. At night we may return to a refreshing shower which disintegrates the costume of the day and gently wraps us in a sleeping garment. Stranger things we have known in these past seventy years and two.

Though we certainly cannot know what the fashion future will bring us, we can enjoy what has passed and we can see that each of our dolls is adequately prepared to represent us in that future. To this end this book is submitted for your use and enjoyment.　　　　　　　　　— February 15, 1972

Earlier editions of this work were greeted with generous praise by doll collectors and costumers alike. I am grateful for their kind approbation; when one works diligently to achieve a goal, appreciation is always welcome.

Several people also shared ideas for improvement, pointed out errors in text, or confessed to confusion in following a certain instruction. One asked for more illustrations of finished garments. As a result of these loving critiques, the book in its present edition has been fine-tuned to include such suggestions to the benefit, it is hoped, of us all.

Johana Gast Anderton
July 15, 1996

Chapter 1

TIPS ON SEWING FOR DOLLS

Since most collectors or doll costumers have at least a speaking knowledge of sewing techniques, we will not begin with a basic sewing course. Rather, having assumed each of us to be acquainted with the ways of needle and thread, a discussion of the peculiarities of sewing for dolls is in order.

One of the first and most common mistakes made in sewing for dolls is not allowing sufficient width of trouser legs or sleeves. All too often, when the garment is completed and ready to be placed on the doll, the seamstress discovers the dress or shirt will not pass over the doll's extremities. The rule must be **"CHECK THE FIT, RE-CHECK IT, AND CHECK IT AGAIN"**.

As work progresses on a garment, keep the doll at hand and fit as you stitch. Since dolls, for the most part, do not move, it is usually not necessary to allow for movement and give in fitting doll fashions. If the doll is a walking doll or a performing doll, by all means switch it on and check the fit while the doll is in action.

Another oft-repeated mistake in making doll clothes is in the selection of fabrics. How saddening to see a beautiful doll, dressed in a fine outfit which has obviously cost the dressmaker many hours, but made of such stiff, heavy fabric as to be completely out of proportion to the size of the doll.

Fine fabrics drape more easily and becomingly than heavy ones. Tiny prints are more in proportion to small garments and doll measurements. Stripes should be narrow, checks minute, and plaids softly defined. Laces should be of proportionate widths, ruffles not tightly gathered as to appear ludicrous on a small doll. Buttons and other fasteners ought to be doll-sized.

Bear in mind that we are not talking here about the 44 inch ball-jointed bisque doll or a 32 inch vinyl Pollyana. These, of course, will require larger, even normal-sized fasteners and patterns. The small and average-sized doll, however, requires fine thread and delicate buttonholes, the narrowest of bias tape and ribbon, and carefully trimmed seams to avoid bulkiness.

Just as we consider our own features, coloring of hair, skin, and eyes, when selecting colors and fabrics for our own wardrobe, we should do the same when choosing for our dolls. A red-haired bisque with high coloring could look well in a cooling green or blue. Or a pink chosen for its precise shade may be just the right color to highlight the red hair. If time is valuable and much running to and fro with samples is not possible, then pack up the doll in question and carry it with you to the fabric shop. A possible combination may occur which otherwise would not have been considered had the doll been left at home.

When an old doll is found in an original or very old dress which is tattered and quite soiled, it is often a temptation to throw everything out and begin anew. What a tragic mistake to destroy such valuable evidence! Many collectors tell stories of their zeal as beginning collectors in making every doll spotless and perfect.

There are times, of course, when it is wise to renew or replace an old dress. Often the underwear is in good condition and only the dress needs redoing. In such cases,

the old dress may be copied carefully, cleaned as carefully and safely as possible, then filed away with a full description of the doll to which it belongs. Some collectors even pin these old garments to the underclothes of the the doll.

In keeping with the wish for authenticity, consideration should be given to the age of each individual doll. As fashion changes, so too the face of fashion undergoes sometimes striking transformations. Eyebrows are considered important one year, and are dusted to diminish their effect the next. Lashes are blackened, curled, and even lengthened with new products designed to perform such magic. This season the eyes may be slanted at the corners with a bit of pencil; next year they may be required to appear quite round.

In each decade there is a face, representative of the aspirations of every young lady or gentleman who wishes to appear *au courant*. Dolls usually reflect this image even in the facial contours. In an age when obviously well-fed children were considered the most attractive, dolls were plump, well-stuffed dumplings. Slender, active, outdoor children have their counterparts in the long-legged, slim, almost boyish, girl dolls of another decade.

It is often with results bordering on the ridiculous that dolls are dressed in fashions not of their period. Equally ludicrous is the child doll dressed in the velvet, brocades, and laces of a matronly lady. A study should be made of the child fashions of each period as well as the adult designs. Consideration of the doll's proportions will give the final clue as to the age-type the doll represents.

Hair styles are another point at which mistakes may be made in the finishing of a doll's couture. Do not create, for a girl doll, the piled-up pompadour of a lady of fashions. Pigtails, ponytails, bangs, bobs, long curls, and loose, flowing tresses are all suitable for the girl doll of several decades. All these may be tied up with bows and ribbons, or tucked under a flop hat or beanie, depending upon the period.

Human hair has been considered one of the finest materials ever used in the making of dolls' wigs. The next most satisfactory material which lends itself to careful combing and to realistic styling. Mohair has a soft, low sheen especially flattering to the composition dolls.

Newer, man-made materials have been introduced which have much durability and may be shampooed easily and combed, brushed, and curled. These fibres, dynel, Saran, nylon, and various blends, are of various qualities and features. Saran is rather coarse, has high luster, and is a good quality material. Chatty Cathy and other early dolls from Mattel featured Saran wigs rooted in the vinyl heads. Saran does not seem to break off easily as do some of the other synthetic fibers.

Dynel is a finer, softer fibre with a duller sheen than Saran, and is more suitable for smaller dolls. Nylon has a sheen somewhat higher then Dynel and is a tough fibre, although both these and some of the blends do have the tendency to break off rather badly. These fibres also tend to frizz when exposed to heat.

A general rule for replacing wigs is to replace with a wig of similar material to that with which the doll was first produced: Human hair or mohair, sometimes fur, wigs for bisque, china, and composition dolls; Saran, dynel, nylon, and synthetic blends for hard plastic, vinyl and soft vinyl dolls. Hard plastic dolls were sometimes issued with mohair wigs; the choice for these is a matter of taste. Styling of the wig may be matched to the old wig as nearly as possible.

Coat for a little lady from four to eight years, made of broadcloth and trimmed with stitched bands. It is cut circular; the back has a narrower yoke than the front, and has a wide box-plait down the centre.

Simple Embroidery Stitches

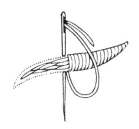

SATIN STITCH may be padded or not. It consists of regular smooth stitches taken close together side by side across a space, either straight across or on a slant. This is the most important stitch in French Embroidery.

RUNNING OUTLINE is made by running a row of short stitches along the line of stamping and then going back, putting the needle under every stitch, always putting in under from the same side.

VOIDED SATIN STITCH is made in exactly the same manner, working two sections side by side. Often a space is voided only a part of the way, then the two portions converge into one. This stitch is especially useful in working broad spaces which seem too wide for a single stitch.

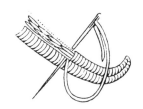

SIMPLE OUTLINE is made from left to right, putting the needle forward a short distance along the line of stamping and bringing it up at the end of the last stitch. Always keep the thread on the same side of the line.

BULLION STITCH. Bring the thread up at the base of the petal, insert the needle at the apex and bring the point out at the base again; wrap the thread a number of times around the needle and draw through, then carry down at the apex.

LONG EYELET. Run a thread around the stamped line, slit the space, roll back the edges on the wrong side, and whip over and over with short, close stitches.

BUTTONHOLING may be padded or not and is worked from left to right. Holding the thread down with the left thumb, a stitch is taken across the space to be covered, and the loop formed when the thread is drawn up makes a purling on the edge of the space.

A **SHADED EYELET**, one which is heavier on one side, is padded between the double lines, and otherwise worked in the ordinary way.

ROUND EYELET. Run stamped line with fine stitches, punch with stiletto, clip material if it does not separate easily, hold edges under, and work in over-and-over stitch from right to left with thread below needle as in illustration.

SIMPLE EMBROIDERY STITCHES

ITALIAN CUT WORK consists of long, narrow spaces buttonholed on the sides with buttonhole bars across and the material cut away beneath. The bars are put in before the edges are buttonholed.

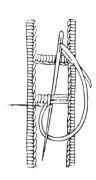

CHAIN STITCH is a form of outlining which is also used for filling large spaces. It is really a succession of buttonhole stitches made along a single line, putting the needle back into the last stitch each time and working towards one.

LONG AND SHORT BUTTONHOLING is made like simple buttonholing except that the stitches are of unequal length. This stitch is used when an irregular effect is desired.

SATIN OUTLINE is made over a single run thread, or over simple outlining, if a more cordlike effect is desired. After running the padding thread, work over and over with very short, close stitches, keeping these stitches at right angles to the stamped line. This stitch is used in French embroidery.

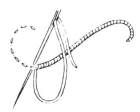

SNAIL TRAIL, is made from right to left along a single line of stamping. The thread is held on the line while a short buttonhole stitch is made over it.

FRENCH KNOTS. Bring the thread out on the right side, then, holding it with the left hand, wrap once, twice, or several times around the needle; insert the needle near where it was brought up and hold the thread taut while the needle is carried through.

WOVEN BAR, used in Italian cut work. Carry two threads across the space, fasten securely in edge of material, and weave over and under the threads. Buttonhole or satin-stitch the edges before cutting away linen beneath the bars.

GERMAN KNOT, is made from left to right. Take a short tight stitch at right angles to the stamped line, put a loose simple stitch and a loose buttonhole stitch into the first stitch. Repeat at intervals.

FAGOTING, usually employed for joining two edges, consists of buttonhole-stitches taken on first one edge and then the other, letting the work progress towards one. When two bands are fagoted together, they are first basted on stiff paper and then the stitches added.

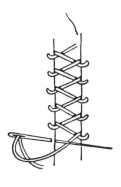

COUCHING, consists of sewing down a cord or several strands of thread by taking short stitches across at regular intervals.

SIMPLE EMBROIDERY STITCHES

LAZY DAISY or **BIRD'S-EYE STITCH** is another form of buttonholing. Long loop stitches, beginning and ending at the same place, are caught down with a short stitch in the end of the loop.

CROSS STITCH consists of two short stitches crossing at right angles. The top threads should all run in the same direction.

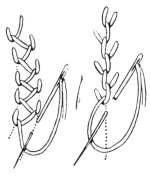

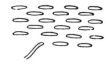

SPACED BUTTONHOLING or **BLANKET STITCH** is made in the same manner as simple buttonholing, except that a short space is left between stitches.

BRIAR STITCH and **FEATHER STITCH** are both forms of buttonholing made toward the worker. The first is made along two lines by taking a short buttonhole-stitch first on one line and then on the other. Feather-stitch is made with short, slanting buttonhole-stitches taken alternately on the left and right of a single line.

DARNING consists of parallel rows of short, regular stitches; the stitches of each row alternate with those of the last. It is used for filling large spaces or backgrounds.

PADDING FOR SATIN STITCH is one of the most important factors in producing beautiful work. Pad by rows of close stemstitching or outlining, running lengthwise the design, taking up as little material as possible on the wrong side. Make padding compact, but do not draw stitches so tightly as to pull the linen. Pad sufficiently to give good relief.

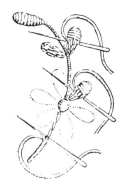

HONEYCOMB STITCH, which is used for filling irregular spaces or backgrounds, is a simple loose buttonhole stitch worked into the preceding row and the fabric beneath. The illustration shows the method of working very plainly.

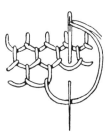

Simple Embroidery Stitches

SEED STITCH consists of one, two, or more short stitches taken over and over at regular intervals to fill a space. The work progresses from right to left with the needle pointed towards the left.

BUTTONHOLED SCALLOPS WITH PICOT BARS.
Buttonhole one complete scallop and to the bar on the next; carry thread across to first scallop and back three times, the buttonhole back over the threads and continue second scallop. Make three buttonhole stitches in the top of one stitch in the center to form the picot

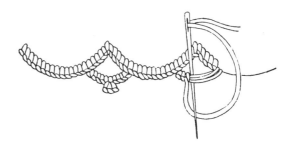

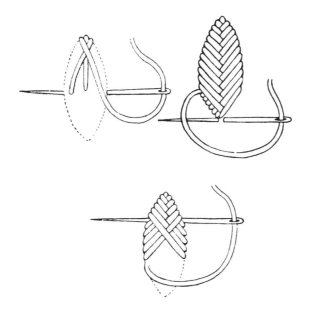

Self-Padding Stitch. Bring the needle through at upper point of leaf, take a long stitch across centre from right to left, carry thread again to the point and take a short stitch just below it from side to side, then another long stitch at centre just below previous long stitch and repeat until leaf is filled.

Chapter 2

MAKING PAPER PATTERNS FROM THE BOOK

Every effort has been made to keep the patterns as clear and easy to follow as possible. Patterns are all full size and ready to be traced. Only occasionally has it been necessary, because of size, to break the lines of a pattern. In such instances, the end of each line is keyed to match the end of the line where the pattern continues. With one exception, (the Buddy Lee overalls), the broken lines are continued on the same page, placed at a different angle.

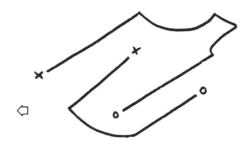

To trace patterns, never use a ball-point pen. The rolling ball-point will press through the tracing paper and have a tendency to cut into the book pages. When the book pattern is traced more than once, there will be gradual damage to the printed page. The ideal method of tracing patterns is to use a lead pencil or a soft-tipped fibre pen, good quality artists' tracing paper, available at art supply shops padded in several sizes, and a clear, acetate shield to protect the book page. This acetate shield may be slipped under the edge of the dustjacket in the back of the book where it will be available for future use.

To trace patterns with broken lines, place paper and shield over the page and trace one section, carefully following the lines and ending exactly where the printed line ends. Lift the paper and move it about to determine where the corresponding lines take up. Replace the paper, aligning the marks, and complete the pattern tracing.

Seam and hem allowances are not drawn on the pages. After the pattern is traced and before cutting it out, draw seam allowances on the paper. Cut out paper pattern with hem and seam allowances. Mark all instructions on your pattern, including matching instructions and fold indications. Also mark each pattern piece with the size, type, and any other pertinent information. While this may seem time-consuming, a few minutes at this point may save hours later. Mark each piece: "From Anderton's *Sewing for Twentieth Century Dolls*, P.(no.)," fold pattern pieces together neatly, and place in individual envelope with description on the outside. Keep all such pattern envelopes in a special box and you will be ready at all times for a session of doll clothes sewing without the fuss of finding patterns and instructions.

Further use may be made of the individual pattern envelopes as you sew. Any alterations for a particular doll, and special effects, or other items of importance may be duly noted on the reverse of the envelope and will be available to anyone using the pattern in the future.

Chapter 3

FITTING PATTERNS TO YOUR DOLL

The patterns in this book are as accurate in size and fit as it is possible to make them. It is possible, however, that a given pattern will not fit the doll of your choice even though the doll is the "same" or nearly the same as the doll from which the pattern was made.

Wide variations are often found in body styling. This is particularly true in the case of the old ball-jointed bodies. One doll may have a fat "tummy" and a protuberant *derriere* while another doll of the same height will be quite willowy or perhaps bosomy.

Measure your doll by taking the front measurements, underarm across the front to opposite underarm, and back measurements, underarm across the back to opposite underarm. Do not measure simply by placing the measuring tape around the body. This will be misleading since front and back measurements are usually not the same.

Now check the measurements of the pattern you have selected, both with a tape measure and by placing the pattern pieces against the doll. When you are satisfied the pattern actually fits, you are ready to cut the fabric.

There are several methods of enlarging and decreasing patterns. One of the simplest methods, when a minimal alteration is required, is bisecting the pattern laterally and vertically, and cutting it apart on those lines. This gives four pattern pieces from one. These four pieces may either be moved apart to enlarge the pattern piece or slightly overlapped to decrease the pattern. A bit of transparent tape will hold them together at the new measurement.

As previously stated, this method works only if the adjustment is a minor one. For alterations requiring major size changes, the most efficient method is one which takes a little practice, but which is actually quite easy to accomplish. Without cutting out the paper pattern you have traced from the book, divide it carefully into one inch squares.

Now for some computation: Let us suppose your doll is 18 inches tall whereas the pattern is for a 12 inch doll. Your doll is one and one-half times as tall as the doll of the pattern. Mark off another larger piece of paper in one and one-half inch squares and transfer the pattern line-for-line, using the squares as guide-lines. This same method, in reverse, may be used to decrease a pattern.

Widening or narrowing of shoulders may be necessary since some dolls, especially some of the ball-jointed ones, have rather wide shoulders owing to the large ball joints, while others may have quite sloping shoulders. Do check carefully to be sure the pattern gives adequate length of skirt for your particular doll. Generally, alterations of doll clothes are the same as for full-size fashions.

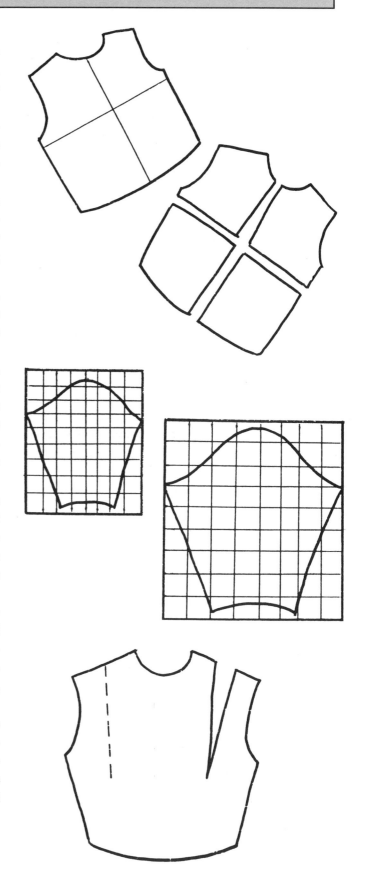

October 1915

The Smartest of the Autumn Hats

They may flare or dip, they may be large or small, but all are feather-trimmed

Selected by GRACE MARGARET GOULD

Illustrated by AUGUSTA REIMER

VELVET. Fur. Feathers — these three proclaim the fashion in millinery for fall and winter. There is scarcely a hat for the autumn that does not show the introduction of velvet, if it is not entirely made of that material: and as for the trimming, it is bound to be of feathers, one kind or another, and often fur, too is introduced.

LARGE and small, high and low, these are the new hats for the autumn. No one definite shape is a necessity, but rather to suit the individuality of the wearer is the mission of the hat this season. Well down on the head it must be placed, with a slight dip to the right side, to be correct. It is worn again this year without even the suggestion of a bandeau.

Chapter 4

HATS AND OTHER ACCESSORIES

Whether your interest in the book stems from a desire to costume a collection or to dress play dolls, consideration should be given to accessories. Although usually the first things lost in a doll's wardrobe, accessories are a great deal of fun. Ingenuity and imagination must be called upon to invent many of the tiny personal oddments which every well-dressed doll counts among her possessions.

Hats are perhaps the obvious place to begin and, indeed, an entire book might be devoted to the construction of really elaborate headgear of every imaginable style. Patterns for hats and bonnets are given throughout the book wherever the original matching *chapeau* was available. If a hat pattern is not given with the style of your choice, simply borrow suitable headgear from another pattern.

1930-31

1913

1915

1915

1913

Underthings are adequately described in each section along with patterns for dresses and other garments. Stockings and shoes have a separate section to which you may refer and are also occasionally included along with certain patterns.

Castoffs are often the source of material for doll clothes; the lone stocking or glove offers many possibilities, for example. From the toe or the top of an ankle sock come skating caps, ear huggers, neck scarves, and beanies. A leather helmet for a boy doll may be made from a discarded glove. Make fur-lined hoods and other accessories from a fur-lined driving glove.

Bits of leather also provide materials for shoes, boots, purses, and vests. The fingers of white kid gloves become upper arms for bisque dolls with kid bodies. Long white dress gloves for teen fashion dolls are made from the fingers of ladies' nylon gloves. The fingers of leather gloves are also excellent as boots for small dolls. The leather may be dampened and shaped to the foot and when dry will retain the boot shape. Protect the doll foot and leg from dampness when using this method.

Discarded underwear often has areas of little wear which provide adequate material for dolls' underthings. Some stockings make excellent seamless undersuits for small dolls.

Old, worn, much-laundered sheets and white shirts give the softness required for slips, petticoats, and underpants.

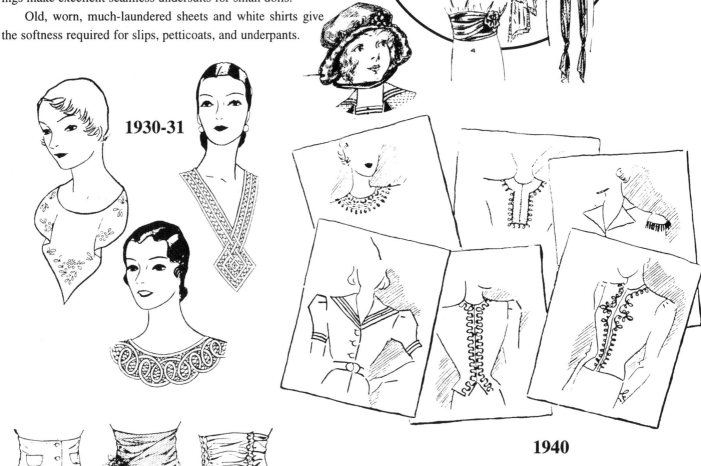

1913

1930-31

1940

1914

The crowns of old straw or felt hats may be cleaned, steamed, and shaped over fruit jars or other forms, and emerge as the best of dolls hats.

In most homes, a button box or special drawer houses a collection of beads, buttons, spools, pins, and other oddities which lend themselves to the creation of doll jewelry. A fancy button, for example, may be just right as a brooch at the throat of a special doll's dress. The remaining pearls of a broken strand may be adequate for a doll necklace; an old ring could become a doll bracelet; map pins or even some hat pins may be changed into perfect dolls' earrings.

The secret is imagination - Yours.

PATTERNS

Chapter 5

BODIES

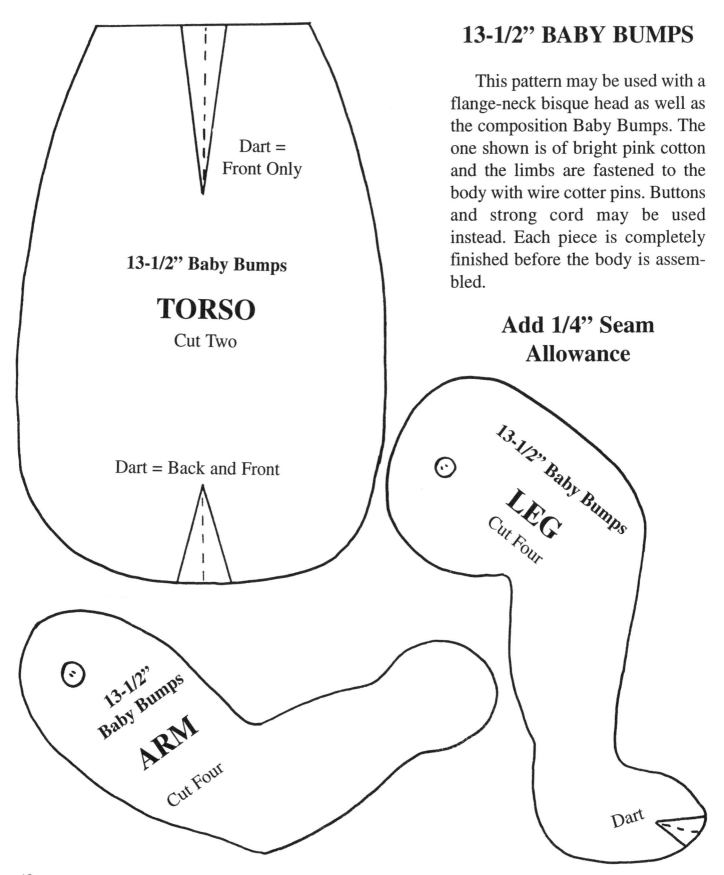

13-1/2" BABY BUMPS

This pattern may be used with a flange-neck bisque head as well as the composition Baby Bumps. The one shown is of bright pink cotton and the limbs are fastened to the body with wire cotter pins. Buttons and strong cord may be used instead. Each piece is completely finished before the body is assembled.

Add 1/4" Seam Allowance

Dart = Front Only

13-1/2" Baby Bumps

TORSO
Cut Two

Dart = Back and Front

13-1/2" Baby Bumps
LEG
Cut Four

13-1/2" Baby Bumps
ARM
Cut Four

Dart

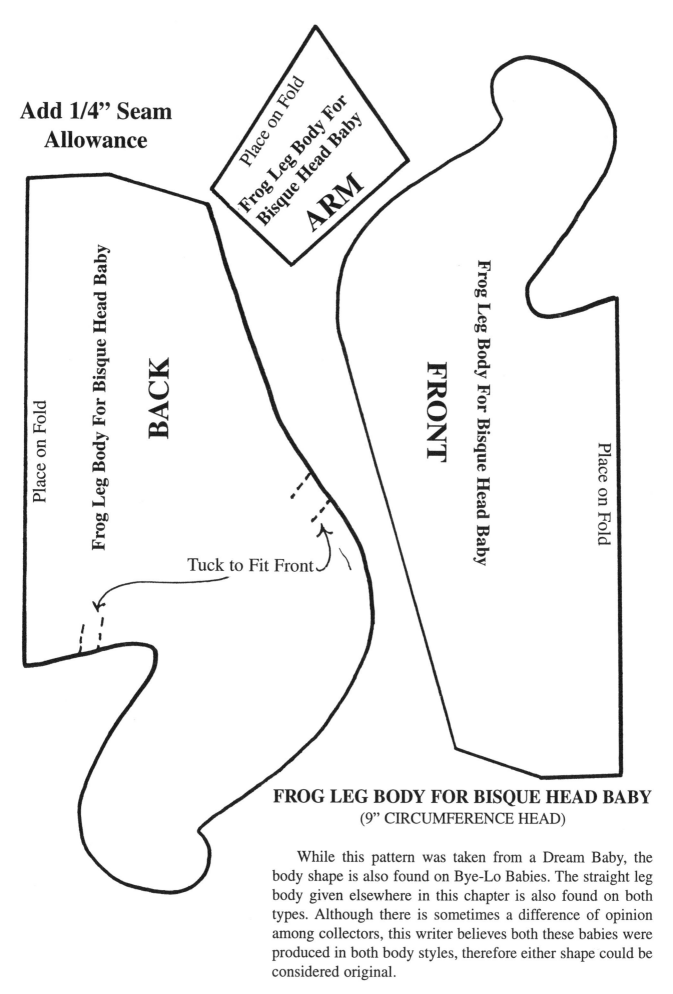

Add 1/4" Seam Allowance

Place on Fold

Frog Leg Body For Bisque Head Baby

ARM

Place on Fold

Frog Leg Body For Bisque Head Baby

BACK

FRONT

Frog Leg Body For Bisque Head Baby

Place on Fold

Tuck to Fit Front

FROG LEG BODY FOR BISQUE HEAD BABY
(9" CIRCUMFERENCE HEAD)

While this pattern was taken from a Dream Baby, the body shape is also found on Bye-Lo Babies. The straight leg body given elsewhere in this chapter is also found on both types. Although there is sometimes a difference of opinion among collectors, this writer believes both these babies were produced in both body styles, therefore either shape could be considered original.

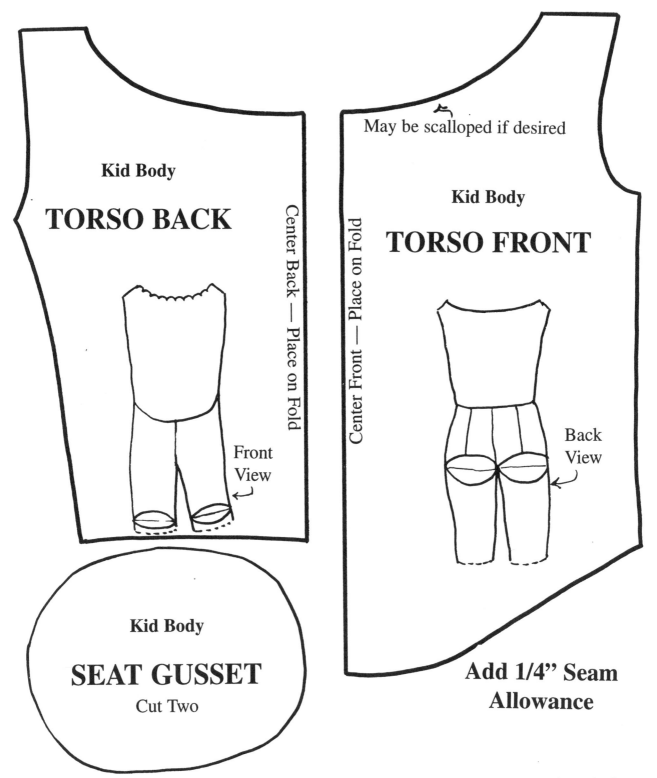

Kid Body

TORSO BACK

Center Back — Place on Fold

Front View

Kid Body

May be scalloped if desired

TORSO FRONT

Center Front — Place on Fold

Back View

Add 1/4" Seam Allowance

Kid Body

SEAT GUSSET

Cut Two

This body may also be made of heavy unbleached muslin or pink sateen. The pattern makes a body approximately 12" from shoulder to mid-calf. Length of leg below knee may require adjustment depending on type of lower limb used. A cloth lower leg and foot may be added in place of bisque, composition, or celluloid.

1. Insert knee gussets in leg sections.
2. Seam each leg section together, matching double and triple dots.
3. Insert seat gusset in each leg section.
4. Seam leg sections together along crotch seam.
5. Sew side seams of torso.
6. Seam leg assembly to torso.

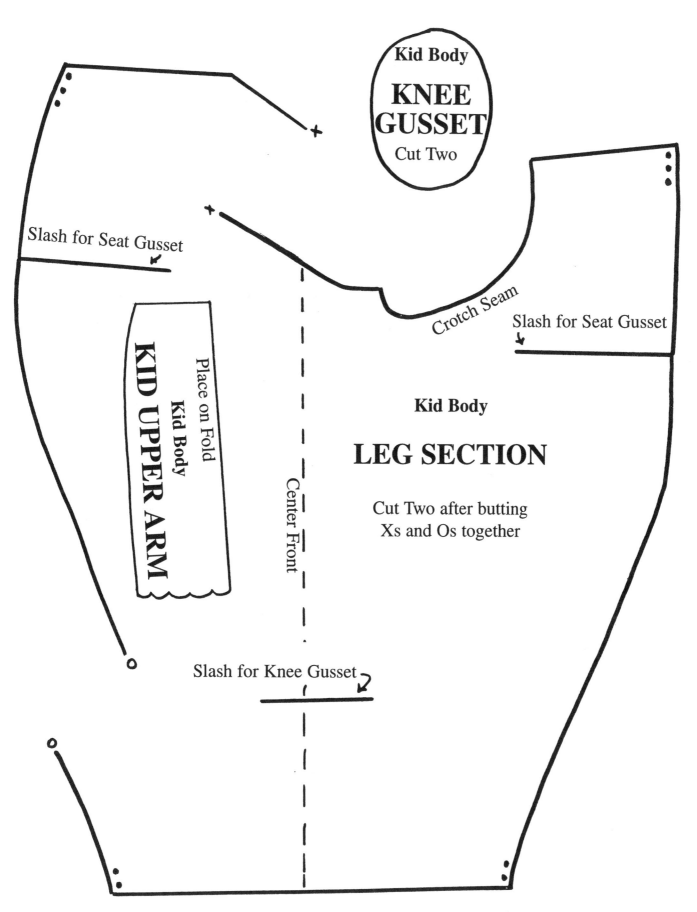

Kid Body

KNEE GUSSET

Cut Two

Slash for Seat Gusset

Place on Fold
Kid Body
KID UPPER ARM

Center Front

Crotch Seam

Slash for Seat Gusset

Kid Body

LEG SECTION

Cut Two after butting
Xs and Os together

Slash for Knee Gusset

Add 1/4" Seam Allowance

BODY FOR 11-1/2" DREAM BABY

(WITH 8" CIRC. HEAD)

Use unbleached muslin or other sturdy cotton. If celluloid, bisque, or composition hands are not available, cut fabric to include hands with arm. Stuff finger area lightly, stitch to define fingers, then stuff hands fatter.

1. Seam, turn and stuff legs.

2. Baste tops of legs closed, matching back seam to front seam.

3. Sew side seams of body, taking tucks in back to fit back to front.

4. With body wrong side out insert stuffed legs with feet toward neck opening. Match seams to O's on pattern front. Check to be sure front of legs and body are together. Baste across lower body, turn and check position of legs in relationship to body. If correct, turn and stitch across lower body twice for added strength.

5. Turn, stuff body, attach head, wrapping several times with heavy thread or cord.

6. Attach arms.

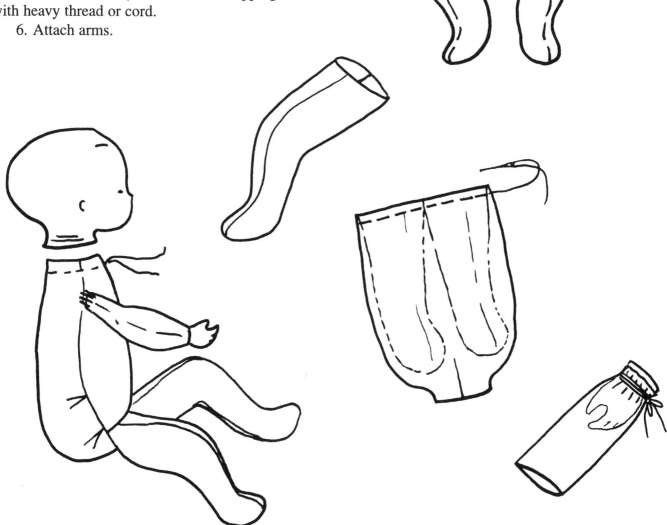

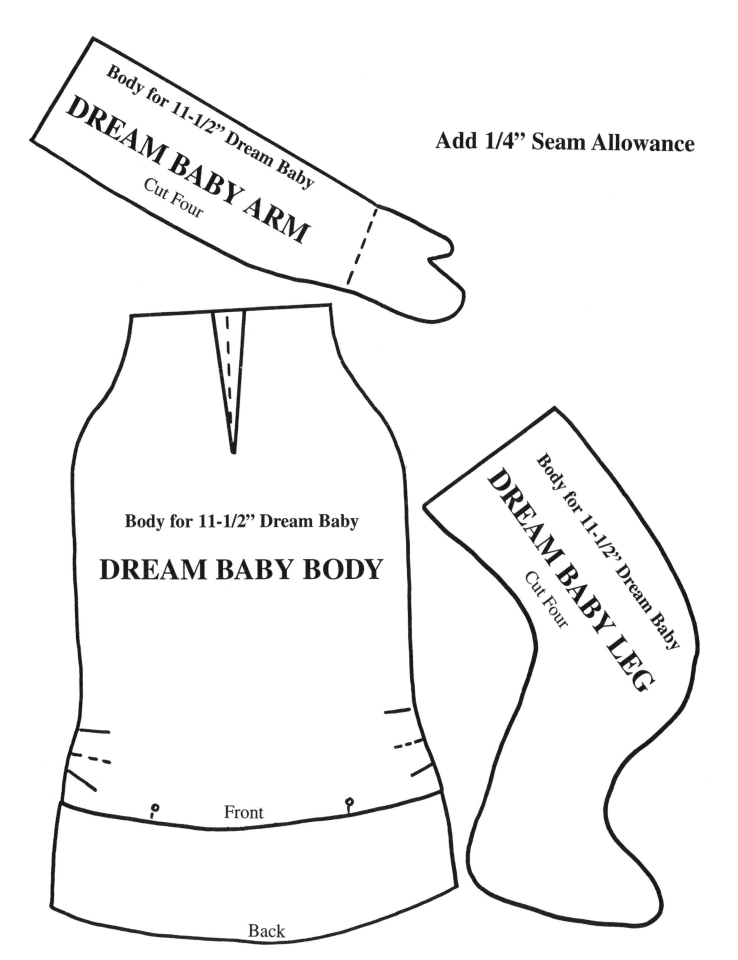

Add 1/4" Seam Allowance

Body for 11-1/2" Dream Baby

DREAM BABY ARM

Cut Four

Body for 11-1/2" Dream Baby

DREAM BABY BODY

Front

Back

Body for 11-1/2" Dream Baby

DREAM BABY LEG

Cut Four

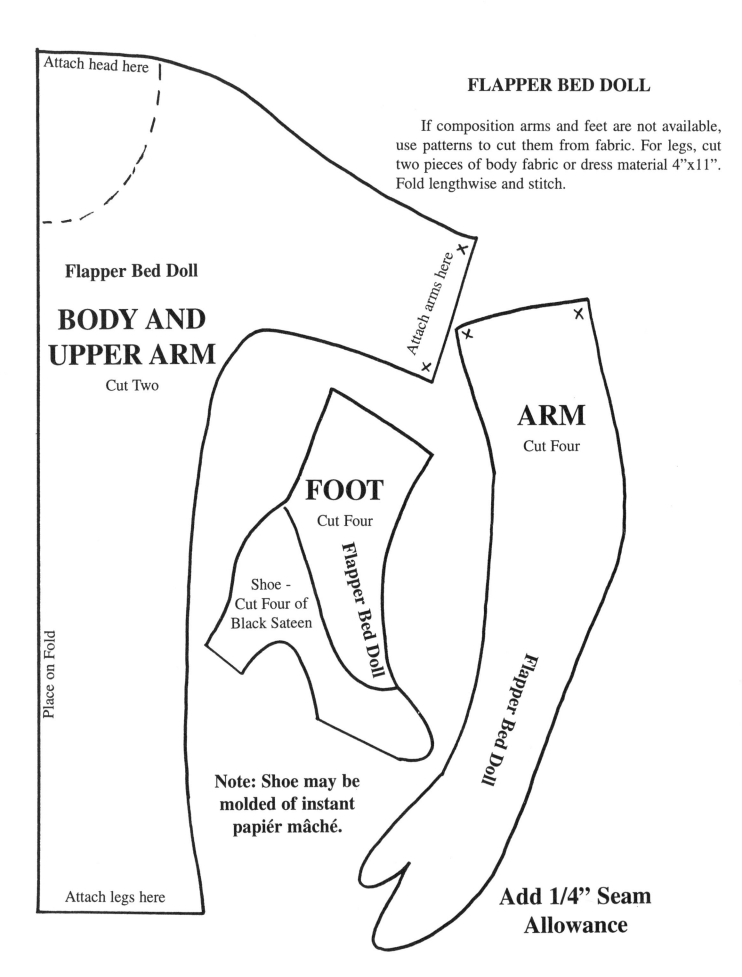

Attach head here

FLAPPER BED DOLL

If composition arms and feet are not available, use patterns to cut them from fabric. For legs, cut two pieces of body fabric or dress material 4"x11". Fold lengthwise and stitch.

Flapper Bed Doll

BODY AND UPPER ARM

Cut Two

Attach arms here

ARM

Cut Four

Flapper Bed Doll

FOOT

Cut Four

Flapper Bed Doll

Shoe - Cut Four of Black Sateen

Place on Fold

Note: Shoe may be molded of instant papiér mâché.

Attach legs here

Flapper Bed Doll

Add 1/4" Seam Allowance

Chapter 6

STOCKINGS AND SHOES

Shoes are not difficult to make if taken step by step. Complete each step on both shoes before proceeding to the next step. This way, the shoes will be a matching pair, and will also be easier to finish.

Stockings, too, are quite simple since they may often be made of old discarded hosiery which has a finished top waiting to be utilized. The Chatty Cathy socks may be cut of any knit such as an old undershirt. Fold over the top along dash line, then stitch the side seam, turn to right side and you have a finished sock.

Several patterns for stockings and shoes are shown elsewhere in this volume. Consult the index to learn their location.

TO MAKE SHOES

1. Cut all pieces and lay out in sets for each shoe. Cut side piece, one innersole and one outer sole, and any other sections.

2. Attach innersole to bottom of doll's foot with a bit of floral clay, sew any seams required for the side of the shoe and place on doll's foot. Put dots of glue all around and glue side to innersole.

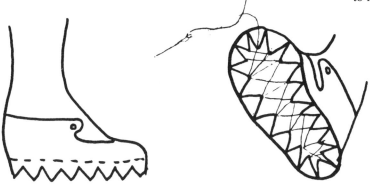

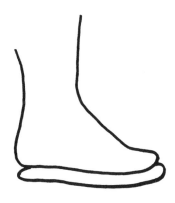

3. Fold over seam allowance, snip to ease all around, dot glue all around outer sole and folded-over section. Allow to set, then glue together. Additional reinforcement may be made by stitching back and forth across bottom of foot before gluing on outer sole and heel if desired.

SANDALS

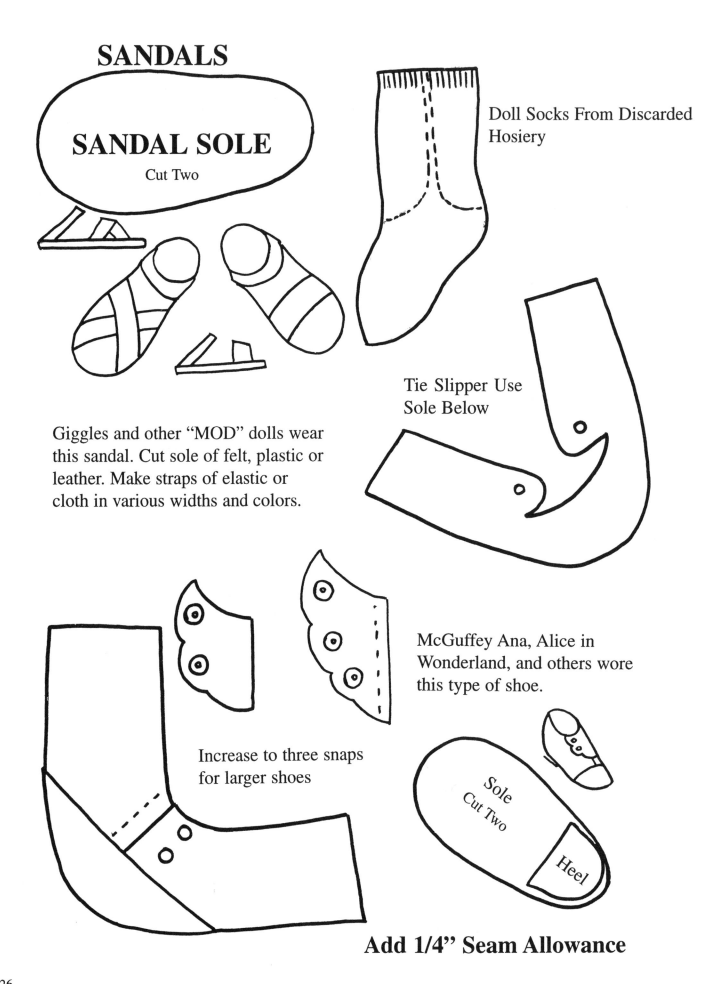

SANDAL SOLE
Cut Two

Doll Socks From Discarded Hosiery

Giggles and other "MOD" dolls wear this sandal. Cut sole of felt, plastic or leather. Make straps of elastic or cloth in various widths and colors.

Tie Slipper Use Sole Below

McGuffey Ana, Alice in Wonderland, and others wore this type of shoe.

Increase to three snaps for larger shoes

Sole
Cut Two

Heel

Add 1/4" Seam Allowance

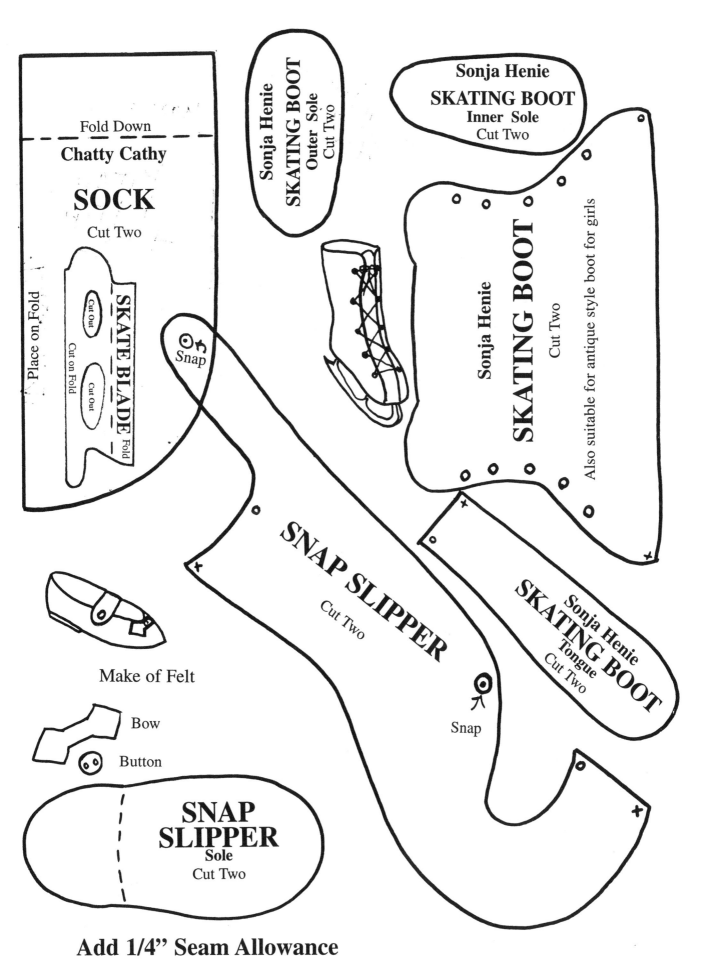

Fold Down

Chatty Cathy

SOCK

Cut Two

Place on Fold

SKATE BLADE

Cut Out

Cut on Fold

Cut Out

Fold

Snap

Sonja Henie
SKATING BOOT
Outer Sole
Cut Two

Sonja Henie
SKATING BOOT
Inner Sole
Cut Two

Sonja Henie
SKATING BOOT
Cut Two

Also suitable for antique style boot for girls

Make of Felt

Bow

Button

SNAP SLIPPER
Cut Two

Snap

Sonja Henie
SKATING BOOT
Tongue
Cut Two

SNAP SLIPPER
Sole
Cut Two

Add 1/4" Seam Allowance

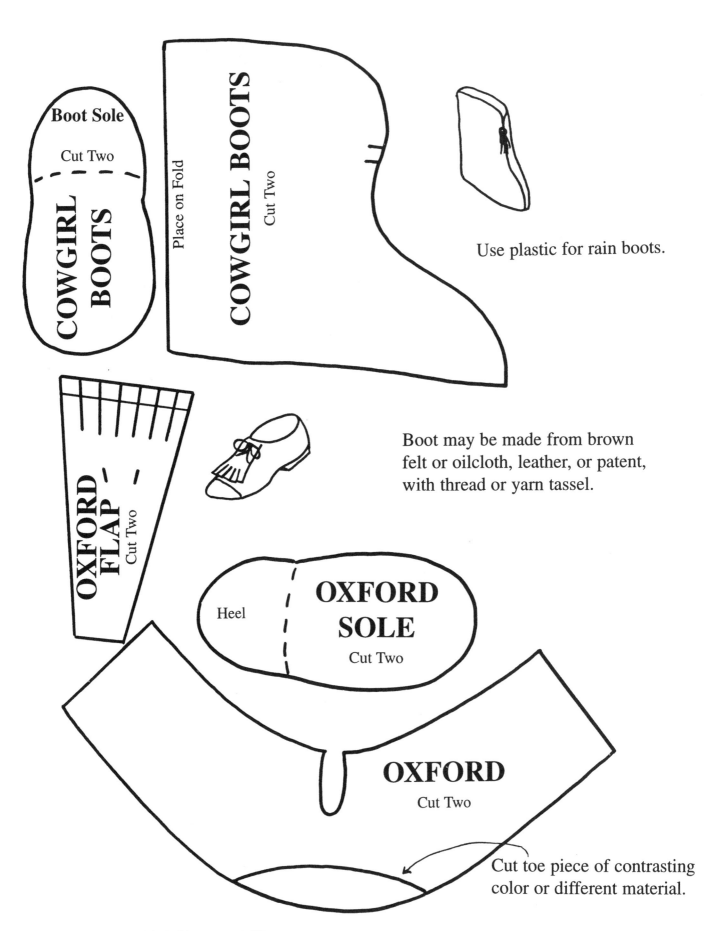

Boot Sole

Cut Two

COWGIRL BOOTS

Place on Fold

COWGIRL BOOTS

Cut Two

Use plastic for rain boots.

Boot may be made from brown felt or oilcloth, leather, or patent, with thread or yarn tassel.

OXFORD FLAP

Cut Two

Heel

OXFORD SOLE

Cut Two

OXFORD

Cut Two

Cut toe piece of contrasting color or different material.

Add 1/4" Seam Allowance

Chapter 7

THE 1900s

Dressy, with Little Trimming

The turn of the Century, although the dawn of a new era, nevertheless saw many 1890s styles holding their own. Sailor collars, always a classic, were still popular for little girls and boys. Sweeping skirts, large sleeves, bustles, and bosom padding remained in style, changing in shape and size from year to year.

Where climate or school buildings permitted, school clothes were made of wash fabrics such as pique, challis, lawn, batiste, and lace. Heavier fabrics in use were navy blue serge, fine striped worsted, cashmere, dark challis and wool batiste. Navy blue was brightened with white or red braid, piping, or gilt buttons. Black and white shepherd's check worsted was highlighted with piping of cardinal, emerald green, cerise, or other light colors, set off with fancy buttons and a colored patent leather belt. Blue dotted French flannel with solid blue bands and a white sailor collar was trimmed with braid and a patent leather belt.

Boy's coats were double breasted, boxy, and of diagonal storm serge, chinchilla cloth, or polo cloth. Suits were of serge, woven checks, or worsted. Early in the decade the Eton collar with soft tie, worn with a suit having a straight jacket and bloused short trousers was proper dress for a young man. This suit was worn with long, dark hose and a vest.

Lace, tucks, cording, piping, and smocking were used as trims on ladies' dresses of challis, lawn, linen, broadcloth, or India mull. Velvet ribbon trims were much in evidence.

A Street Suit with Gored Jacket

1904

A Smart Suit for Street Wear   **Silk Girdle Strewn with Sequins**   **Black Silk with Gold Buckle**   **A Model in Challis**

3428

3071

3208

3265

3196

2791

3371

3045

3144

3735

3449

3668

3727

3618

3585

2686

PICTORIAL
REVIEW

3288

3345

Pictorial Review for December 1910

3166

3634

3219

3262

3710

2512

3522

3145

25" GERMAN BISQUE CHILD
(MARKED DEP11)

Attach Shoulder ruffle here

Back View

This bisque-head doll has a ball-jointed, composition and wood body. Here is an excellent example of differences in proportion among similar types of dolls. This child, though definitely not a toddler type, is proportionately narrow across the back with protuberant chest and stomach. The patterns reflect this proportioning. Her measurements are:

Height	25"
Waist	13-1/2"
Hips	16"
Chest	14-1/2"
Neck to wrist	9"
Front, neck to crotch	12"
Back, neck to crotch	11"

UNDERWEAR

As always, fit and complete the underwear first. Although this child wears only a slip with a double ruffle and a pair of drawers, it would be simplicity itself to construct a vest of the same fine cotton, using the slip bodice pattern lengthened by one and one-half inches.

Diagrams for the drawers are self-explanatory. To finish legs of the drawers, cut two pieces of same cotton fabric 10" long and 3" wide. Sew 5 very narrow tucks along the length of each piece. Hem and trim with lace, one long side on each piece, following sketch of finished drawers. Seam two short sides together, gather remaining long sides to fit lower edges of leg openings. Cover this seam with insertion lace.

For slip, fit and complete slip bodice and set aside.

For skirt of slip, cut a piece of fabric 10" by 28" long. Attach 1" lace to one long side. Seam short sides together to a point 6" from the bottom edge of lace and flounce - sew along a line marked 4" from bottom of lace.

To make flounce, cut a piece of fabric 2" by 40" long. Stitch 2 narrow tucks full length of piece. Attach 2-1/2" wide lace to long side of piece. Gather remaining long side and attach to skirt of slip as above. Attach skirt to bodice.

DRESS

This original dress, in a turn-of-the-Century style, offers a construction challenge yet is quite simply made. Alternating panels of fragile pink silk and ecru lace combine to achieve an artistic, stylish appearance. While the back is straight, the front is slightly bloused, although not as decidedly as the white dress shown for our 28" K★R.

A step-by step approach is basic to the construction of this dress; therefore, do not skip ahead and become confused.

DRESS for a little girl from five to ten years old. It could be made in any of the sheer washable materials or the soft light-weight woolen goods. The collar is of sheer linen batiste.

1904

DRESS REQUIREMENTS

Make the following paper patterns to be cut from dress material and mark each one as it is cut out:

A. Shoulder Ruffle A- 2 pieces ....2-1/4" x 17"

B. Skirt Flounce B - 1 piece ....2-1/2" x 60"

C. Skirt Flounce C - 1 piece ....1-3/4" x 26"

D. Sleeve D - 2 pieces ....Pattern Piece D.

E. Bodice Panel E - 1 piece....................4" x 13".

F. Bodice Panel F - 1 piece ....3" x 13".

G. Bodice Back - 4 pieces ....Pattern Piece G.

H. Bodice Front - 1 piece............Pattern Piece H.

Pin, cut, and set aside above pattern pieces.

Measure and lay out the following pieces of lace: pin an identification slip of notepaper to each:

1. Skirt Ruffle — 1 piece 2" lace, 88" long.

2. Skirt section — 1 piece 1-1/2" lace, 36" long.

3. Shoulder Ruffle — 2 pieces 2" lace, 36" long.

4. Sleeve Ruffle — 2 pieces 2" lace, 15" long

5. Bodice Front — 1 piece 1-1/2" lace, 13" long.

6. Sufficient lengths of lace to construct the Lace Bodice section (see Pattern Piece 6).

7. Narrow lace for neck edge finish and sleeve band.

8. Sufficient 1/2" lace trim for Lace Bodice and for attaching shoulder ruffle.

DRESS CONSTRUCTION

Bodice is lined with fine cotton; dress is fine silk alternating with fine lace. Do not use cotton lace or eyelet for these are too heavy and will not hang properly.

1. Sew tucks in pieces B,E,F, and G. Refer to diagrams and sketches.

2. Using Pattern Piece 6, construct Lace Bodice section.

3. Open out Bodice Front H Lining.

4. Construct bloused over-section following dress diagram and using Pieces E,F, and Lace 5.

5. Gather upper edge of construction (in 4 above) to fit lower edge of Lace Bodice section 6 and seam together.

6. Pin this construction unit to Bodice Front Lining H.

7. Pin one back lining section to each back dress section and assemble bodice and lining front to backs as one.

8. Gather sleeves along dotted lines, fitting upper edge to armhole and lower edge to narrow flat lace cut to fit over doll's hand.

9. Gather Lace Piece 4 to fit Sleeve Band 7 and attach.

10. Construct shoulder ruffle by gathering upper edge of Lace Piece 3 to long edge of dress material section A. Gather remaining long edge of A to fit line marked on pattern with XXXs. Cover this seam with narrow Lace 8.

11. Finish back opening, crochet three button loops and attach three buttons.

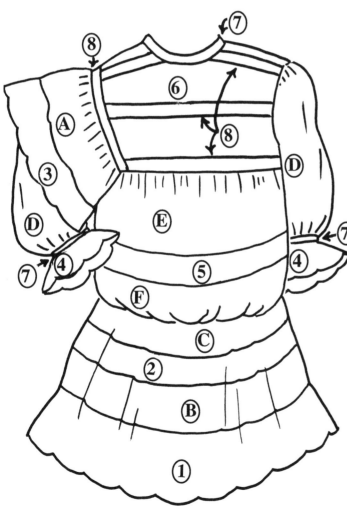

Construction Diagram

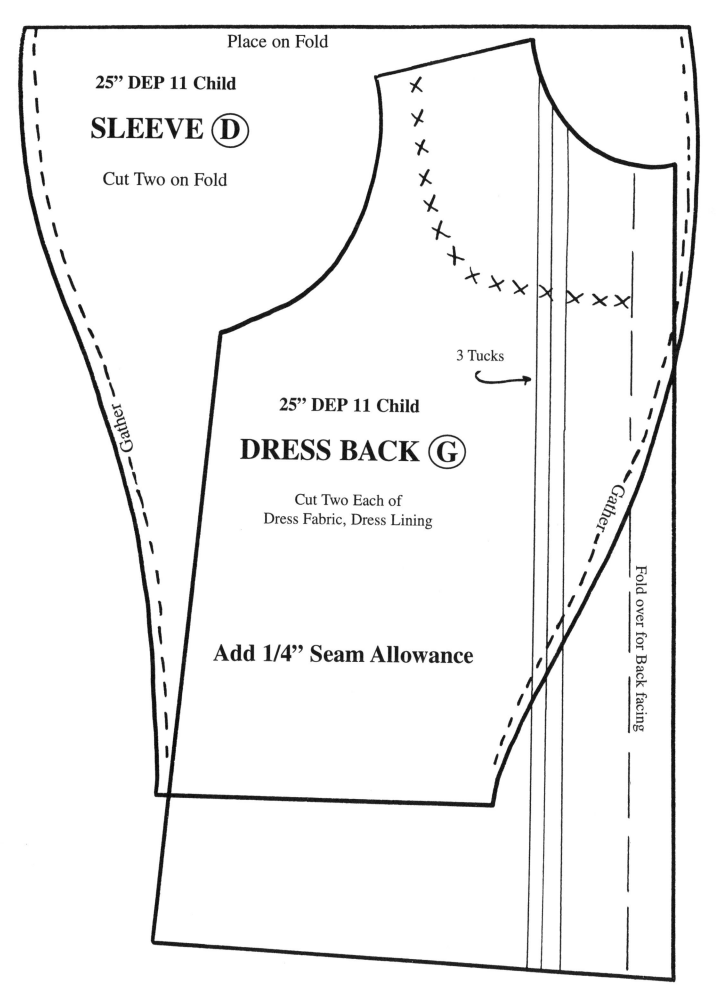

Place on Fold

25" DEP 11 Child

SLEEVE Ⓓ

Cut Two on Fold

Gather

25" DEP 11 Child

DRESS BACK Ⓖ

Cut Two Each of
Dress Fabric, Dress Lining

Add 1/4" Seam Allowance

3 Tucks

Gather

Fold over for Back facing

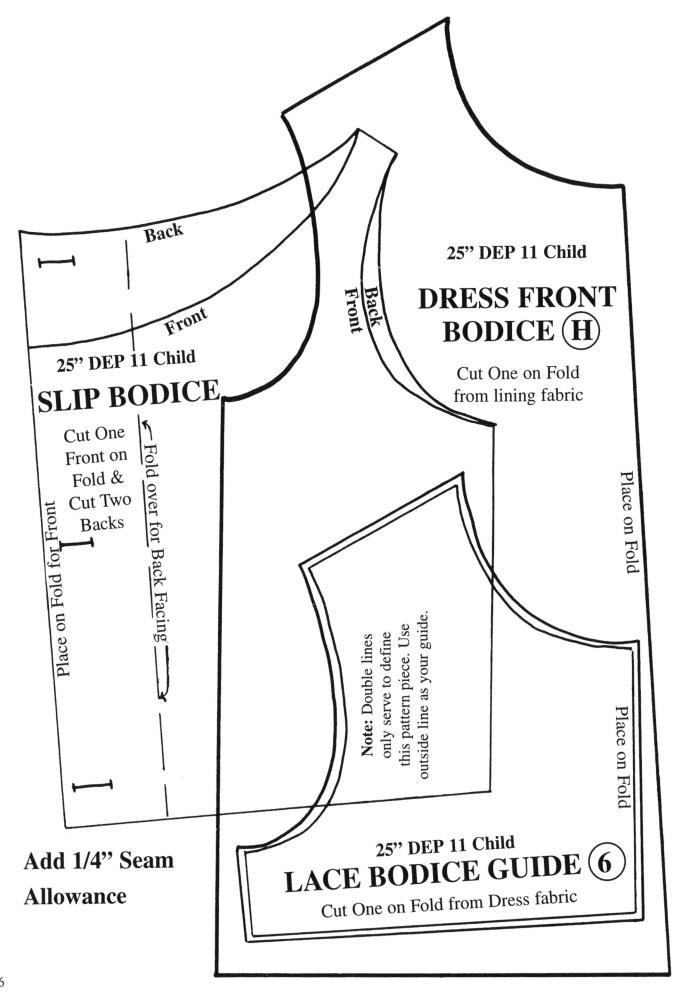

Back

Front

25" DEP 11 Child

SLIP BODICE

Cut One Front on Fold & Cut Two Backs

Place on Fold for Front

← Fold over for Back Facing →

Add 1/4" Seam Allowance

Back
Front

25" DEP 11 Child

DRESS FRONT BODICE Ⓗ

Cut One on Fold from lining fabric

Place on Fold

Note: Double lines only serve to define this pattern piece. Use outside line as your guide.

Place on Fold

25" DEP 11 Child

LACE BODICE GUIDE ⑥

Cut One on Fold from Dress fabric

36

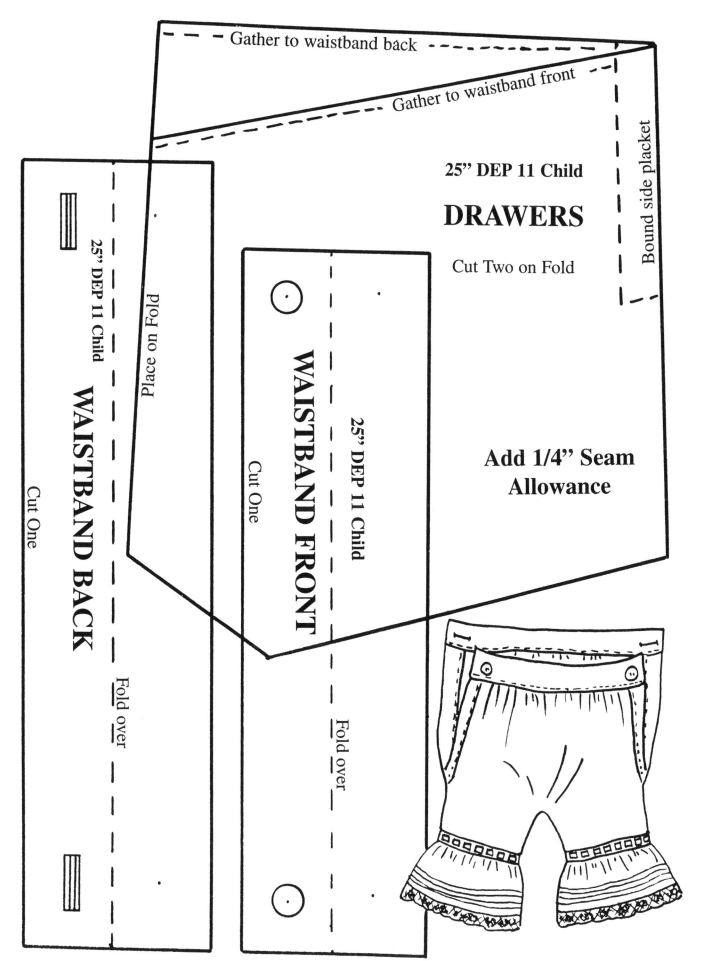

Gather to waistband back

Gather to waistband front

Bound side placket

25" DEP 11 Child

DRAWERS

Cut Two on Fold

Add 1/4" Seam Allowance

25" DEP 11 Child

WAISTBAND BACK

Place on Fold

Cut One

Fold over

25" DEP 11 Child

WAISTBAND FRONT

Cut One

Fold over

37

1904

DRESS for a little girl from six to ten years of age. It would be very pretty if made of a light figured or plain challis and trimmed with narrow black velvet ribbon.

"SLIDELL" - A 21" GERMAN BISQUE
(HANDWERCK 10911)

"Slidell" is named for a little town in Louisiana across Lake Ponchartrain from New Orleans. In a flea market one vacation, we found this doll lying in a box in all her original finery, waiting for us. Rebekka and I knew she must come home with us. We also knew that someday we would share her so that others could enjoy being able to duplicate her costume.

Bright rose-pink cotton made up the dress, with an overdress of some more fragile material, probably silk, which now hangs almost completely in shreds. The narrow black velvet ribbon trim, the underthings, the pink stockings, and the shoes are all in good condition. The shoes are of fine white leather with tiny eyelet's and flat heels, pink shoe laces, and a numeral 6 on the sole of each.

UNDERCLOTHES

Begin with the underthings. Cut them from fine cotton such as lawn or batiste and trim with antique lace or good quality new eyelet or lace. Cotton trim may be salvaged from discarded garments if in good condition. The flounce for the slip is made from a piece of cotton 4" by 30". Sew the two tucks, add 1-1/2" wide lace along one side, then gather to fit body of slip. Cover this seam with insertion lace, topstitched.

THE STOCKINGS

This stocking pattern may seem to make no sense whatever but is actually quite easy to assemble once the cut-out material is in hand.

Cut two on fold from discarded hosiery or fine knit underwear. If positioned properly on old stockings, the top will have a ready-made finished edge.

THE SHOES

See Chapter 6 — STOCKINGS AND SHOES for general directions on constructing these shoes.

THE DRESS

Work the dress and overdress as one, sewing sleeve seams together, etc.

Cut the dress along solid lines of pattern. Cut the back of overdress same as the dress. Cut the front of overdress extending along the dotted lines as shown. Gather overdress front at neck opening and bottom edge to fit dress.

For dress flounce. Cut a piece of fabric 4" by 36" plus hem allowance. Hem one long side; add 3/4" lace along hemmed side. Repeat for overdress flounce, apply narrow ribbon trim (see sketch). (Note: Overdress should be of much lighter, finer material than dress). Gather remaining long sides of dress flounce and overdress flounce as one to fit lower edge of body of dress. Cover this seam with same ribbon.

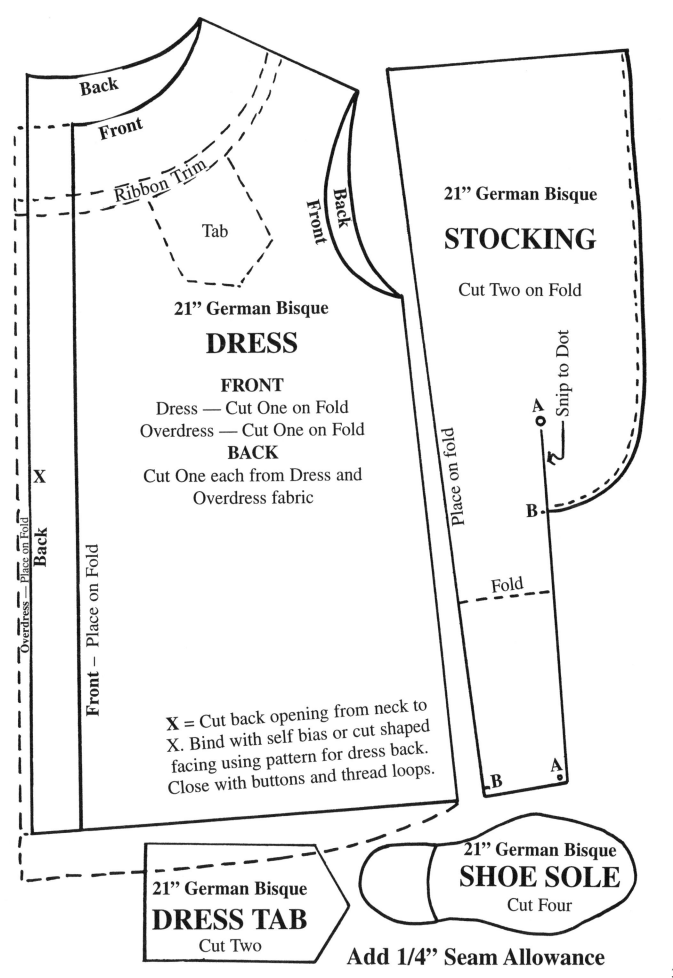

Back

Front

Ribbon Trim

Tab

Back

Front

21" German Bisque

STOCKING

Cut Two on Fold

A ∘ ← Snip to Dot

B

21" German Bisque

DRESS

FRONT
Dress — Cut One on Fold
Overdress — Cut One on Fold
BACK
Cut One each from Dress and
Overdress fabric

Overdress — Place on Fold

X

Back

Front – Place on Fold

Place on fold

Fold

X = Cut back opening from neck to
X. Bind with self bias or cut shaped
facing using pattern for dress back.
Close with buttons and thread loops.

B   A

21" German Bisque

DRESS TAB

Cut Two

21" German Bisque

SHOE SOLE

Cut Four

Add 1/4" Seam Allowance

Add 1/4" Seam Allowance

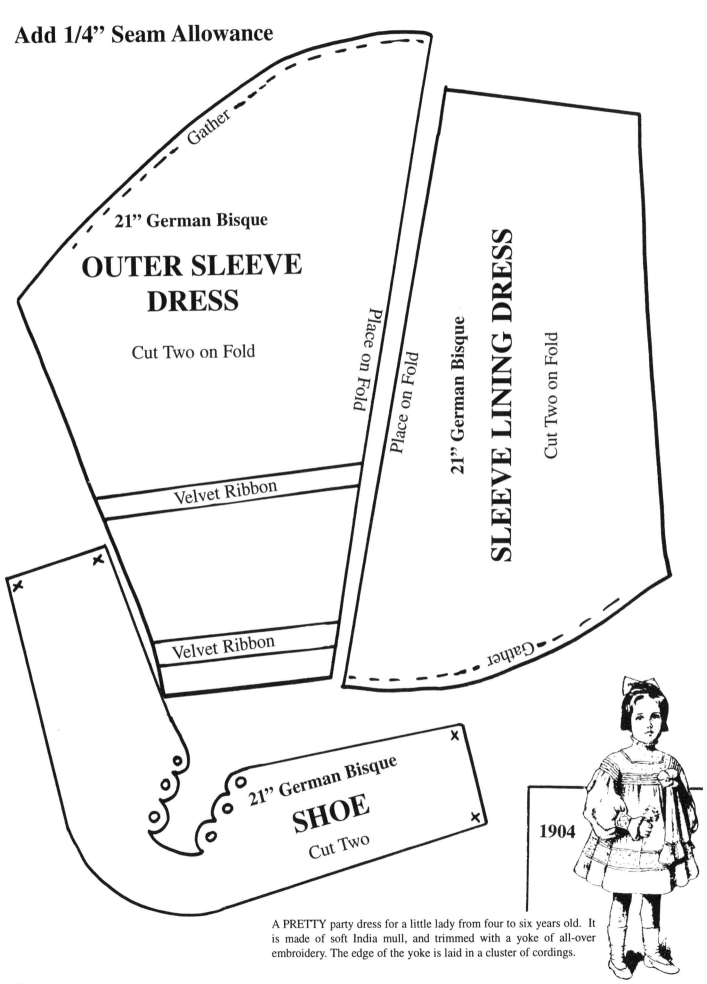

Gather

21" German Bisque

OUTER SLEEVE DRESS

Cut Two on Fold

Velvet Ribbon

Velvet Ribbon

Place on Fold

Place on Fold

21" German Bisque

SLEEVE LINING DRESS

Cut Two on Fold

Gather

21" German Bisque

SHOE

Cut Two

1904

A PRETTY party dress for a little lady from four to six years old. It is made of soft India mull, and trimmed with a yoke of all-over embroidery. The edge of the yoke is laid in a cluster of cordings.

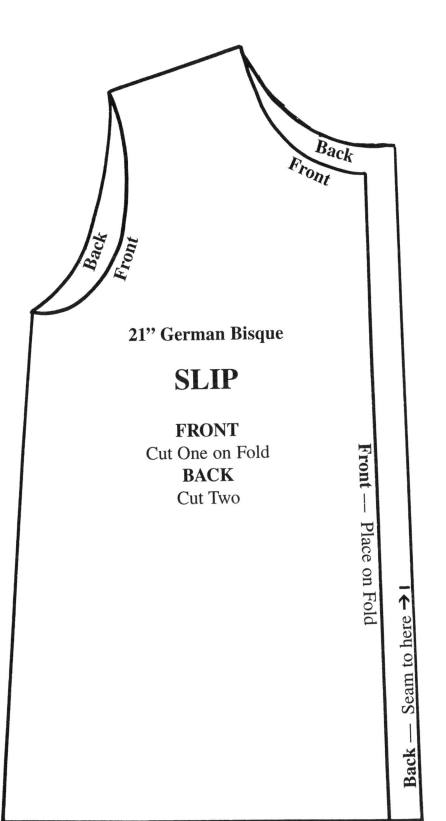

21" German Bisque

SLIP

FRONT
Cut One on Fold
BACK
Cut Two

Back
Front

Back
Front

Front — Place on Fold

Back — Seam to here →

1904

SUIT for a little boy from five to seven years. Could be made of white duck or linen. It has full bloomer trousers, and the blouse has a pointed stitched yoke and fastens at the right side.

This doll lacked underpants when found. Use suitable pattern from elsewhere in this book.

21" German Bisque
STAND-UP COLLAR — DRESS
Fold
Over
Cut One

Add 1/4" Seam Allowance

28" K ★ R - ORIGINAL COSTUME

Always fit and make the underwear first, fitting the clothes one layer over the last.

UNDERWEAR

The undersuit and slip diagrams are largely self-explanatory. Fig. A, page 46, shows method of attaching underwear buttons with tape.

DRESS

A drop-waist style is typical of the 1900 period; this one is of white cotton trimmed with tucks and lace.

Complete the bodice before adding the skirt. Evenly space seven buttons and buttonholes down the back, which is open to the insertion lace. To achieve the stylish, bloused effect, sew tapes inside the bodice, attached at neckline and lower edge of bodice, and underarm and lower edge of bodice. Underarm tapes are 7-3/4" long; and back tapes are 10-1/2 inches long. There is no tape at the front.

The dress flounce or skirt is a piece of dress fabric 4-3/4" (plus hem allowance) by 56" long. The piece of insertion lace which joins the bodice and flounce is 19" long. Sleeves are also gathered to insertion lace cut 4" long. Do measure the arms of your doll to be sure finished sleeve band will pass over the doll's hand.

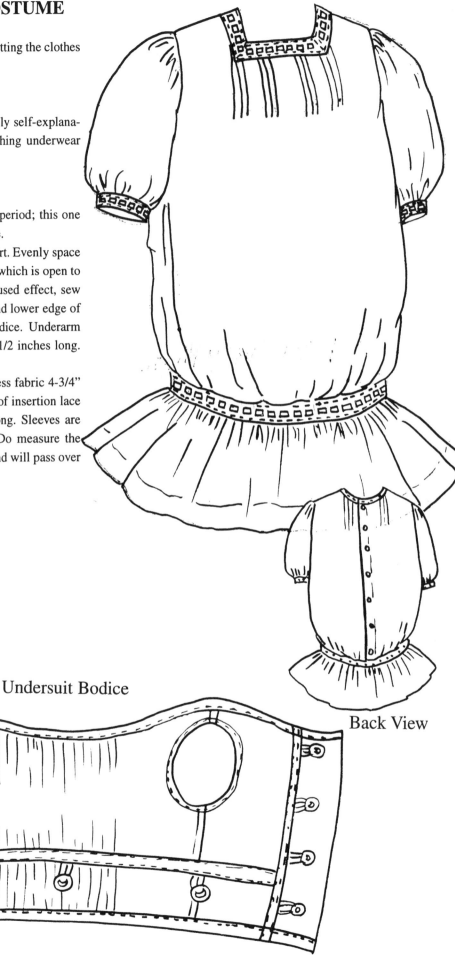

Back View

Undersuit Bodice

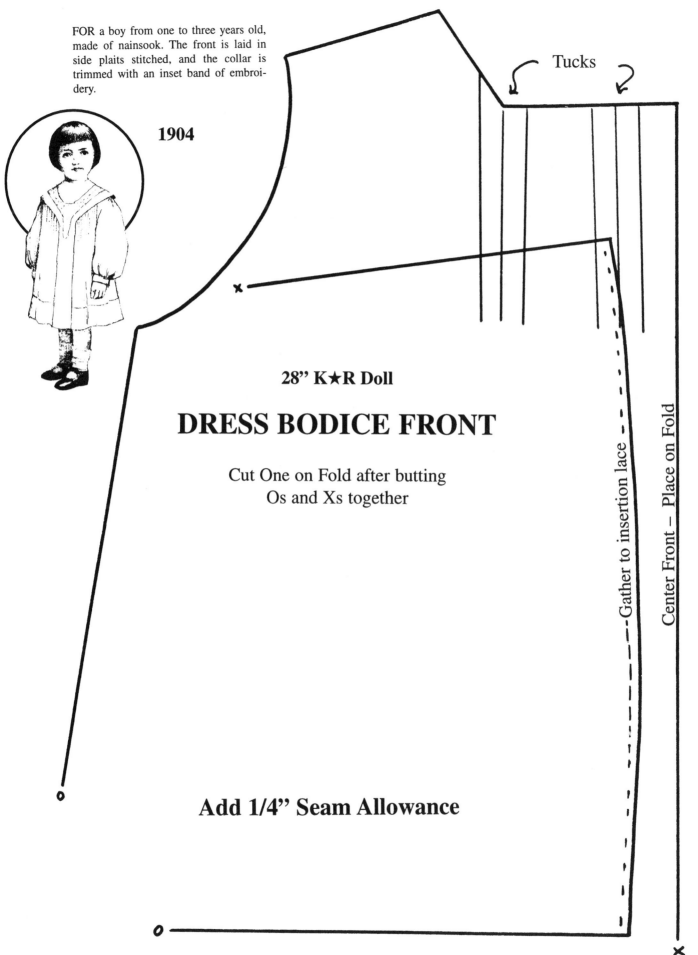

FOR a boy from one to three years old, made of nainsook. The front is laid in side plaits stitched, and the collar is trimmed with an inset band of embroidery.

1904

Tucks

28" K★R Doll

DRESS BODICE FRONT

Cut One on Fold after butting
Os and Xs together

Gather to insertion lace

Center Front – Place on Fold

Add 1/4" Seam Allowance

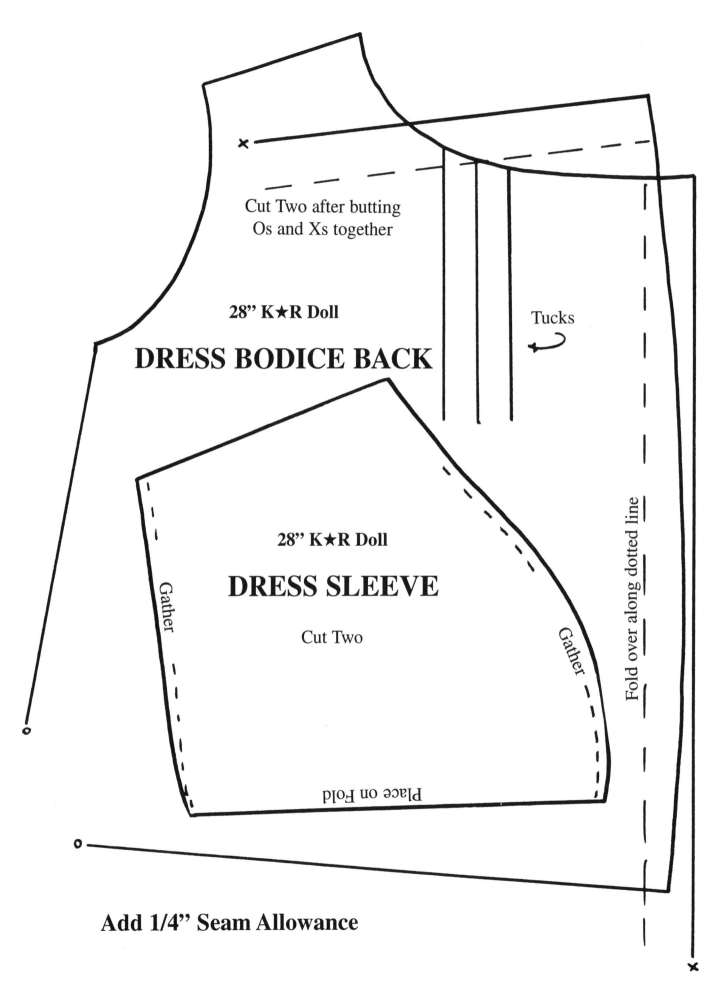

Cut Two after butting
Os and Xs together

28" K★R Doll

DRESS BODICE BACK

Tucks

28" K★R Doll

DRESS SLEEVE

Cut Two

Gather

Gather

Fold over along dotted line

Place on Fold

Add 1/4" Seam Allowance

44

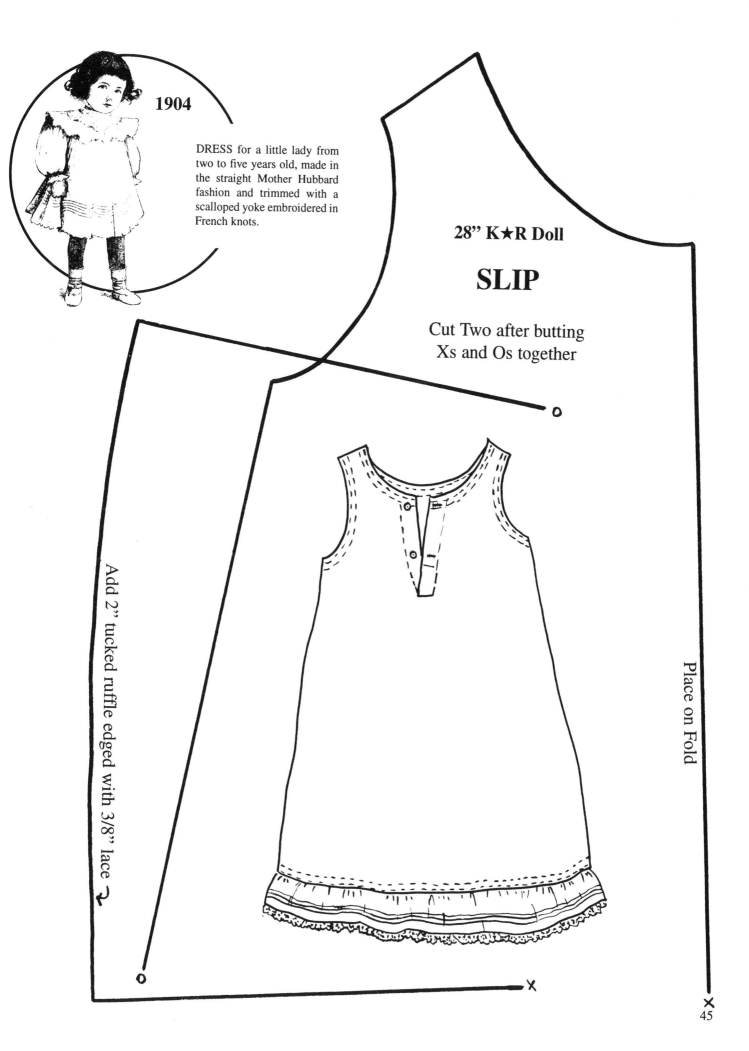

1904

DRESS for a little lady from two to five years old, made in the straight Mother Hubbard fashion and trimmed with a scalloped yoke embroidered in French knots.

28" K★R Doll

SLIP

Cut Two after butting
Xs and Os together

o

Add 2" tucked ruffle edged with 3/8" lace ↩

Place on Fold

o ———————————— X

X
45

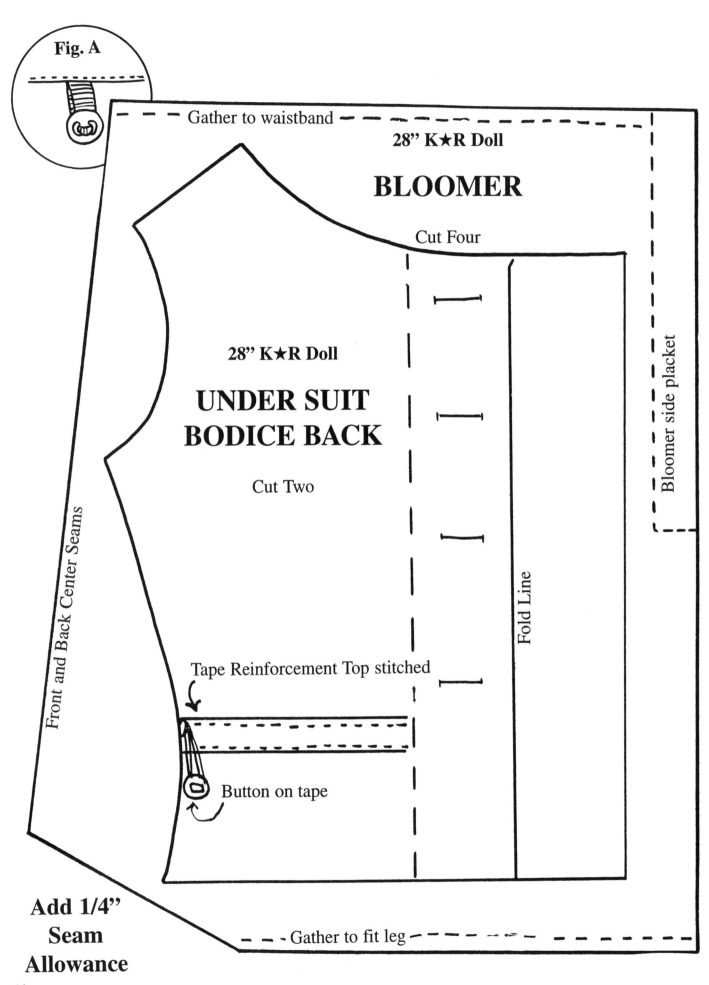

Fig. A

Gather to waistband

28" K★R Doll

BLOOMER

Cut Four

Bloomer side placket

28" K★R Doll

UNDER SUIT BODICE BACK

Cut Two

Front and Back Center Seams

Fold Line

Tape Reinforcement Top stitched

Button on tape

Add 1/4" Seam Allowance

Gather to fit leg

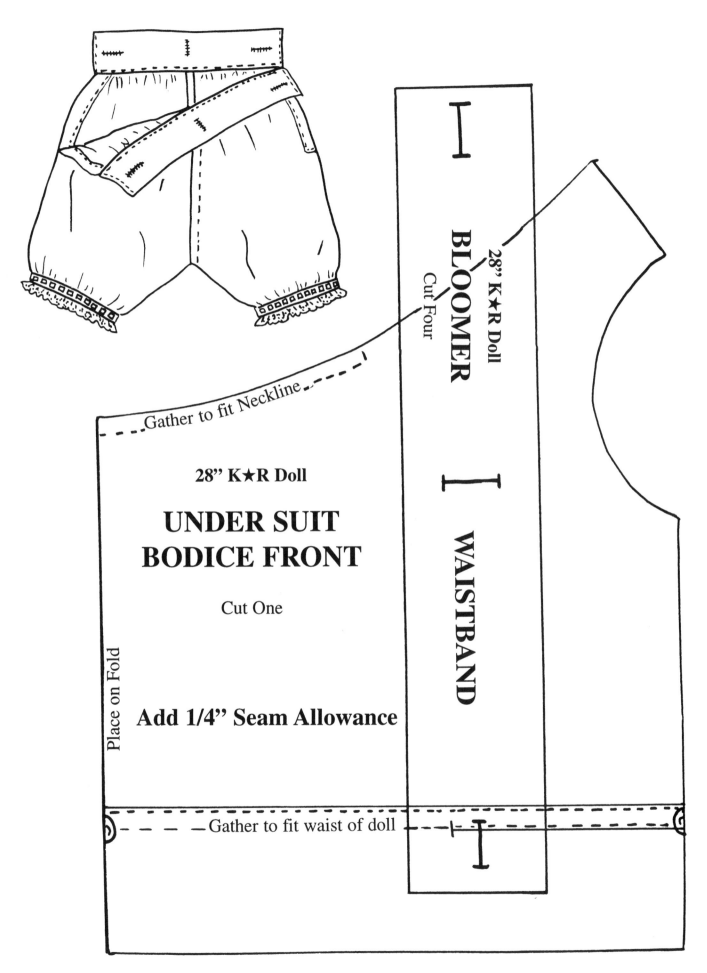

28" K★R Doll

BLOOMER

Cut Four

WAISTBAND

Gather to fit Neckline

28" K★R Doll

UNDER SUIT
BODICE FRONT

Cut One

Place on Fold

Add 1/4" Seam Allowance

Gather to fit waist of doll

Chapter 8

THE 1910S

In 1911, little boys dressed in blouse suits of Galatea, linen, rep, or chambray in light or dark blue, tan or brown tones, trimmed with braid, binding, contrasting stitching, or dickeys of striped material. Muslin, pongee, silk, and flannel were the vogue for night shirts.

In 1913, noting the latest trends, *Pictorial Review* Stated:

"It is not alone woman's outer garments that are affected by style changes, but her underclothing as well. For, whenever a radical change is made in dress, like the introduction of the present fashion in clinging garments, it becomes necessary that the underwear be made to conform with the new lines."

The article goes on to describe the latest in corset covers "designed to preserve the slender lines of the figure." Nainsook, long cloth, and crepe de Chine were popular fabrics for lingerie.

In 1914 this same magazine describes the latest in small boys' apparel as being of "deepest pink and rose tints from his tiny sister's rainbow of colors". Another innovation is the belt for his suits in the fabric of the suit rather than a leather belt as in former years. Older boys were dressing like father in mannish tweeds and polos.

Boys' clothes reflected the influences of war in the years 1917 through 1919; many soldier's uniforms for boys were shown. The military note was present in girls' clothes as well as in their mother's, although generally women's clothes were soft and feminine.

In 1919, little girls wore their hair in long curls with large hairbows perched at the crown. Sweaters were long; dresses slightly high-waisted, belted, made of cotton serge, chambray, closely woven cotton Galatea cloth, poplin, plaid ginghams, and lawn. Silk chiffon was for party dresses. Children wore three-piece knit suits for outdoor play consisting of a long sweater, below the hips, leggings, and hat.

Rompers, creepers, and bloomers were of flannelette, cotton knit, and duckling-fleeced cotton, seersucker, chambray, and percale. Underwear was muslin, nainsook, cotton cambric, flannel, or knit flannelette, and undershirts had diaper tabs. Dresses for toddlers were "walking length" with machine embroidery, gathered from the neck, front, and back.

Coats were of cream color cotton bedford cord, cream white belted chinchilla cloth, white on Liberty Blue velour-finished corduroy, double breasted, black or burgundy velour, walking length, belted with false flap pockets. A cream white cashmere long cloak for Baby had a yoke cape in silk embroidery, with matching embroidery on the cloak skirt.

Baby dresses were predominantly of nainsook and lawn. Fresh air was highly thought of and a must was an outdoor sleeping bag of heavy blanket fleece. Undershirts were "vests". Boys and little fellows wore corduroy suits, belted long jackets and caps to match, long stockings, and high-lace shoes. Small boys were resplendent in Buster Brown suits and Lord Fauntleroy suits of dark blue velveteen.

The Little Boy's Blouse Suit

The Ladies' Home Journal for March 1, 1911   Designs by Selina Yorke

1913

5297   5331   5320

5331

5320

5261   4980

5315   5261   4980   4152

5317

4499

5315   4499   4152   5297   5317

49

Paris says—

*Puffs, frills, pantalettes, laced sleeves,
Sleeveless bodices and high, high collars*

PLAITED tulle opens fan-like above a white satin choker. Colored velvet ribbon spans the back, held in front with tiny flowers.

Drawings by
EDWARD POUCHER

JUST enough of 1860 and 1915 mingled! A dress from Martial et Armand shows a tight-fitting bodice and a bouffant skirt. Like most evening dresses, front and back are flat, the sides distended.

"BUSTLES now!" says Premet. Sometimes he compromises on a huge wired sash bow, one loop black, one red, the ends reversed for oddity.

CAN this narrow velvet ribbon be a belt? Jenny says so, and lets the ends fly loosely under the upstanding loops.

FUR from top to toe—and out to finger tips! Black kid and white fur deck these gloves.

UNDENIABLY they are pantalettes, Paris-sponsored, dark for daytime, with fur and lace for dancing.

MME. ROBERTS lights up a somber waist with brocaded silk, and uses jet buttons for a note of contrast. The inside of the collar, revers and chemisette are starched white organdie, and a cord marks the waist line.

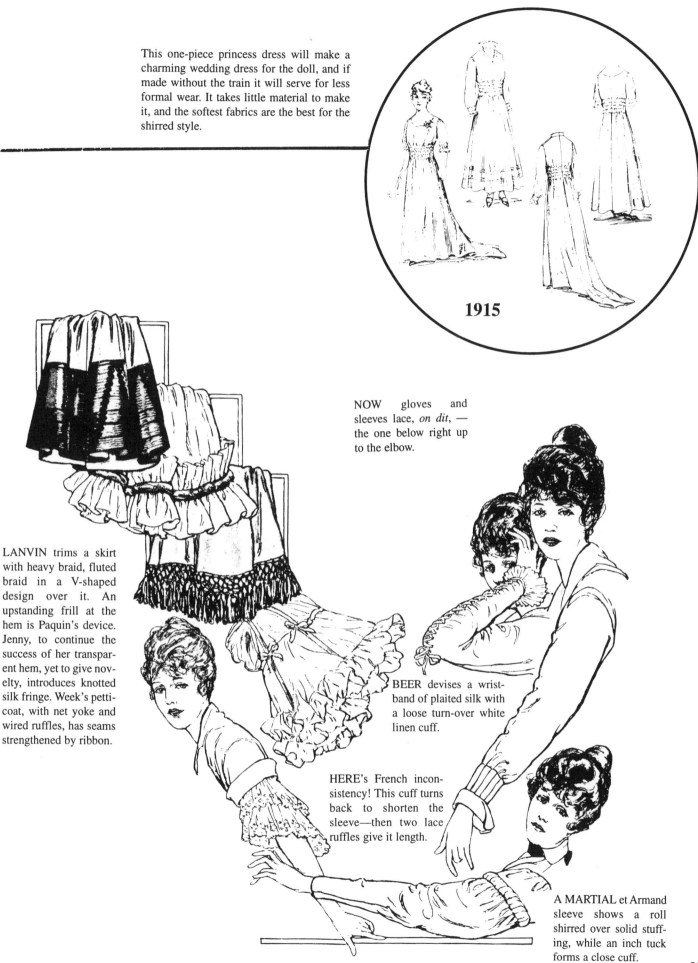

This one-piece princess dress will make a charming wedding dress for the doll, and if made without the train it will serve for less formal wear. It takes little material to make it, and the softest fabrics are the best for the shirred style.

1915

NOW gloves and sleeves lace, *on dit*, — the one below right up to the elbow.

LANVIN trims a skirt with heavy braid, fluted braid in a V-shaped design over it. An upstanding frill at the hem is Paquin's device. Jenny, to continue the success of her transparent hem, yet to give novelty, introduces knotted silk fringe. Week's petticoat, with net yoke and wired ruffles, has seams strengthened by ribbon.

BEER devises a wristband of plaited silk with a loose turn-over white linen cuff.

HERE's French inconsistency! This cuff turns back to shorten the sleeve—then two lace ruffles give it length.

A MARTIAL et Armand sleeve shows a roll shirred over solid stuffing, while an inch tuck forms a close cuff.

51

Reefer 9735

Dress 9180

Suit 9525

Jumper 9733

Suit 9588

1918

CLOTHES OF TO-DAY FOR MEN OF TO-MORROW

MAN's work is never done — and for the saving of clothes, which is no small matter these days, there is a comfortable jumper (design 9733) that can be slipped right on over the suit. It is a splendid protection to a man's clothes. It is very simple in construction and inexpensive to make. The pockets are very convenient. Use denim, duck, khaki or flannel.

A 36 breast measure requires 3-7/8 yards denim 27 inches wide.

Design 9733, 10 sizes, 30 to 48 inches breast measure.

Suit 9383

Suit 8930

Dress
1188

Suit 9588

Suit 1429

Suit 9998

Military Suit
1403

FEBRUARY, 1919

53

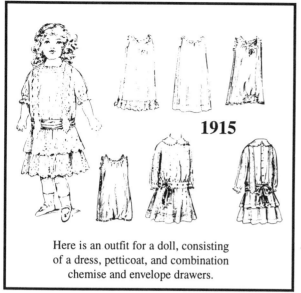

Here is an outfit for a doll, consisting of a dress, petticoat, and combination chemise and envelope drawers.

1915

1913

1913

WARDROBE FOR A 16"-18" DOLL OF ABOUT 1910

This doll had a trunk-full of beautiful clothes; so many in fact it was difficult to decide which garments to show in our limited space. At every opportunity I have drawn multi-purpose patterns to take full advantage of a page.

One of the most important articles of apparel in a doll's wardrobe was a raincape, judging from the fact that one appeared in nearly every large grouping of doll clothes examined by this writer. The pattern given may be varied with a fur collar and heavy lining for a winter cape.

A cream flannel petticoat was a must in the days of unreliable heating and long, cold winters. In addition there must be a fine tucked lawn petticoat, often edged with lace. Other petticoats were sometimes worn with dress-up clothes, or for added warmth.

This doll had a full array of hats and several are given here. She also had a muff and a neckpiece called a "tippet" which was worn over the coat collar. This was not only warm but also decorative. Remnants of fur "tails" hung from the end of this accessory. Any fur item may be duplicated with ease since the advent of the "fake furs" made of synthetic fibers.

Underwear included drawers with ruffles and bloomers. There was also a romper; however, these are all covered sufficiently elsewhere in the book.

Although the doll for which these clothes were made had a bisque head, the styles and size are correct for Schoenhut dolls.

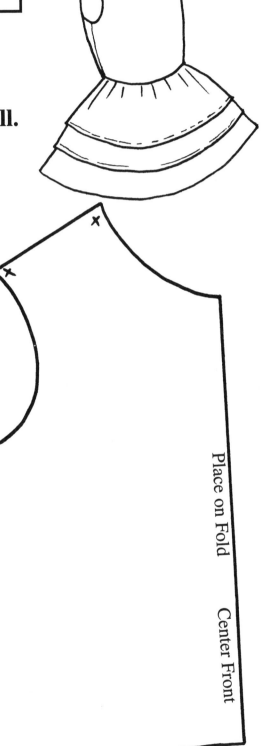

**16"-18" Bisque Head or
Schoenhut Doll**

PETTICOAT

Cut One of: 5" x 18" Flannel
5-1/2" x 26" Lawn

**Flannel petticoat has feather-stitch
trim; lawn one has tucks.**

**Add 1/4" seam allowance for 18" doll.
Seams allowed for 16" doll.**

**16"-18" Bisque Head or
Schoenhut Doll**

TOP

Place on Fold

Center Front

Attach Petticoat

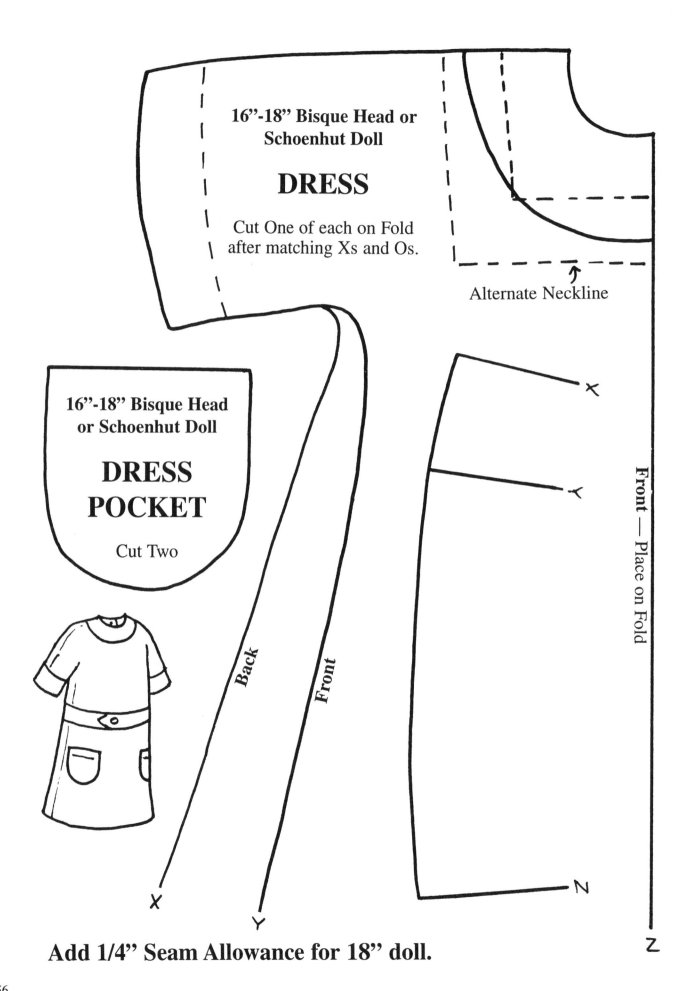

16"-18" Bisque Head or Schoenhut Doll

DRESS

Cut One of each on Fold after matching Xs and Os.

Alternate Neckline

16"-18" Bisque Head or Schoenhut Doll

DRESS POCKET

Cut Two

Back

Front

Front — Place on Fold

X

Y

N

Z

Add 1/4" Seam Allowance for 18" doll.

16"-18" Bisque Head or Schoenhut Doll

COAT

BACK
Cut One on Fold from Coat and Lining fabric

FRONT
Cut Two each from Coat and Lining fabric

Back

Front

Place on Fold

Front Facing Pattern Line ↳

Back — Place on Fold

COAT COLLAR
Cut One and Lining On Fold

COAT CAPE
Cut One and Lining On Fold

Add 1/4" Seam Allowance for 18" doll.

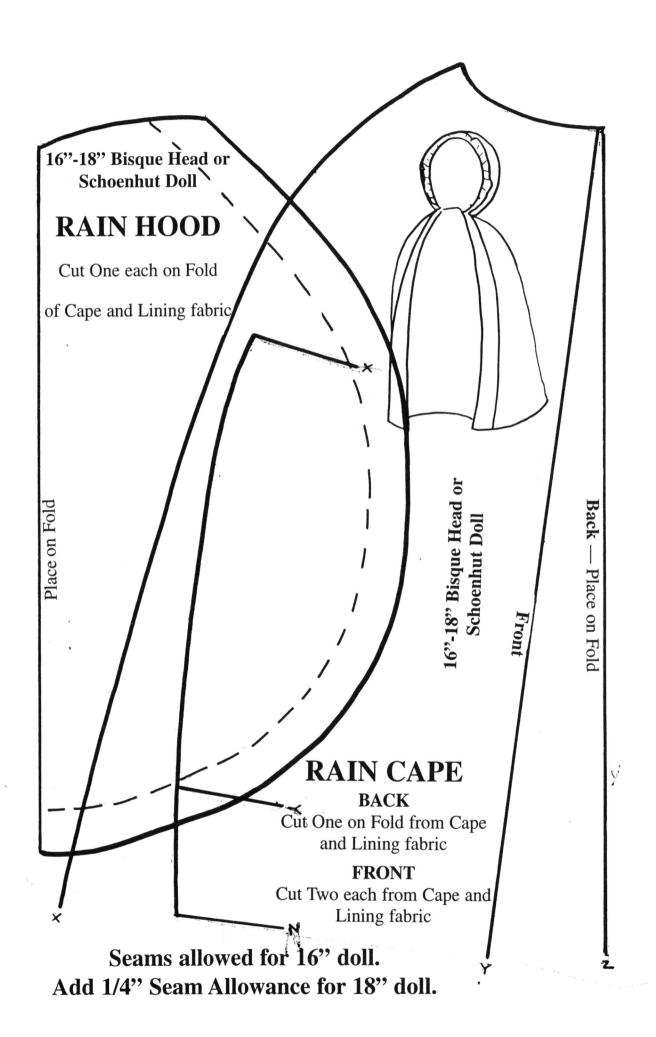

16"-18" Bisque Head or Schoenhut Doll

RAIN HOOD

Cut One each on Fold

of Cape and Lining fabric

Place on Fold

16"-18" Bisque Head or Schoenhut Doll

Front

Back — Place on Fold

RAIN CAPE

BACK

Cut One on Fold from Cape
and Lining fabric

FRONT

Cut Two each from Cape and
Lining fabric

Seams allowed for 16" doll.
Add 1/4" Seam Allowance for 18" doll.

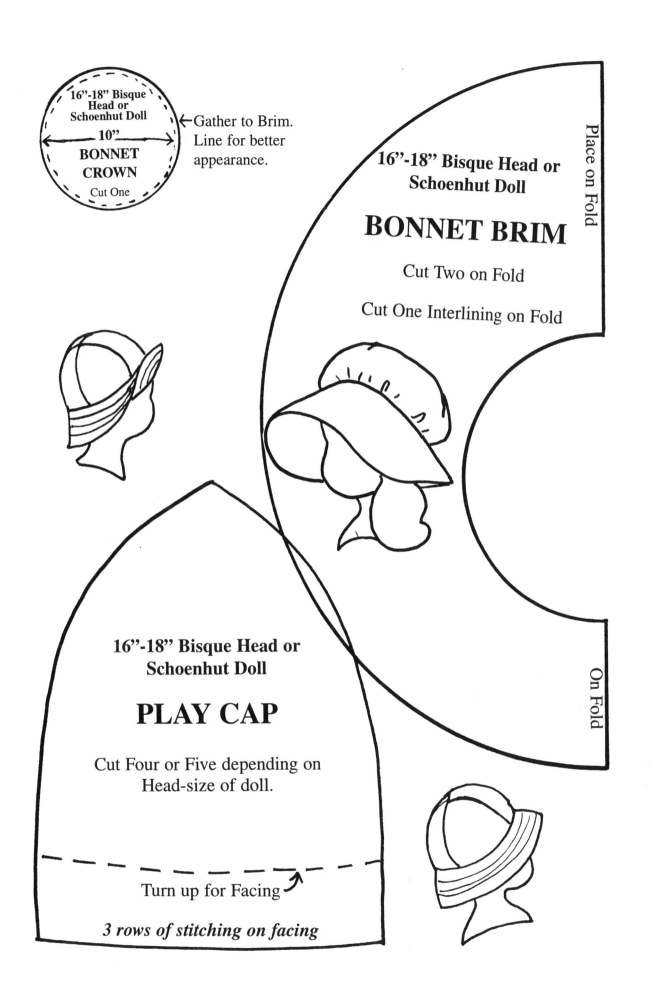

16"-18" Bisque
Head or
Schoenhut Doll

10"

BONNET
CROWN

Cut One

←Gather to Brim.
Line for better
appearance.

16"-18" Bisque Head or
Schoenhut Doll

BONNET BRIM

Cut Two on Fold

Cut One Interlining on Fold

Place on Fold

On Fold

16"-18" Bisque Head or
Schoenhut Doll

PLAY CAP

Cut Four or Five depending on
Head-size of doll.

Turn up for Facing

3 rows of stitching on facing

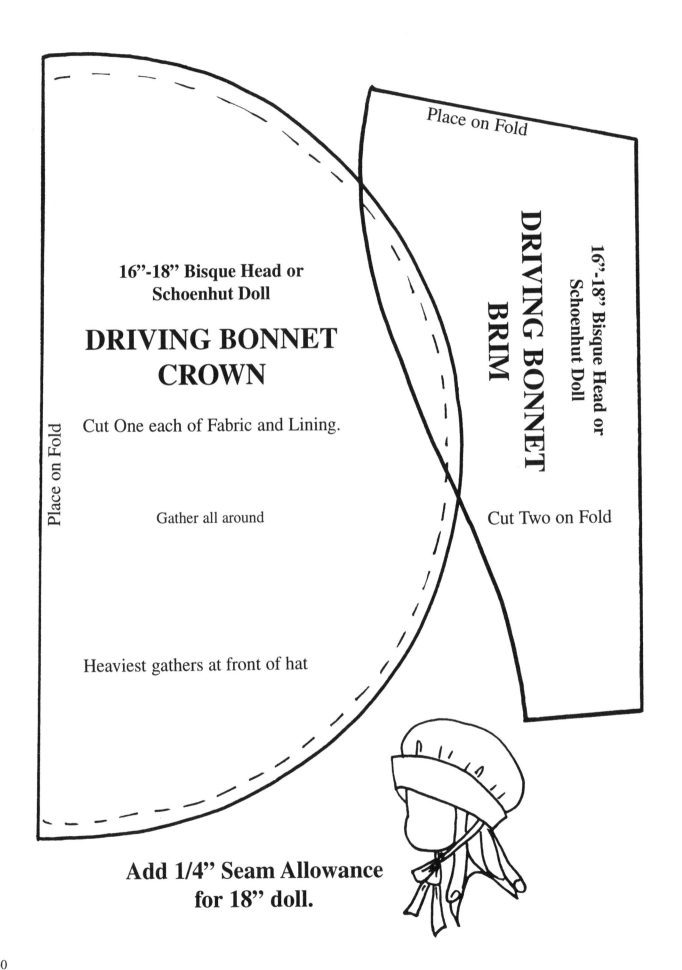

Place on Fold

16"-18" Bisque Head or
Schoenhut Doll

DRIVING BONNET
CROWN

Cut One each of Fabric and Lining.

Gather all around

Heaviest gathers at front of hat

Place on Fold

**DRIVING BONNET
BRIM**

16"-18" Bisque Head or
Schoenhut Doll

Cut Two on Fold

**Add 1/4" Seam Allowance
for 18" doll.**

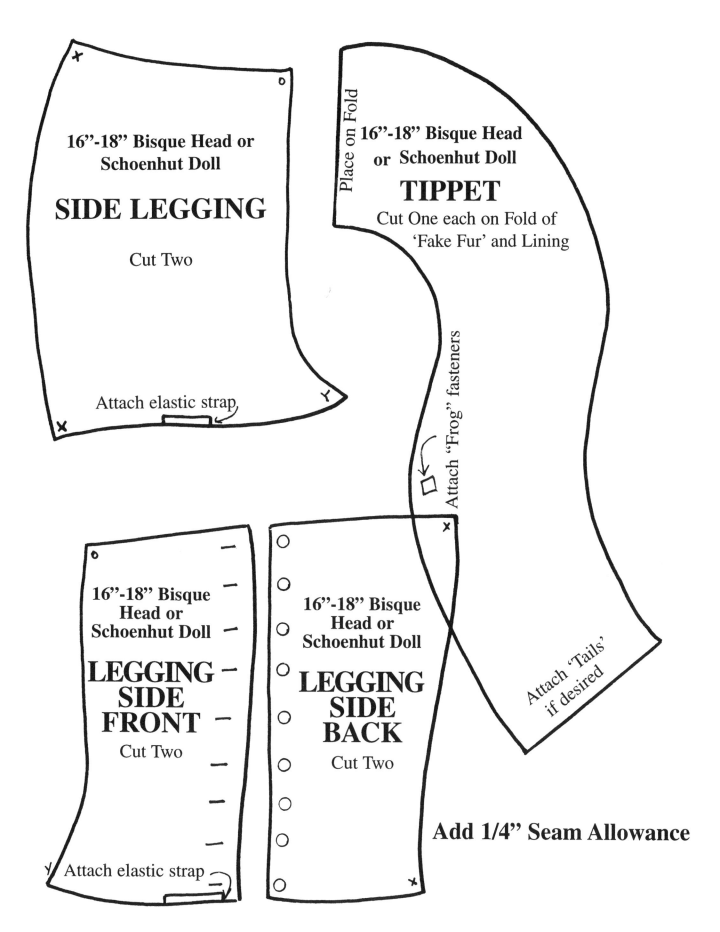

16"-18" Bisque Head or Schoenhut Doll

SIDE LEGGING

Cut Two

Attach elastic strap

Place on Fold

16"-18" Bisque Head or Schoenhut Doll

TIPPET

Cut One each on Fold of 'Fake Fur' and Lining

Attach "Frog" fasteners

16"-18" Bisque Head or Schoenhut Doll

LEGGING SIDE FRONT

Cut Two

Attach elastic strap

16"-18" Bisque Head or Schoenhut Doll

LEGGING SIDE BACK

Cut Two

Attach 'Tails' if desired

Add 1/4" Seam Allowance

Tuck and add lace
Front of Shirt

11" Billy Boy

White Lacey
SHIRT

Cut Two Front
Cut One Back

NOTE: Original Clothes:
★Shirt is sleeveless, white cuff
is attached to jacket sleeve.

Front

Back — Place on Fold

Add 1/4" Seam Allowance

Place on Fold

11" Billy Boy

JACKET
BACK

Cut One of Black Velvet

Cut Two of
Black Velvet

11" Billy Boy

JACKET
SLEEVE

★

Place on Fold

11" Billy Boy
SHIRT COLLAR
Cut One and edge with narrow lace

Place on Fold

Back

Front
11" Billy Boy

TROUSERS

FRONT & BACK
Cut One each of
Black Velvet

For Billy's Velvet Beret,
Cut 6-1/2" dia. circle of
velvet, run gather thread
around, gather to fit head,
finish with 3/8" band.

Place on Fold

For tie use
bit of black
ribbon.

Cut Two of Black Velvet

11" Billy Boy

JACKET
FRONT

11" BILLY BOY
BY GEM

62

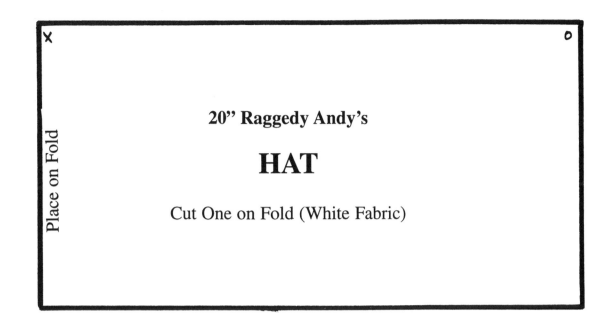

20" Raggedy Andy's

HAT

Cut One on Fold (White Fabric)

Place on Fold

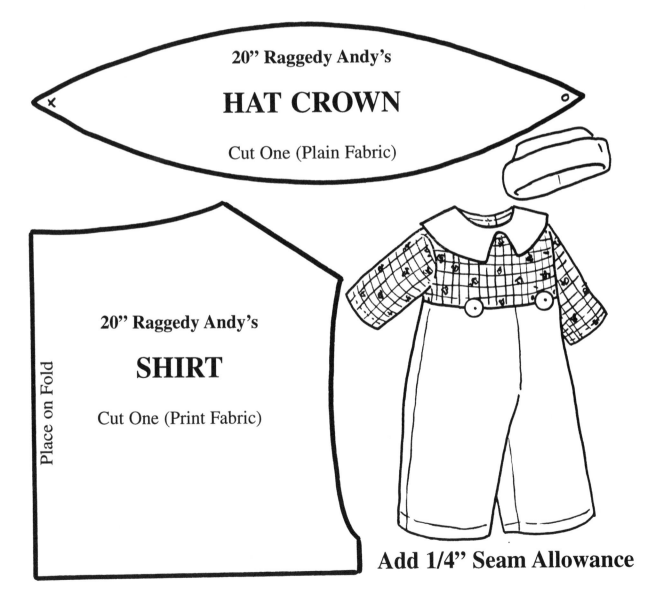

20" Raggedy Andy's

HAT CROWN

Cut One (Plain Fabric)

20" Raggedy Andy's

SHIRT

Cut One (Print Fabric)

Place on Fold

Add 1/4" Seam Allowance

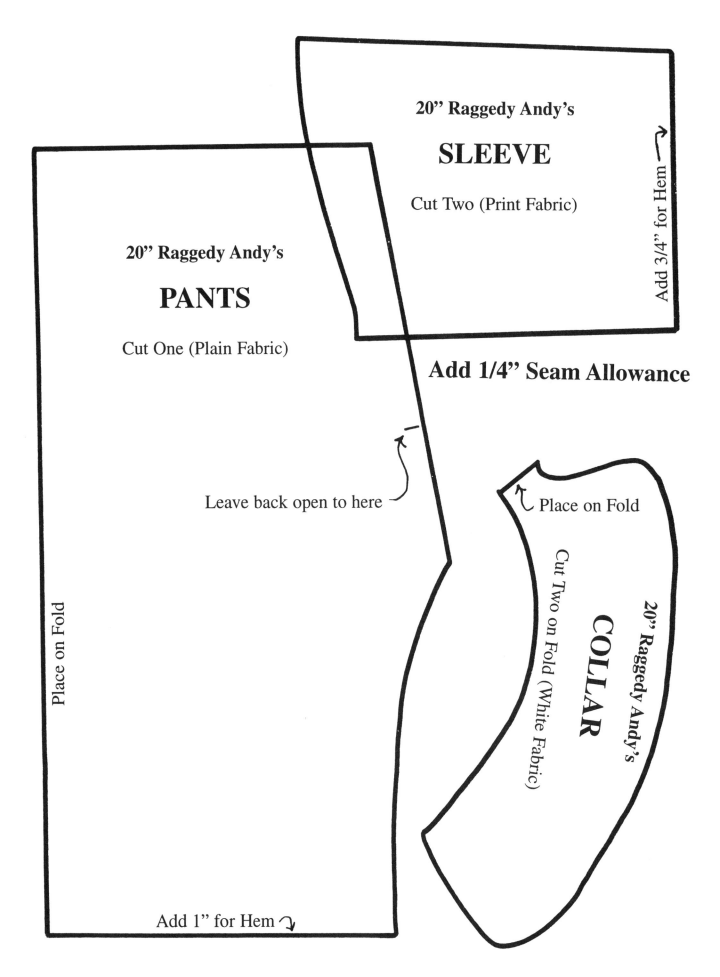

20" Raggedy Andy's

SLEEVE

Cut Two (Print Fabric)

Add 3/4" for Hem

20" Raggedy Andy's

PANTS

Cut One (Plain Fabric)

Add 1/4" Seam Allowance

Leave back open to here

Place on Fold

Place on Fold

Cut Two on Fold (White Fabric)

20" Raggedy Andy's

COLLAR

Add 1" for Hem

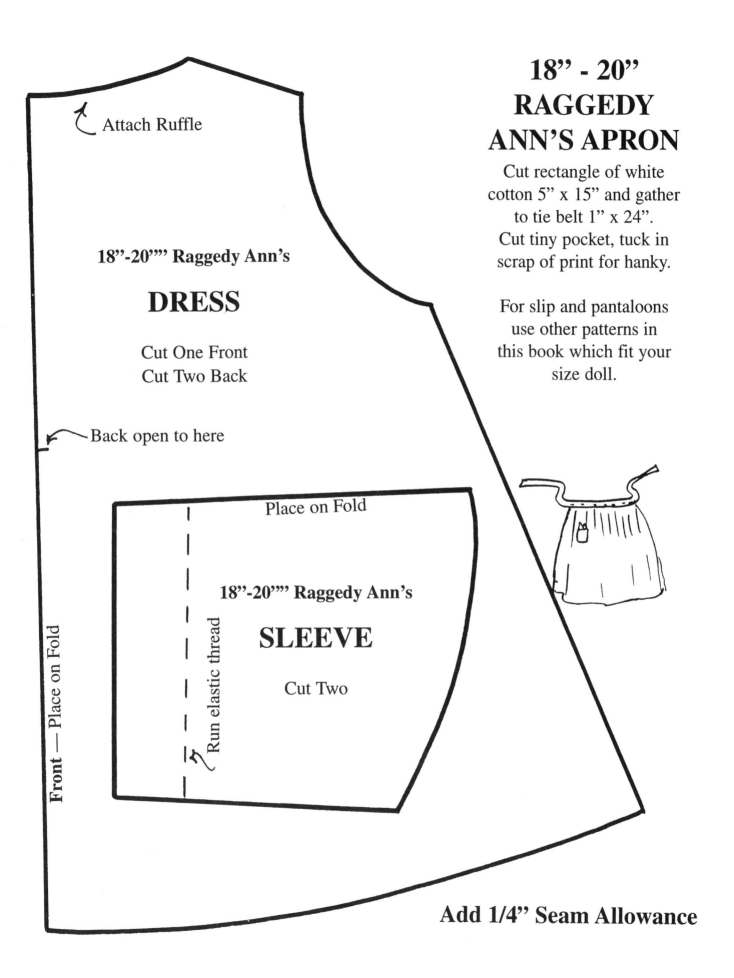

Attach Ruffle

18"-20"" Raggedy Ann's

DRESS

Cut One Front
Cut Two Back

Back open to here

Front — Place on Fold

Place on Fold

Run elastic thread

18"-20"" Raggedy Ann's

SLEEVE

Cut Two

18" - 20"
RAGGEDY
ANN'S APRON

Cut rectangle of white
cotton 5" x 15" and gather
to tie belt 1" x 24".
Cut tiny pocket, tuck in
scrap of print for hanky.

For slip and pantaloons
use other patterns in
this book which fit your
size doll.

Add 1/4" Seam Allowance

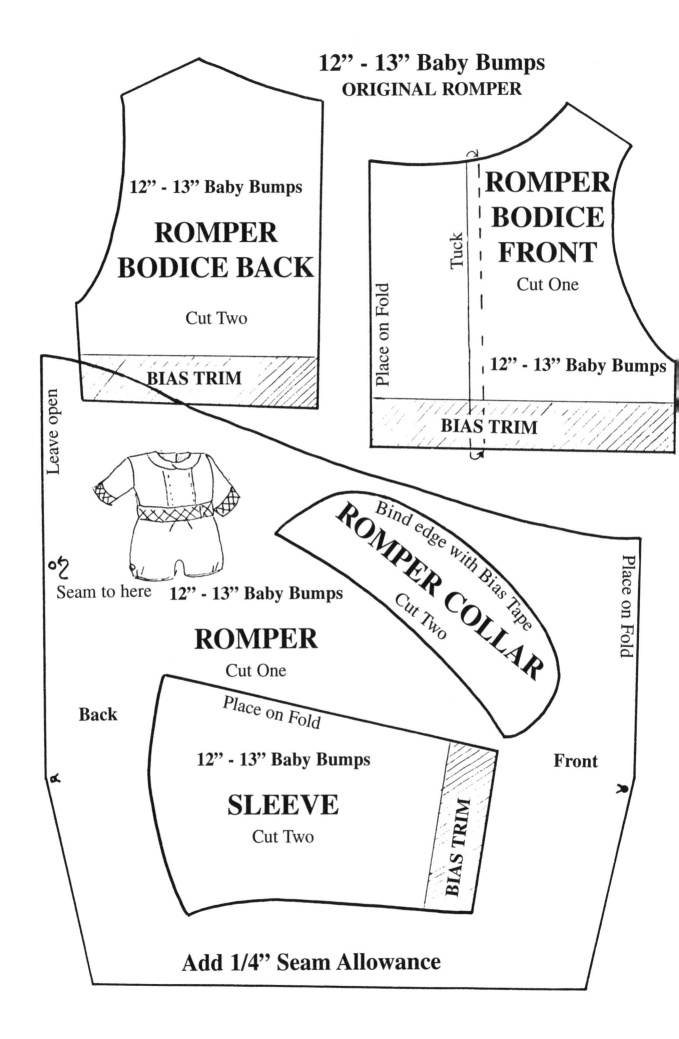

12" - 13" Baby Bumps
ORIGINAL ROMPER

12" - 13" Baby Bumps

ROMPER BODICE BACK

Cut Two

BIAS TRIM

ROMPER BODICE FRONT

Cut One

Place on Fold

Tuck

12" - 13" Baby Bumps

BIAS TRIM

Leave open

Seam to here

12" - 13" Baby Bumps

ROMPER

Cut One

Bind edge with Bias Tape

ROMPER COLLAR

Cut Two

Place on Fold

Back

Place on Fold

Front

12" - 13" Baby Bumps

SLEEVE

Cut Two

BIAS TRIM

Add 1/4" Seam Allowance

THE SCHOENHUT DOLLS

Here is a virtual panorama of original clothes for Schoenhut boy and girl dolls. The patterns I have drafted are all-purpose ones which may be used selectively to create many different dresses and suits. Each pattern piece is numbered, the costumes are numbered, and a list of required pattern pieces for each outfit is given along with a description of original fabrics and colors. The doll figures are taken from an old Schoenhut catalog. Patterns are drafted for a 16-17" doll, by adding seam allowances. They will fit a 14" doll as drawn.

Baby dresses and rompers are covered adequately elsewhere in this book, as are drawers, petticoats, stockings, shoes, and other wardrobe items. A Pattern is given for the Schoenhut underwear since it is almost a trade-mark of these dolls. Made of fine knit, the girls' undersuit is lace-edged with a lace inset at front; the boys' undersuit is plain. Both have three buttons in back.

Space has not been used to give patterns for skirts of dresses when a pattern is merely a rectangle of proper size, such as in dress numbers 561 and 562. Some of these skirts are gathered to the bodice or to a belt, and some are pinch-pleated while others are box-pleated.

Note different belt treatments: number 569 is a separate belt with rounded ends; 570 is a ribbon tie; 530 is narrow, loose, and buttoned; 561,562,563 and others have sewn-in belts, topstitched; and 569 has a loose belt with buttonholes on both ends which is buttoned first to dress, then the dress is buttoned, and finally the right end of the belt goes over the same button.

None of the views shows sailor bellbottom trousers, but many collectors like to dress their Schoenhut boys in this style and I have given the pattern along with three other trouser effects.

---

560 — Pink or blue chambray, white linene trim. Collar 2, dress pattern page 56, sleeve 1, belt 2 or 5, cuff 1.

561 — Pink or blue percale, colored chambray trim. Collar 3, bodice 3, 2, sleeve 1, cuff 1, belt 1.

562 — Pink or blue chambray, white linene trim, snap buttons. Collar 1, bodice 4,6, sleeve 1, belt 4, cuff 1.

563 — Pink and blue gingham, embroidery and fancy braid trim. Collar 5, bodice 8,7, sleeve 1, belt 1, dickey 1.

564 — Fancy striped, or blue plaid gingham, colored piping, white tucked guimpe. Blouse (guimpe) bodice 4, 6, sleeve 1, dress 1, belt 2.

565 — Pink and blue gingham, pink or blue chambray trim. Collar 3, bodice 1,2, belt 6, cuff 1.

566 — Pink or blue chambray, braid and button trim, fancy white waist. Blouse, bodice 11, 12, collar 2, vest, bodice 9, 7.

567 — Pink plaid or pink striped zephyr gingham, plain pink or white lawn trim. Dress, page 56, collar 3, overdress, bodice 7,8, belt 1.

568 — Pink or fancy striped zephyr gingham, braid and embroidery trim. Dress, page 56, collar 4, vest, bodice 11, 12.

569 — Pink and blue striped zephyr gingham, braid trim, fancy guimpe. Dress, page 56, collar 4, overdress bodice 10, 13, belt 1.

570 — Blue and pink or yellow and pink flowered lawn, lace trim and fancy guimpe. Bodice 8, 13, blouse, bodice 5, 7, collar 4.

530 — White and blue linene, blue trim, red stars and tie. Dress, page 56, with front neck opening 9, collar 5, belt 4, sleeve 1.

580 — White, embroidery insertion, lace and ribbon trim. Bodice 1,2, sleeve 2 with lace ruffle.

532 — White, embroidery insertion, tucking, beading, ribbon trim. Adapt dress, page 42.

581 — Fancy white dress, skirt, yoke of embroidery, lace, ribbon trim. Bodice 4, 6, sleeve 2 with ruffle.

582 — Fancy white dress, skirt and waist of embroidery, embroidery and ribbon trim. Dress, page 56, collar 4, sleeve 2.

583 — Fancy white dress, fine lawn, fine lace insertion, lace edge, ribbon trim. Bodice 1, 2, sleeve 2 with ruffle, lace ruffle over shoulders.

584 — Same as 583 with trim varied

820 — Assorted Oliver Twist suits of blue or brown pants with blue and white or plain white waists. Bodice 11, 12, collar 1, sleeve 1, trousers 1.

821 — Same description as 820. Same as 820 except collar 2, trousers 2.

819 — Assorted Buster Brown Suits of blue and white or red and white striped seersucker, white trim and tie. Jacket 1, 2, sleeve 1, collar 1, trouser 3, elastic at hem.

812 — Assorted Russian Suits of white linene with pink or blue collars, shield, belt, and tie. Jacket 3, 2, sleeve 1, belt 4, dickey 1, collar 6.

813 — Assorted Russian Suits of blue and white stripe Galetea, white shield and tie. Same as 812

818 — Fancy Suit of white linen pants, white shirt, red cloth coat, silk tie. Jacket 4, 2, collar 7, sleeve 1, trousers 3.

560   561   562   563

564   565   566   567

569   568   570   530

580   532   581   582

583   584   820   821

819   812   813   818

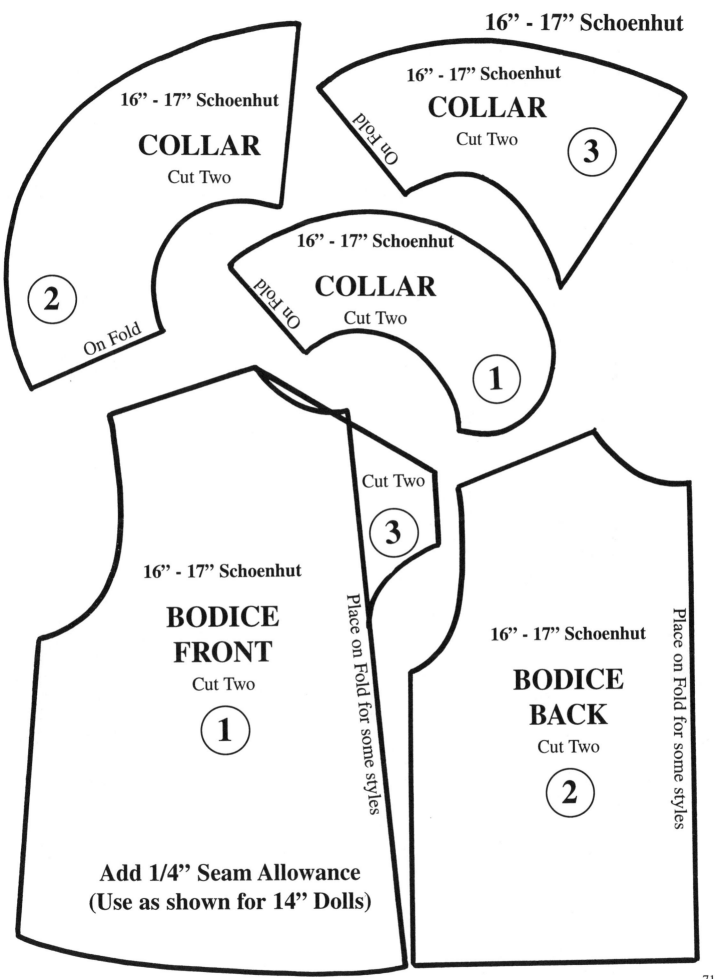

16" - 17" Schoenhut

COLLAR
Cut Two

②

On Fold

16" - 17" Schoenhut

16" - 17" Schoenhut

COLLAR
Cut Two

③

On Fold

16" - 17" Schoenhut

COLLAR
Cut Two

①

Cut Two

③

16" - 17" Schoenhut

BODICE
FRONT

Cut Two

①

Place on Fold for some styles

16" - 17" Schoenhut

BODICE
BACK

Cut Two

②

Place on Fold for some styles

Add 1/4" Seam Allowance
(Use as shown for 14" Dolls)

71

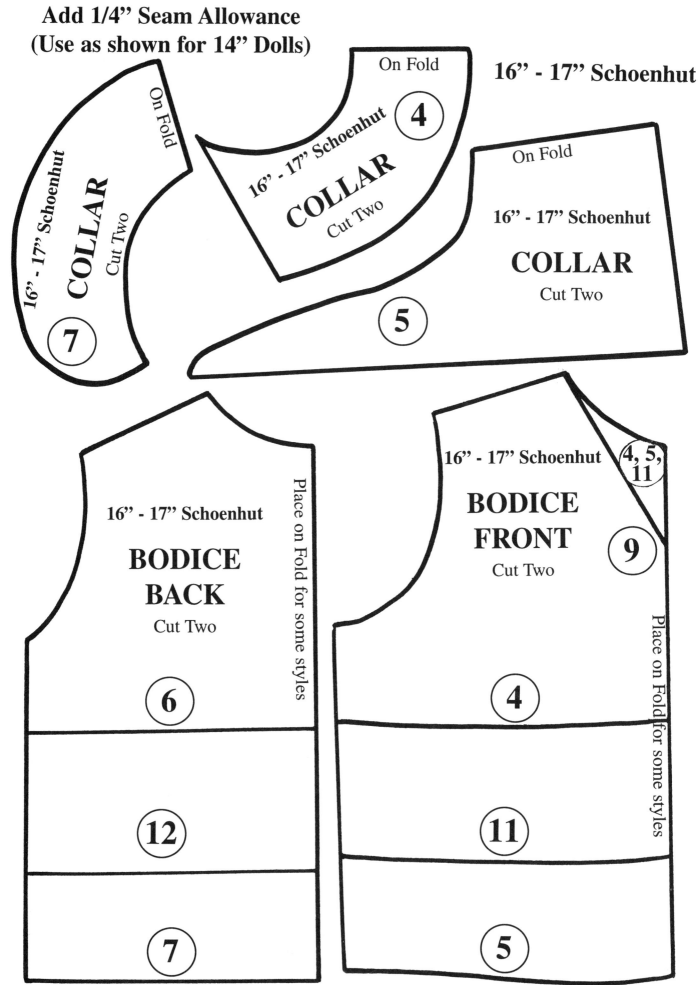

Add 1/4" Seam Allowance
(Use as shown for 14" Dolls)

On Fold

16" - 17" Schoenhut

16" - 17" Schoenhut
COLLAR
Cut Two
④

16" - 17" Schoenhut
COLLAR
Cut Two
⑦

On Fold

16" - 17" Schoenhut
COLLAR
Cut Two
⑤

On Fold

16" - 17" Schoenhut
BODICE
BACK
Cut Two
⑥

Place on Fold for some styles

⑫

⑦

16" - 17" Schoenhut
BODICE
FRONT
Cut Two
④

4, 5, 11,
⑨

Place on Fold for some styles

⑪

⑤

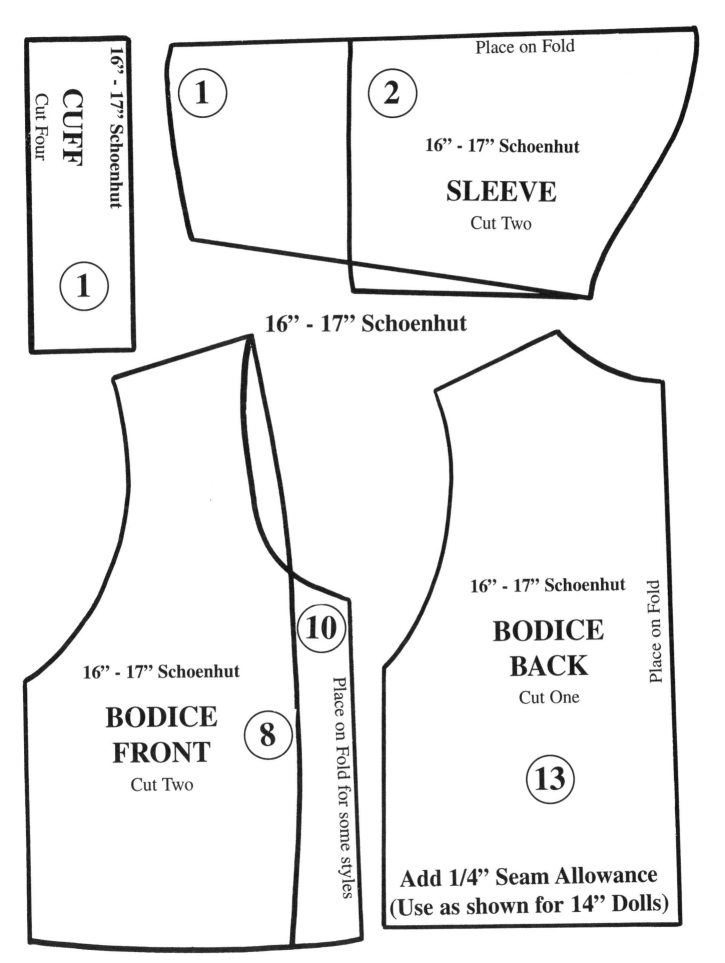

CUFF
Cut Four

16" - 17" Schoenhut

1

1

2

Place on Fold

16" - 17" Schoenhut

SLEEVE

Cut Two

16" - 17" Schoenhut

BODICE
FRONT

Cut Two

16" - 17" Schoenhut

10

8

Place on Fold for some styles

16" - 17" Schoenhut

BODICE
BACK

Cut One

Place on Fold

13

Add 1/4" Seam Allowance
(Use as shown for 14" Dolls)

73

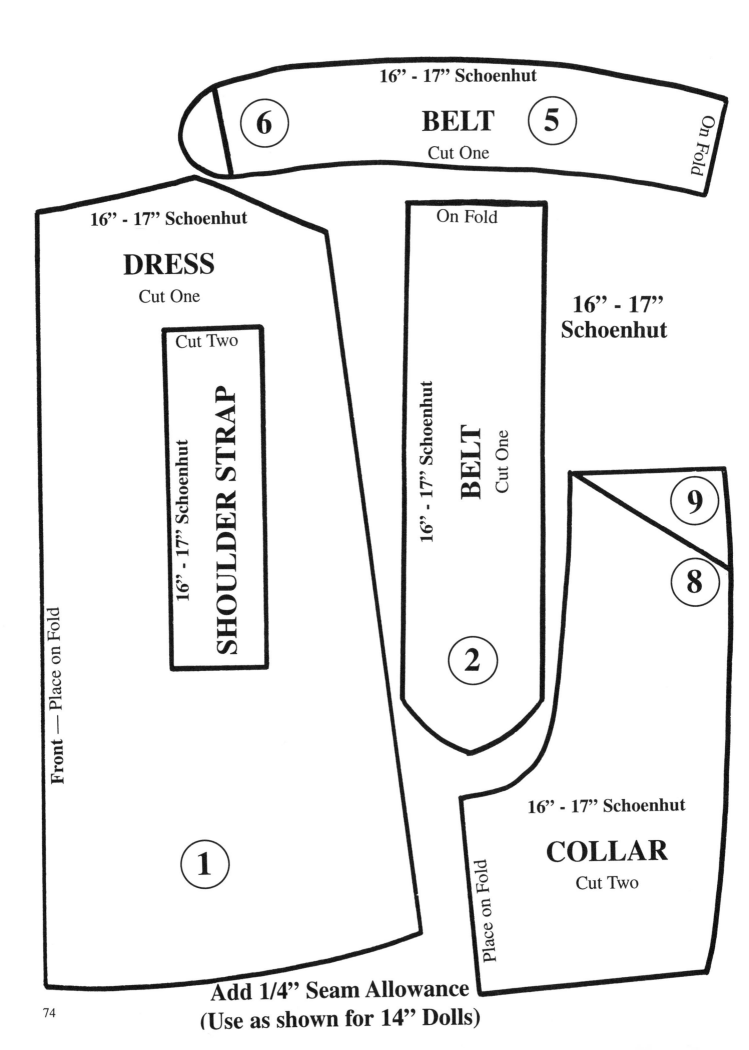

16" - 17" Schoenhut

BELT
Cut One

⑥ ⑤ On Fold

16" - 17" Schoenhut

DRESS
Cut One

On Fold

16" - 17"
Schoenhut

Cut Two

16" - 17" Schoenhut
SHOULDER STRAP

16" - 17" Schoenhut
BELT
Cut One

⑨

⑧

②

Front — Place on Fold

①

16" - 17" Schoenhut

COLLAR
Cut Two

Place on Fold

**Add 1/4" Seam Allowance
(Use as shown for 14" Dolls)**

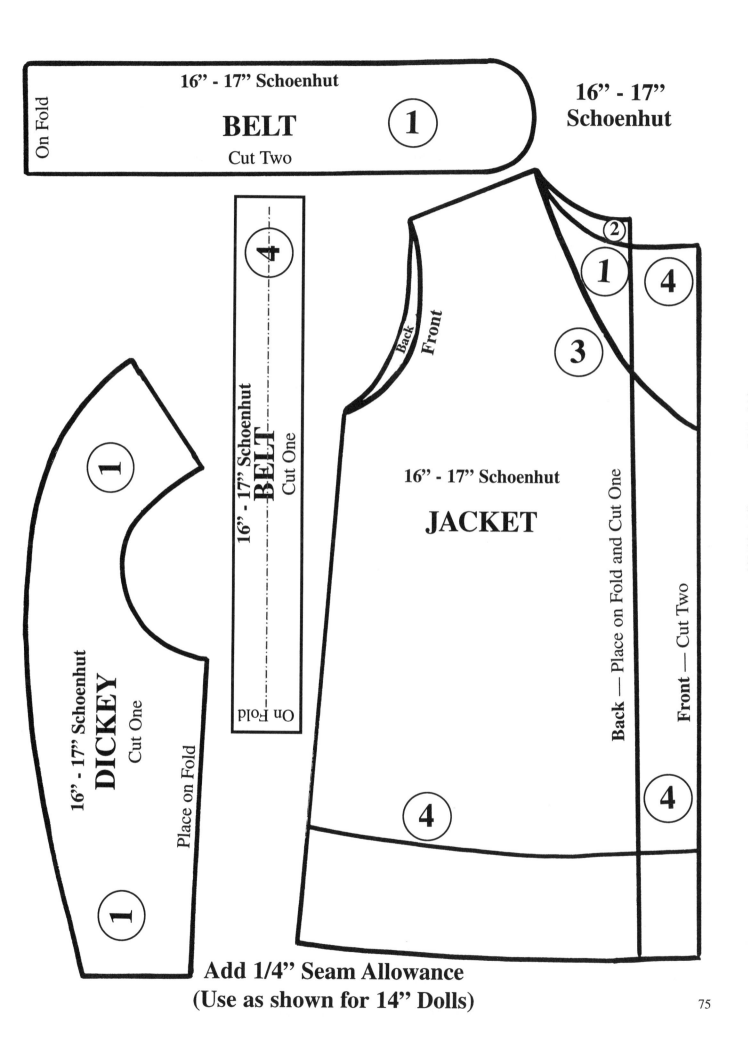

16" - 17" Schoenhut

BELT
Cut Two

① On Fold

16" - 17"
Schoenhut

④ 16" - 17" Schoenhut
BELT
Cut One
On Fold

16" - 17" Schoenhut
DICKEY
Cut One
Place on Fold

① ①

②
① ④
③

Back Front

16" - 17" Schoenhut

JACKET

Back — Place on Fold and Cut One

Front — Cut Two

④ ④

④

Add 1/4" Seam Allowance
(Use as shohwn for 14" Dolls)

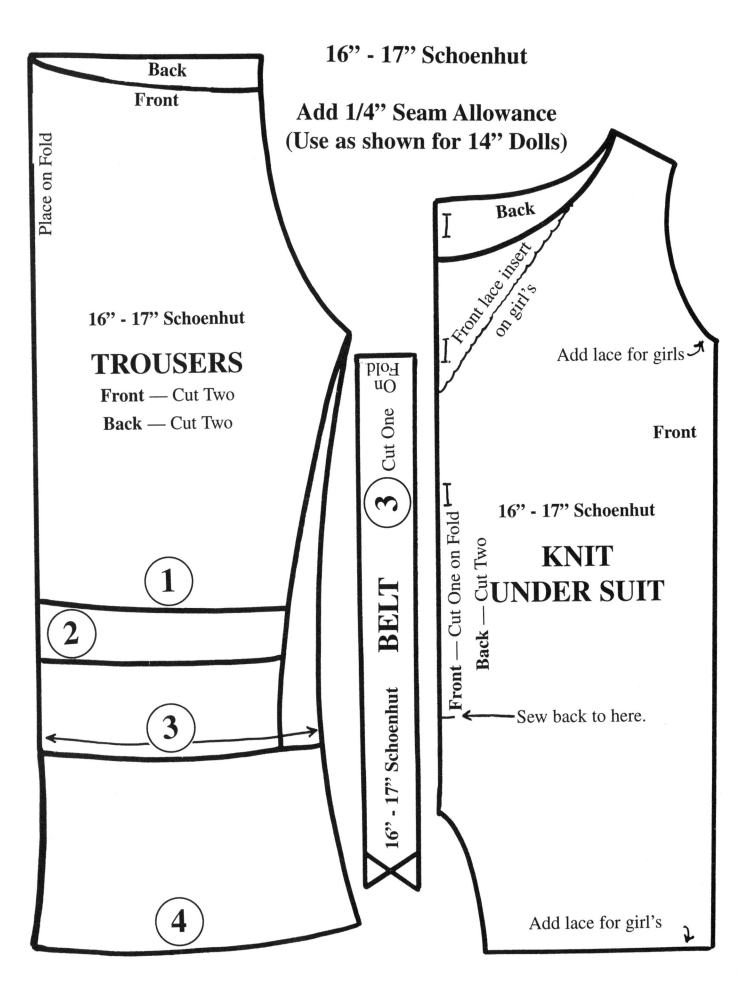

16" - 17" Schoenhut

Add 1/4" Seam Allowance
(Use as shown for 14" Dolls)

Back
Front

Place on Fold

16" - 17" Schoenhut

TROUSERS

Front — Cut Two
Back — Cut Two

① ② ③ ④

On Fold

③ Cut One

BELT

16" - 17" Schoenhut

Front — Cut One on Fold
Back — Cut Two

Back

Front lace insert on girl's

Add lace for girls

Front

16" - 17" Schoenhut

KNIT UNDER SUIT

← Sew back to here.

Add lace for girl's

Chapter 9

THE 1920S

Dolls reflect, more than ever, the styles of their human counterparts. One 20" doll wears a "mushroom style" straw hat with tailored white cotton linene suit in 1921. Some have lawn dresses with matching hats trimmed with roses and ribbons. Dolls were being made with deep shoulder plates by 1923 to allow for the low neckline styles.

Shorter skirts for children were shown in 1926 with toddlers wearing balloon-shaped romper suits with belts or half-belts. Three-piece knitted suits were for cool days. Women's dresses were also shorter and trousers were shown for women. Sailor suits and two-piece Norfolk suits were popular for little boys. Also shown for the small male were cowboy, baseball, Indian, and Forest Ranger suits.

Styles were becoming very straight and narrow with much simpler lines and more sports apparel by 1927. Home sewing is evidenced by the number of patterns being offered for children's and adult's clothing. 1929 brought the flapper styles and larger quantities of children's clothes than previous years.

Tams and cloches, straight-from-the-shoulder coats, both double-breasted and single-breasted, some with collar capes, were seen. Smock and sailor style dresses were shown for little girls. Small boys wore one-piece playsuits while small girls' play costumes were dresses with matching bloomers. Boys proudly wore aviator caps reminiscent of Charles Lindbergh's.

Clothing styles were breaking away from the inconvenience and discomfort of former decades and were moving towards more freedom, better fit, and greater comfort

2120
Emb
706

2118
Emb
718

These figures from *Needlecraft Magazine*, August, 1924, give clues to construction of the fashions of that day. The simple lines lent themselves admirably to simple construction. These dresses could be finished without a pattern by an experienced seamstress, using only the layouts given.

2079
Emb
706

Emb
705

2127

Emb
700
1814

Emb
710
2060

1795

2125
Emb
706

2067

2113
Emb. 708

2109

2109

2067

2113

2079

2060

2109

2113

2060

The Fashion Book

For Spring, illustrating Pictorial Review Fashions

THE PICTORIAL REVIEW COMPANY

Seventh Avenue and Thirty-ninth Street, New York

OFFICERS

William P. Ahnelt
President and Treasurer

Chas. W. Nelson
First Vice-President

Everett D. Trumbull
Second Vice-President

Jay A. Weber
Secretary

Paul Block
Advertising Director

Max Herzberg
Art Director

BRANCH OFFICES

Pacific Coast Branch—
985 Market Street,
San Francisco, Cal.

Southwestern Branch—
505 North Seventh Street,
St. Louis, Mo.

Southern Branch—
82-84 North Broad Street,
Atlanta, Ga.

New England Branch—
116 Bradford Street,
Boston, 11, Mass.

Western Branch—
200-206 South Market Street,
Chicago, Ill.

Canadian Factory and Sales Office—
263-267 Adelaide Street, West,
Toronto, Ontario.

European Factory and Sales Office—
163-165 Great Portland Street,
London, W 1.

HERALDS OF SPRING MODES

SPRING fashions lean towards picturesque expressions, and there are three important silhouettes that carry out these charming styles: the generally becoming straight, slender effect, for daytime wear: the draped silhouette, which clearly defines the figure and brings with it the longer skirt and a waist-line low enough to be smart for the individual figure and the material used: and, finally, there is the slender silhouette, that is broken by the introduction of godet plaits and swaying draperies. Circular effects are added to skirts in various widths, often starting from the knee-line; these godets and circular movements appear at the front of a costume, leaving the back flat. The tight-fitting basque shares honors with the bloused bodice. Often skirts are entirely plaited, or there are inserted or floating knife-plaited panels, and a too tight skirt may add panels of this kind to bring it up to date. The new shoulder yokes are smart, and collars, it is rumored, will be round and low. Ribbons finely plaited may be worked into conventional flower designs. Braided rolls, bias folds, or cordings are all attractive, used for neck, sleeves, and belt adornments. Sleeves are tight and long, flowing or short, according to what the type of gown demands. Materials are fascinating, and in silk, satin, crêpe, and silk-and-wool show Oriental designs, and in a number of instances blistered, crinkled, and ratiné surfaces. Double-bordered effects are lovely, and, with a good pattern, women may make stunning frocks from these effects by using the border at lower skirt for the bodice, and cut in half to deeply band the sleeves. Cotton fabrics are quite as smart for Summer costumes as many of the more expensive fabrics, and the new ginghams and voiles, in lovely colorings in the new, broken checks, dotted, and lace designs, make frocks of real distinction.

BUDDY LEE DOLLS

The H. D. Lee Company, Inc. originated Buddy Lee dolls in 1920-21 as an advertising piece. The doll was first shown in a Lee price list in 1922.

The first Buddy Lee dolls were dressed in Lee overalls and displayed in the window at Dayton Company Department Store on Nicollet Avenue, Minneapolis, Minnesota.

Engineer Doll — Dressed in bib overalls of blue denim with striped white denim jacket, shop cap and bandanna.

Cowboy Doll — Dressed in denim cowboy pants, plaid shirt, belt, bandanna, cowboy hat, and lariat.

Industrial Dolls — Dressed in many colors of shirts, pants, belts, caps, bow ties, or overhand ties, and Union-Alls™.

All-new material may be used for these clothes, or if preferred, worn denims and old, soft workshirts might be utilized. The shirt does not have to be plaid; in advertising photographs furnished this writer by the Company, Buddy Lee wears a shirt with a printed design (see *Twentieth Century Dolls*, p. 32, ADV-L2).

Striped pillow ticking is quite successful in creating the Engineer's outfit. A search of fabric departments will turn up many suitable fabrics for these clothes; however, the look of denim should be considered important in achieving an authentic appearance.

Hats for the Industrial Doll and the Cowboy Doll were buy-outs and there are, therefore, no patterns available for these. The band on the Cowboy hat reads; "Ride 'Em in Lee Rider Overalls" and on others: "Ride 'Em in Lee Copper-Riveted Riders' Overalls". Label on Engineers' hat reads "LEE/UNION MADE". Large circles on Industrial uniform are individual company patches; these were made for a wide variety of companies, including Coca Cola™.

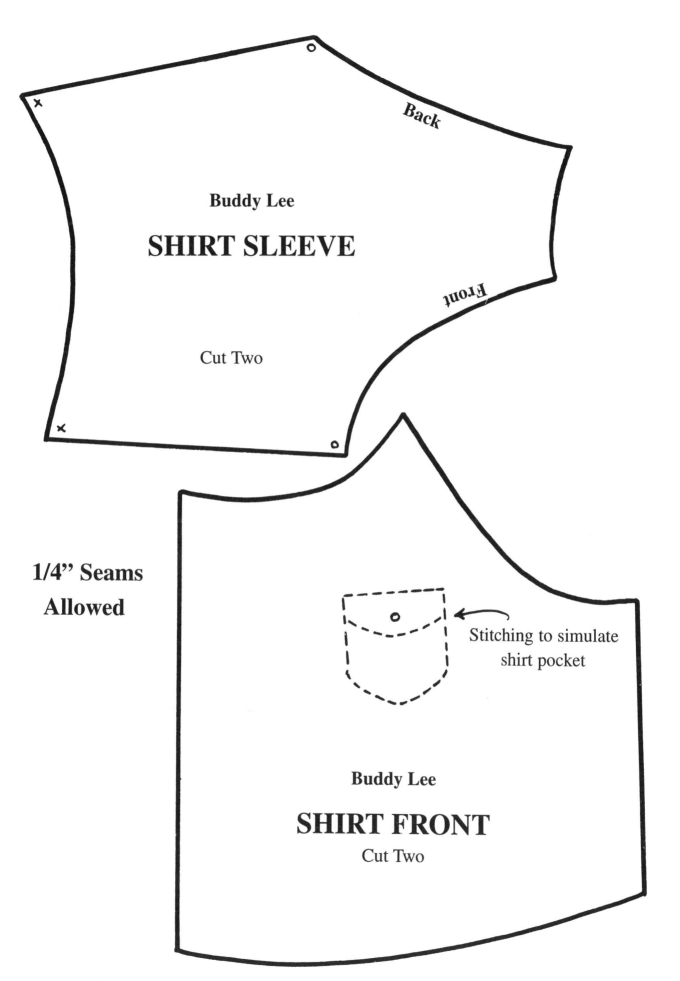

Buddy Lee

SHIRT SLEEVE

Cut Two

Back

Front

**1/4" Seams
Allowed**

Stitching to simulate
shirt pocket

Buddy Lee

SHIRT FRONT

Cut Two

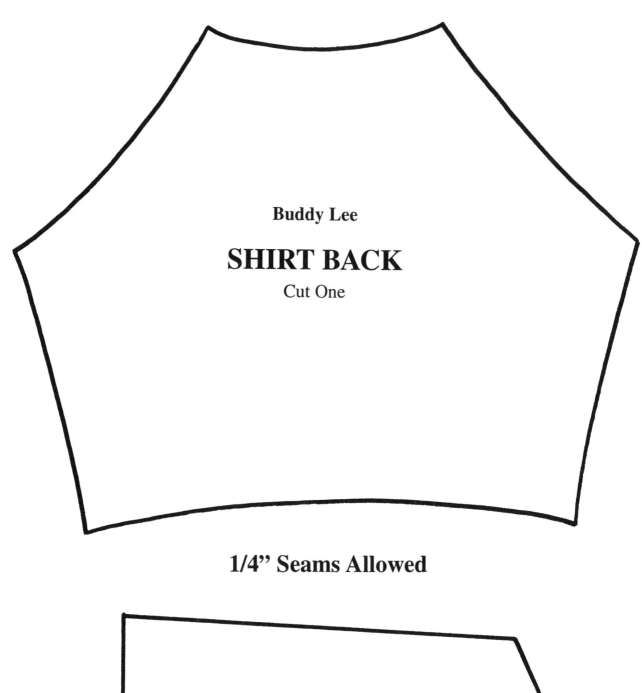

Buddy Lee

SHIRT BACK

Cut One

1/4" Seams Allowed

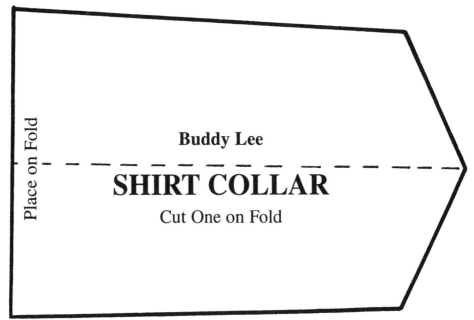

Place on Fold

Buddy Lee

SHIRT COLLAR

Cut One on Fold

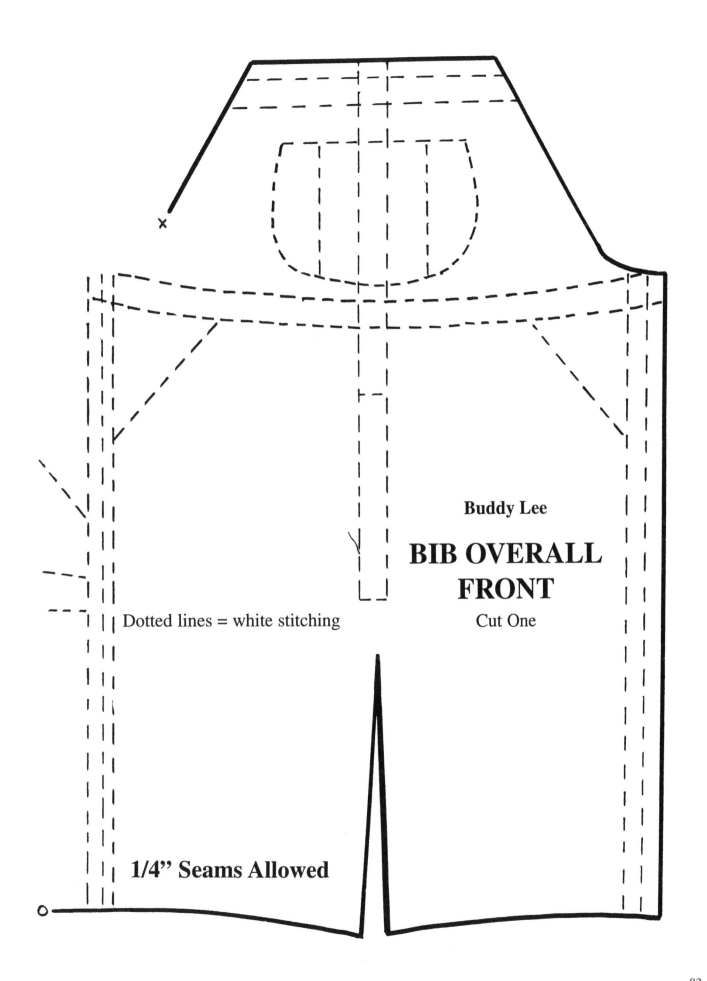

Buddy Lee

BIB OVERALL
FRONT

Cut One

Dotted lines = white stitching

1/4" Seams Allowed

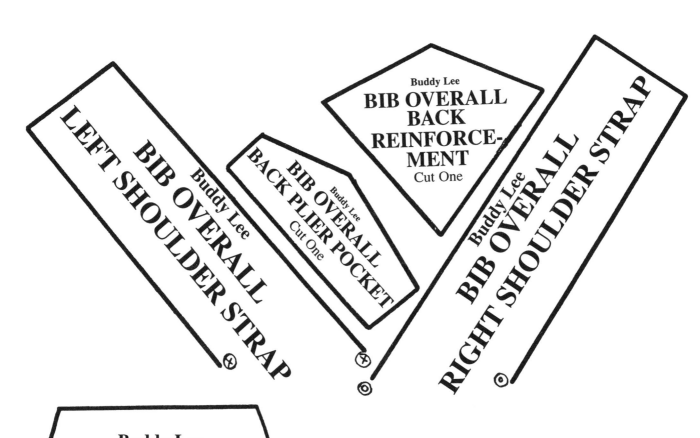

Buddy Lee

BIB OVERALL
FRONT POCKET

Cut One

1/4" Seams Allowed

1/4" Hem all edges

Buddy Lee

BANDANNA

Cut One

Place on Fold

Buddy Lee

BIB OVERALL
HIP POCKET

Cut Two

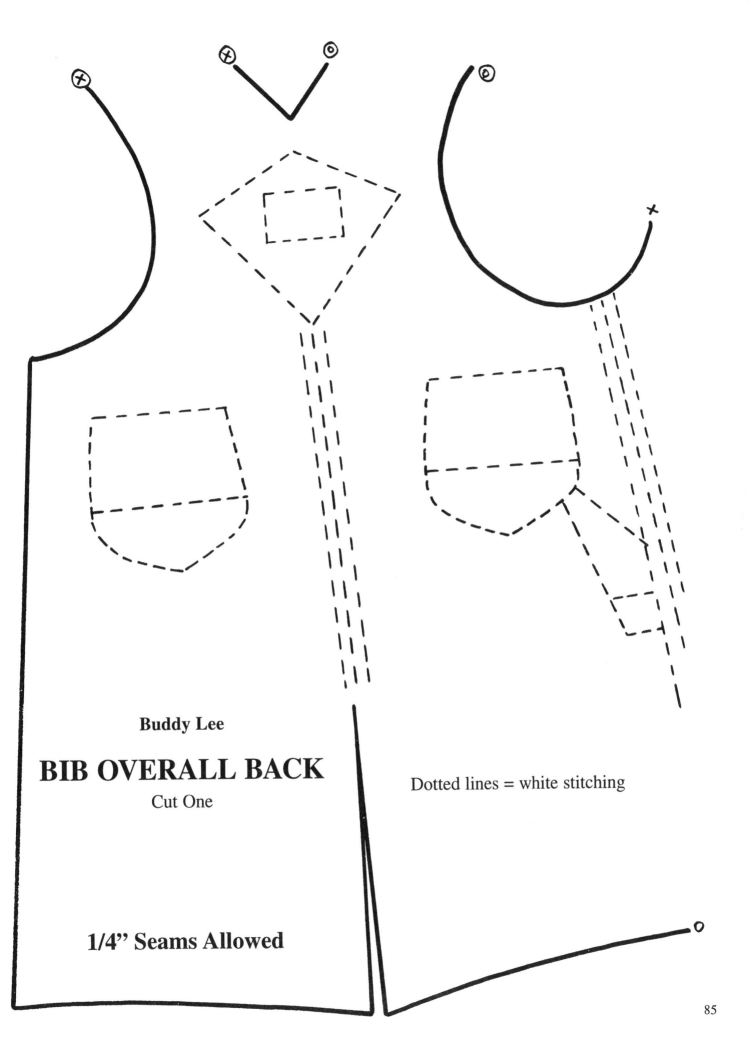

Buddy Lee

BIB OVERALL BACK

Cut One

Dotted lines = white stitching

1/4" Seams Allowed

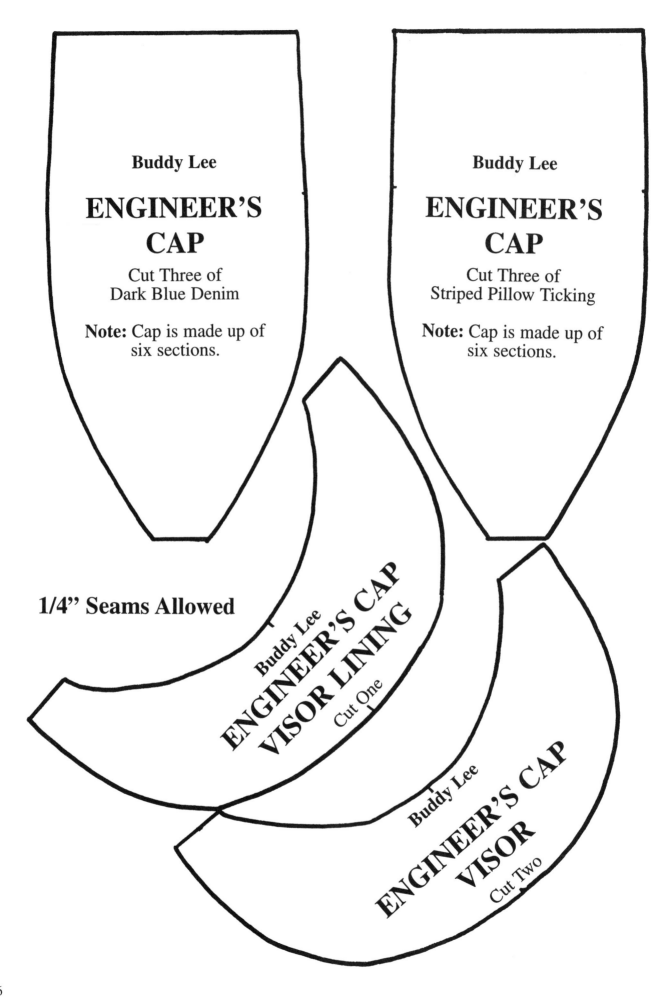

Buddy Lee

ENGINEER'S CAP

Cut Three of
Dark Blue Denim

Note: Cap is made up of
six sections.

Buddy Lee

ENGINEER'S CAP

Cut Three of
Striped Pillow Ticking

Note: Cap is made up of
six sections.

1/4" Seams Allowed

Buddy Lee
ENGINEER'S CAP
VISOR LINING
Cut One

Buddy Lee
ENGINEER'S CAP
VISOR
Cut Two

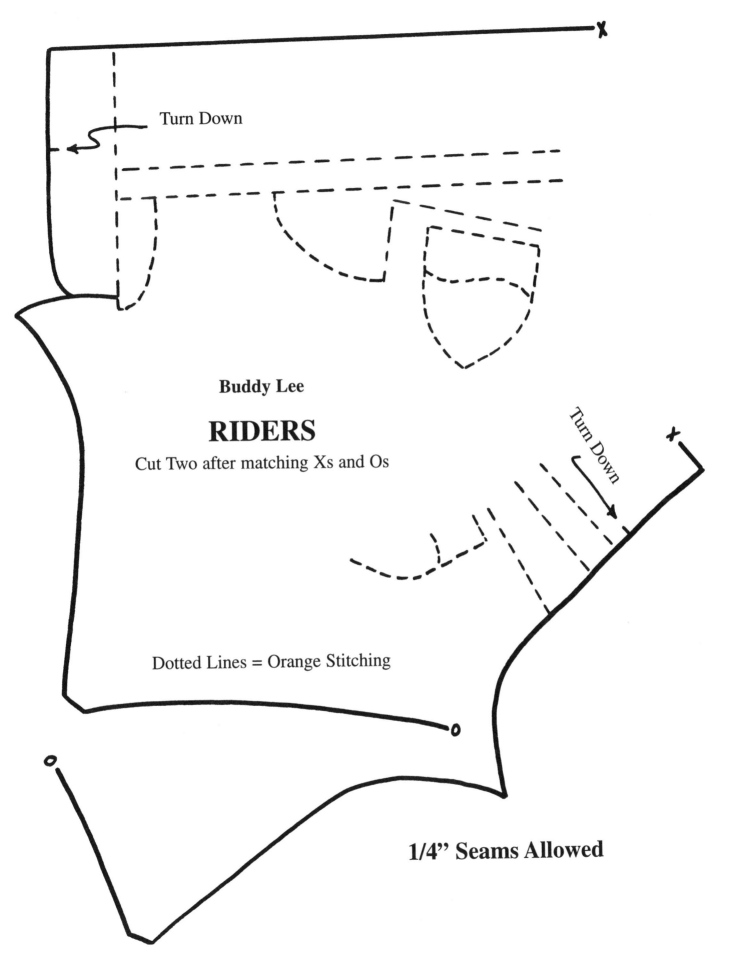

Turn Down

Buddy Lee

RIDERS

Cut Two after matching Xs and Os

Turn Down

Dotted Lines = Orange Stitching

1/4" Seams Allowed

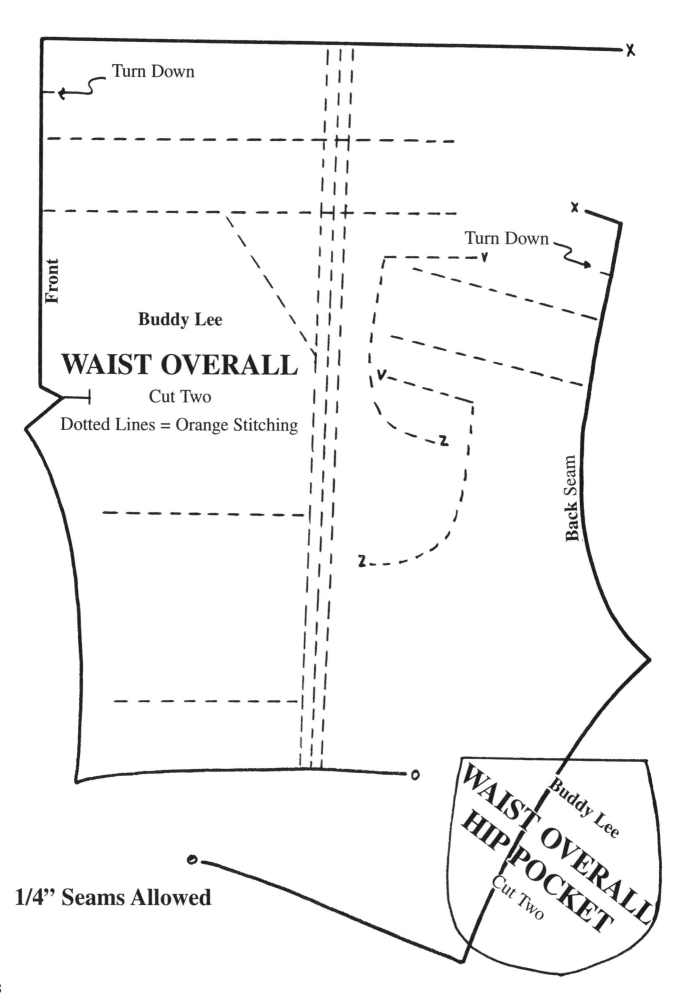

Turn Down

Front

Buddy Lee

WAIST OVERALL

Cut Two

Dotted Lines = Orange Stitching

Turn Down

Back Seam

X

X

o

o

2

2

V

V

1/4" Seams Allowed

Buddy Lee

WAIST OVERALL HIP POCKET

Cut Two

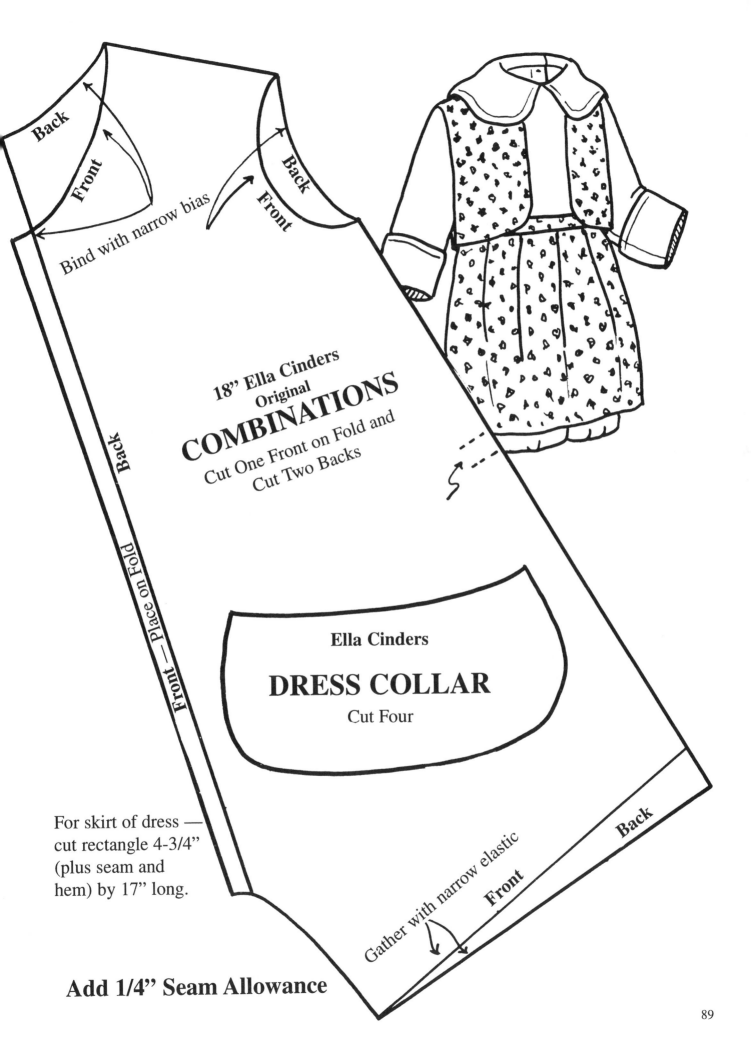

Back

Front

Bind with narrow bias

Back

Front

18" Ella Cinders
Original
COMBINATIONS
Cut One Front on Fold and
Cut Two Backs

Back

Front — Place on Fold

Ella Cinders

DRESS COLLAR

Cut Four

For skirt of dress —
cut rectangle 4-3/4"
(plus seam and
hem) by 17" long.

Gather with narrow elastic

Back

Front

Add 1/4" Seam Allowance

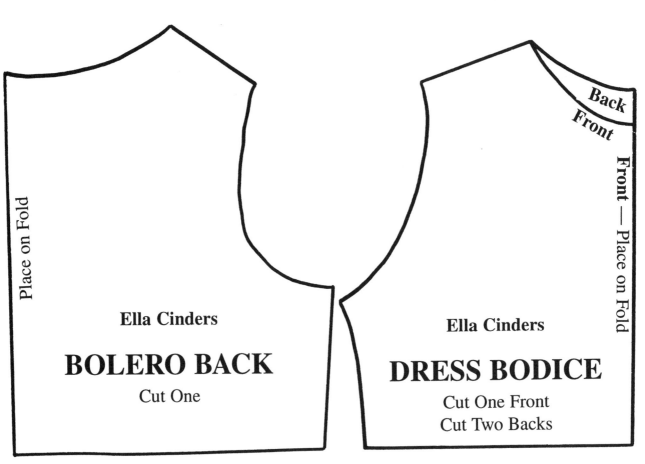

Place on Fold

Ella Cinders

BOLERO BACK

Cut One

Ella Cinders

DRESS BODICE

Cut One Front
Cut Two Backs

Back

Front

Front — Place on Fold

Add 1/4" Seam Allowance

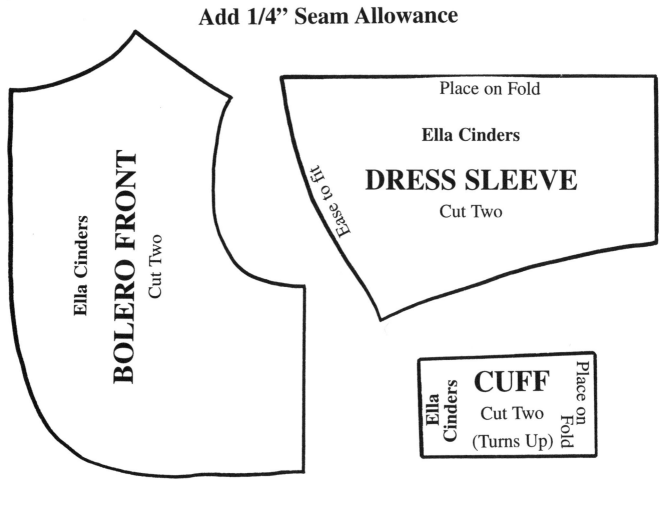

Place on Fold

Ella Cinders

DRESS SLEEVE

Cut Two

Ease to fit

Ella Cinders

BOLERO FRONT

Cut Two

Ella Cinders

CUFF

Cut Two
(Turns Up)

Place on Fold

ENSEMBLE FOR 10-1/2"
BISQUE HEAD BABY

This baby wears all original clothes, although not its own. There is a diaper, a pair of cotton combinations, a cotton short slip (or long shirt, if you will), a long slip, and finally, a long embroidered organdy dress over all.

Fit and complete the underthings beginning with the diaper and working out. This diaper is a strip of flannel cut to fit around the doll and 2 to 2-1/2" wide. Attached to this in the center of one long side is a tab measuring 1-1/4" wide and 4" long. The whole is lace-edged.

The combinations and short slip are cut from a fine-textured cotton and the patterns are self-explanatory.

The long slip is also of this fine cotton, but if desired may be of the organdy used for the dress. The slip hem is edged with 3/4" lace.

For the skirt of the long baby dress, cut a piece of organdy 13-1/2" wide and 27" long. Turn up a 1/2" hem on one long side, then sew 1/2" lace to bottom edge of this hem. Assemble the bodice, gather top edge of skirt to fit the bodice. Sew waist seam, then top stitch 1/4" satin ribbon over seam on right side.

Neck opening and cuffs of sleeves are finished in the same manner as bottom hem of dress. Then satin ribbon is top-stitched over the seam. If desired, the dress may be embroidered with pastel flowers, as is the original. A drawing of the flowered design is shown.

Layette from pages of *Pictorial Review*, 1913

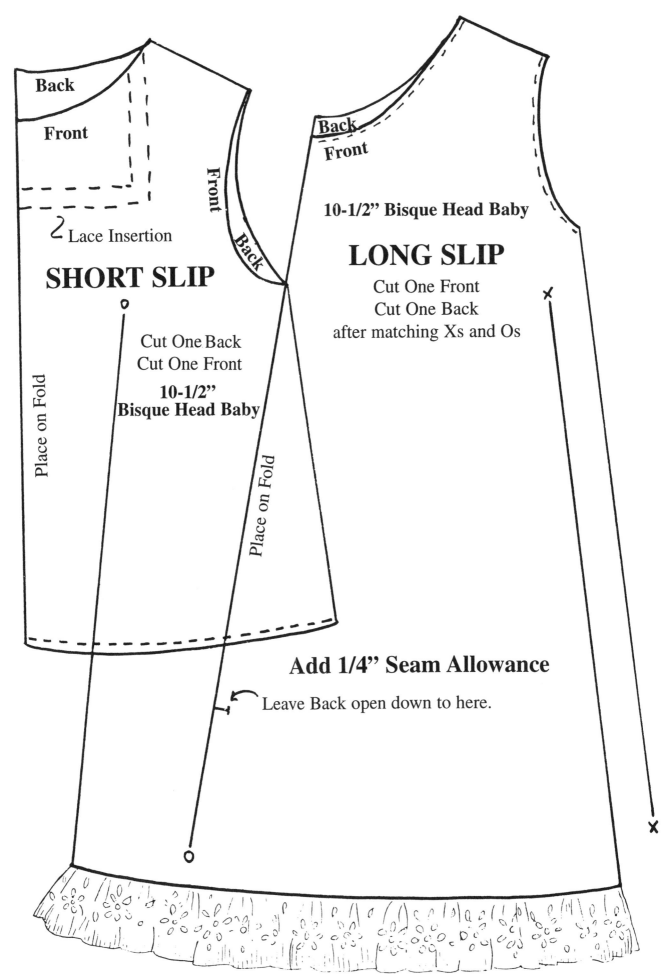

Back

Front

Lace Insertion

SHORT SLIP

Cut One Back
Cut One Front

**10-1/2"
Bisque Head Baby**

Front

Back

Place on Fold

Place on Fold

Back

Front

10-1/2" Bisque Head Baby

LONG SLIP

Cut One Front
Cut One Back
after matching Xs and Os

Add 1/4" Seam Allowance

Leave Back open down to here.

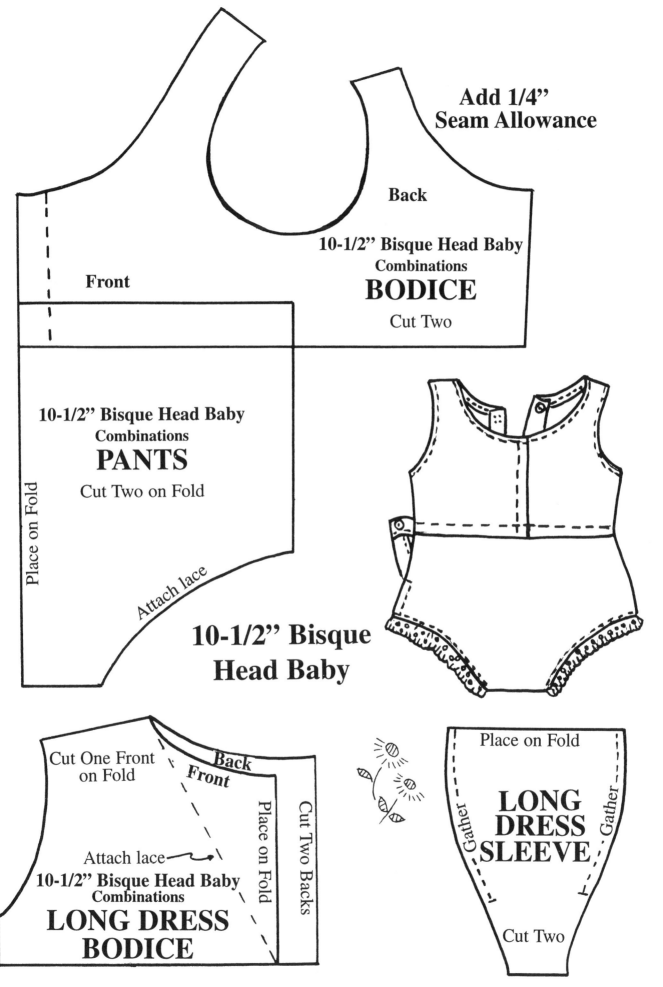

Add 1/4"
Seam Allowance

Front

Back

10-1/2" Bisque Head Baby
Combinations
BODICE

Cut Two

10-1/2" Bisque Head Baby
Combinations
PANTS

Cut Two on Fold

Place on Fold

Attach lace

**10-1/2" Bisque
Head Baby**

Cut One Front
on Fold

Back
Front

Place on Fold

Cut Two Backs

Attach lace

10-1/2" Bisque Head Baby
Combinations
**LONG DRESS
BODICE**

Place on Fold

Gather

**LONG
DRESS
SLEEVE**

Gather

Cut Two

93

14" Bubbles
DRESS BACK SKIRT
Cut Two

← Tuck

Bind neck with bias

Finish with double ruffle →

14" Bubbles
DRESS BODICE BACK
Cut Two

Attach 2-1/2" cotton eyelet ruffle →

14" Bubbles by Effanbee

B --- Gather --- A

14" Bubbles
DRESS FRONT SKIRT
Cut One

Place on Fold — Center Front

Finish with double ruffle ↙

14" Bubbles
DRESS BODICE FRONT
Cut Two

Place on Fold

B

Attach 2-1/2" wide cotton eyelet ruffle ↘

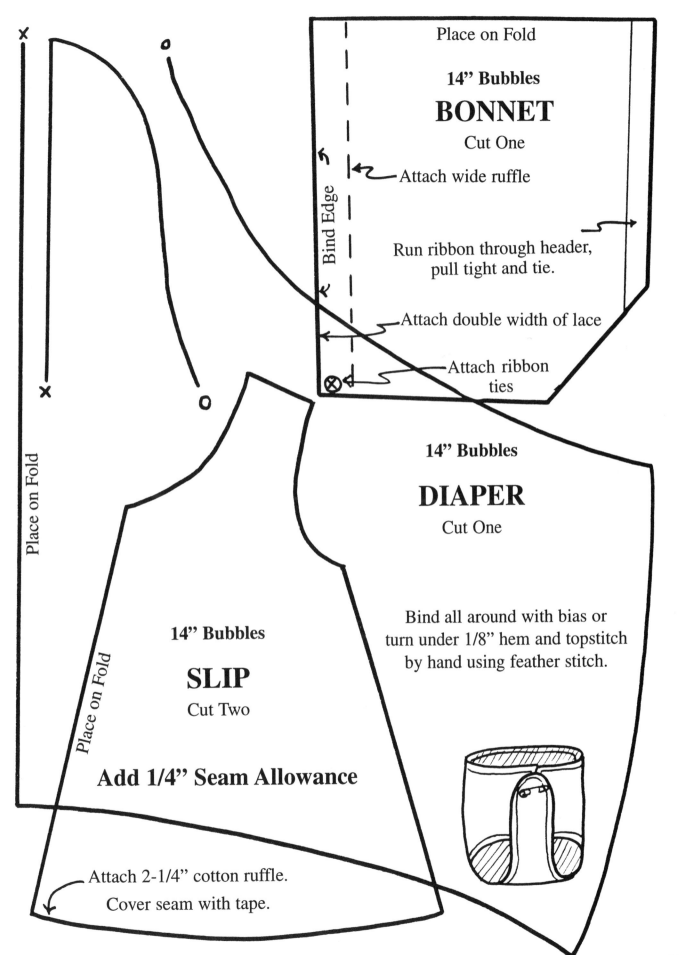

Place on Fold

14" Bubbles

BONNET

Cut One

Attach wide ruffle

Bind Edge

Run ribbon through header,
pull tight and tie.

Attach double width of lace

Attach ribbon
ties

Place on Fold

14" Bubbles

DIAPER

Cut One

Bind all around with bias or
turn under 1/8" hem and topstitch
by hand using feather stitch.

14" Bubbles

SLIP

Cut Two

Place on Fold

Add 1/4" Seam Allowance

Attach 2-1/4" cotton ruffle.
Cover seam with tape.

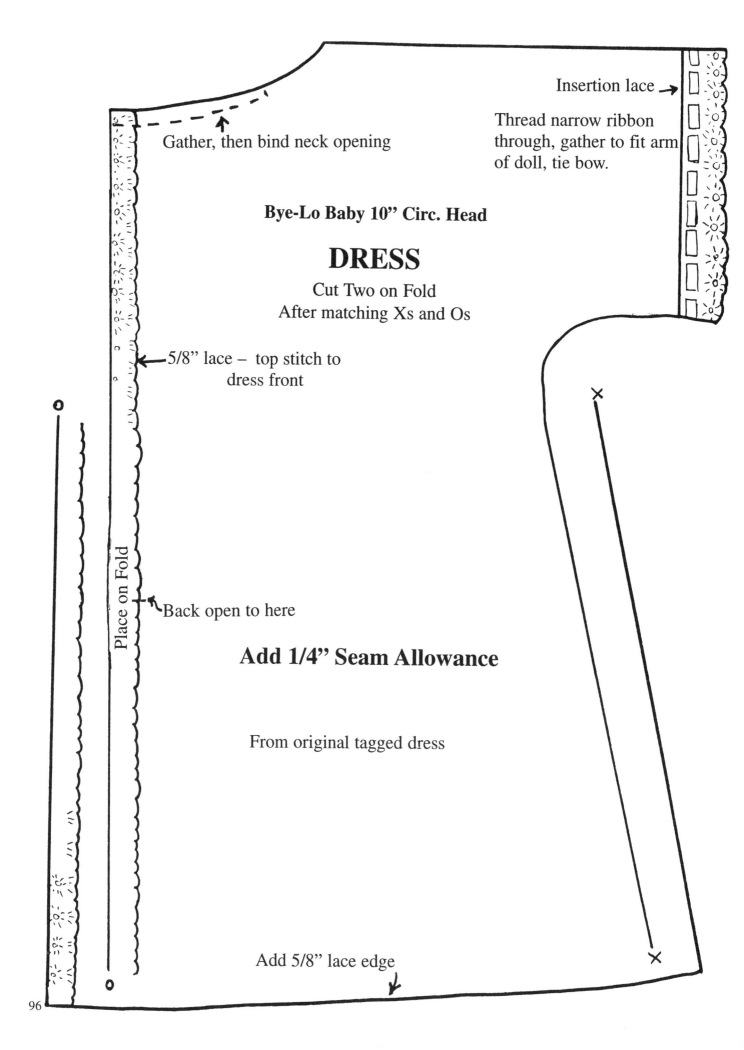

Insertion lace

Thread narrow ribbon through, gather to fit arm of doll, tie bow.

Gather, then bind neck opening

Bye-Lo Baby 10" Circ. Head

DRESS

Cut Two on Fold
After matching Xs and Os

5/8" lace – top stitch to dress front

Place on Fold

Back open to here

Add 1/4" Seam Allowance

From original tagged dress

Add 5/8" lace edge

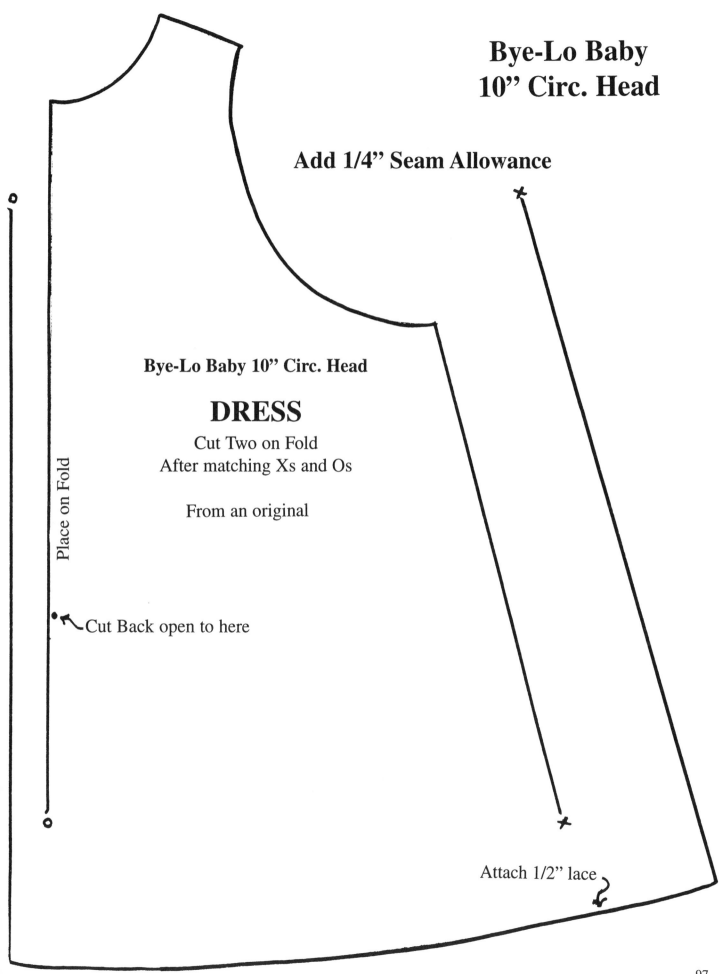

Add 1/4" Seam Allowance

Bye-Lo Baby 10" Circ. Head

DRESS
Cut Two on Fold
After matching Xs and Os

From an original

Place on Fold

Cut Back open to here

Attach 1/2" lace

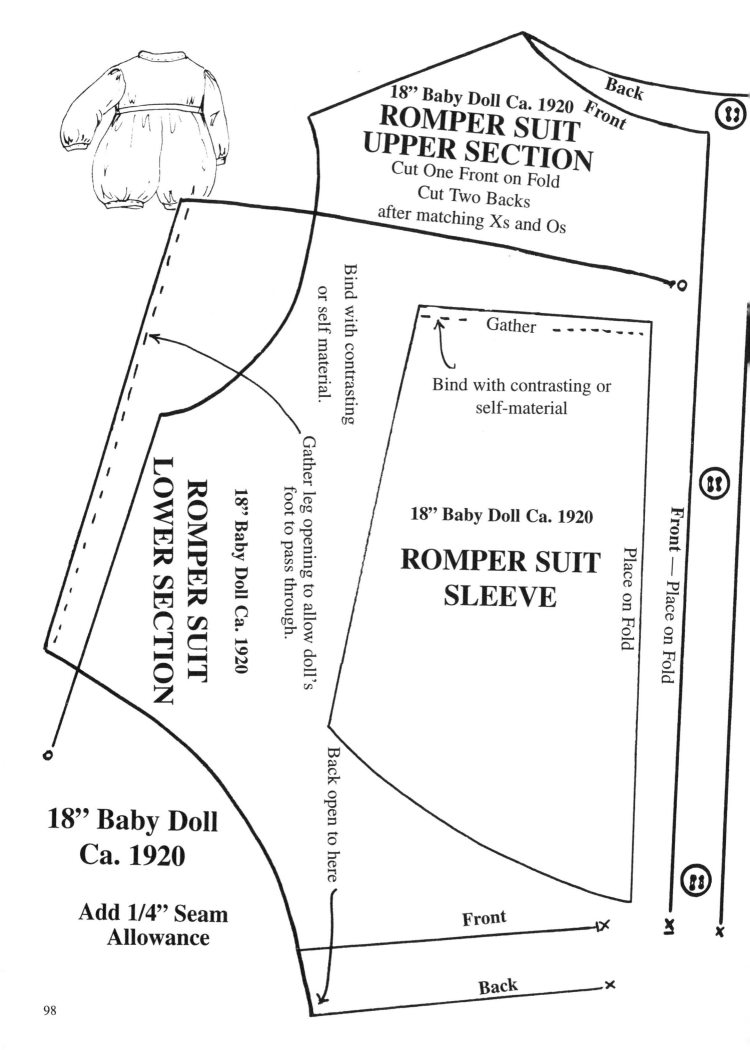

18" Baby Doll Ca. 1920 Front | **Back**

ROMPER SUIT
UPPER SECTION
Cut One Front on Fold
Cut Two Backs
after matching Xs and Os

Bind with contrasting
or self material.

Gather leg opening to allow doll's
foot to pass through.

Gather

Bind with contrasting or
self-material

ROMPER SUIT
LOWER SECTION

18" Baby Doll Ca. 1920

18" Baby Doll Ca. 1920

ROMPER SUIT
SLEEVE

Place on Fold

Front — Place on Fold

Back open to here

18" Baby Doll
Ca. 1920

**Add 1/4" Seam
Allowance**

Front

Back

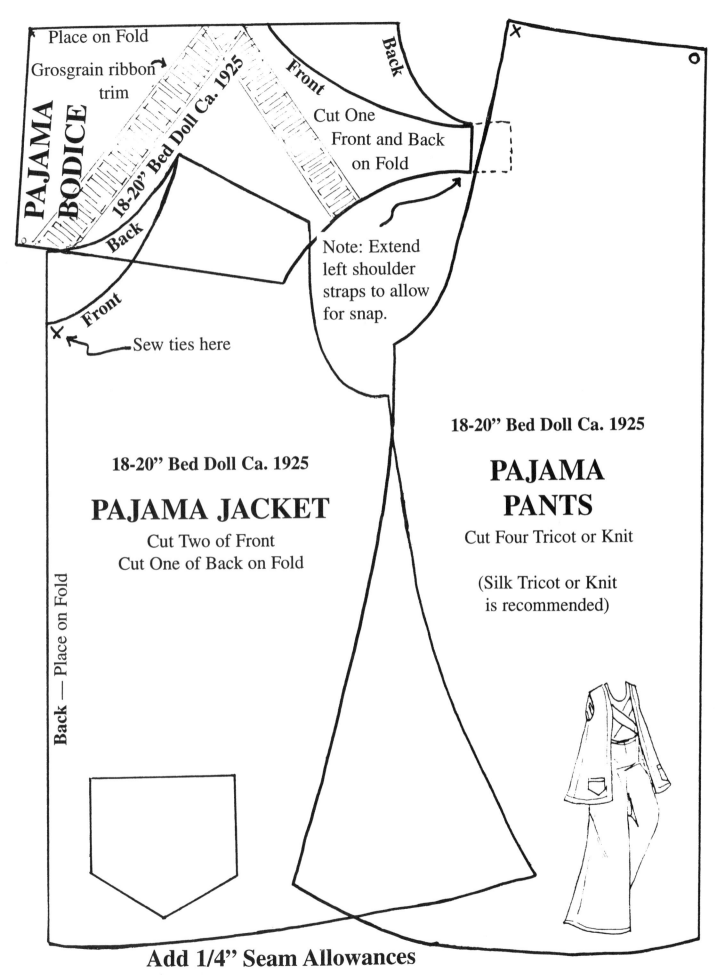

Place on Fold

Grosgrain ribbon trim

PAJAMA BODICE

18-20" Bed Doll Ca. 1925

Back

Front

Front

Back

Cut One
Front and Back
on Fold

Note: Extend
left shoulder
straps to allow
for snap.

Sew ties here

18-20" Bed Doll Ca. 1925

PAJAMA JACKET

Cut Two of Front
Cut One of Back on Fold

Back — Place on Fold

18-20" Bed Doll Ca. 1925

**PAJAMA
PANTS**

Cut Four Tricot or Knit

(Silk Tricot or Knit
is recommended)

Add 1/4" Seam Allowances

18" Käthe Kruse

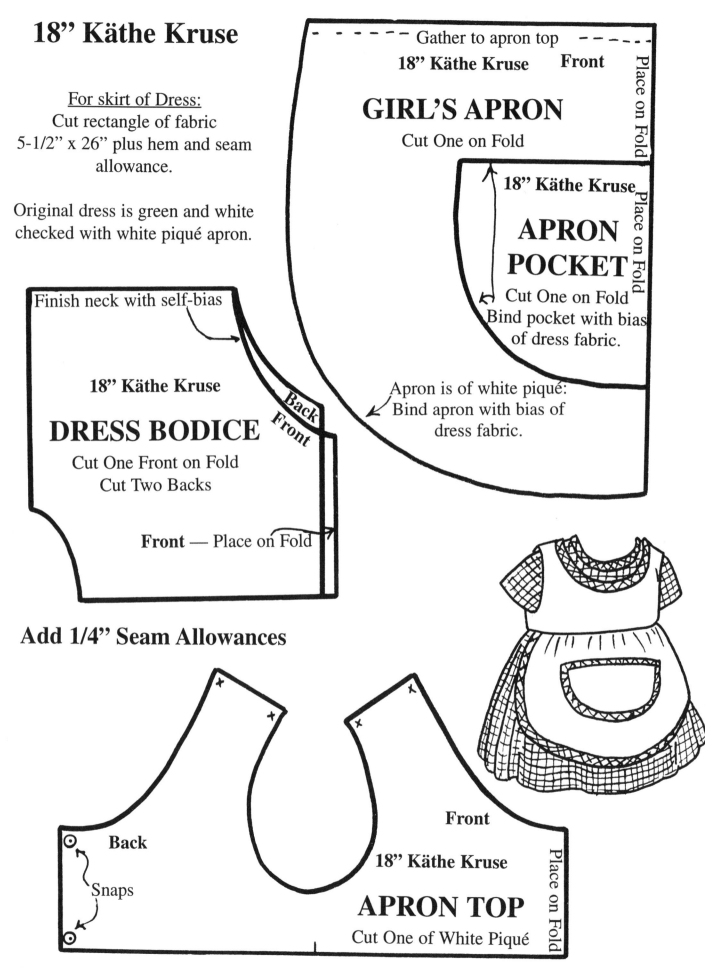

For skirt of Dress:
Cut rectangle of fabric
5-1/2" x 26" plus hem and seam allowance.

Original dress is green and white checked with white piqué apron.

Gather to apron top

18" Käthe Kruse   Front

GIRL'S APRON

Cut One on Fold

Place on Fold

18" Käthe Kruse   Place on Fold

APRON POCKET

Cut One on Fold
Bind pocket with bias of dress fabric.

Finish neck with self-bias

18" Käthe Kruse

DRESS BODICE

Cut One Front on Fold
Cut Two Backs

Back

Front

Front — Place on Fold

Apron is of white piqué:
Bind apron with bias of dress fabric.

Add 1/4" Seam Allowances

Back

Snaps

Front

18" Käthe Kruse

APRON TOP

Cut One of White Piqué

Place on Fold

18" Käthe Kruse

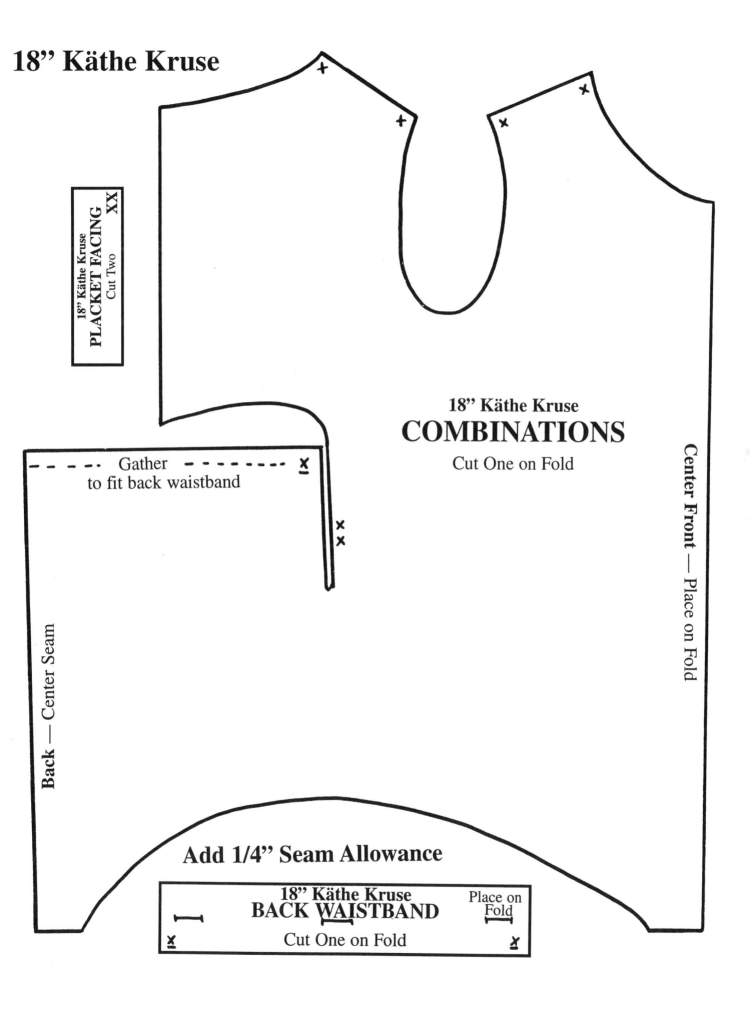

18" Käthe Kruse
PLACKET FACING XX
Cut Two

18" Käthe Kruse
COMBINATIONS
Cut One on Fold

Center Front — Place on Fold

Gather
to fit back waistband

Back — Center Seam

Add 1/4" Seam Allowance

18" Käthe Kruse
BACK WAISTBAND
Cut One on Fold

Place on
Fold

1764

1738

1765

1828

1828

No. 1764. Panniers and rosebuds and lace ribbons bedeck this enchanting costume of a typical Southern Belle. You will get a lot of fun out of making it. The patterns for the organdie dress, the velvet hat and the organdie underwear are so perfect to cut by, and the directions so simple. Designed to fit the average 30-inch French doll. 30 cents.

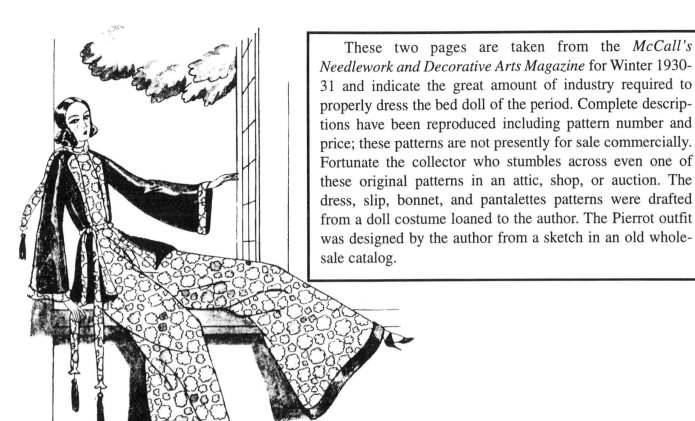

These two pages are taken from the *McCall's Needlework and Decorative Arts Magazine* for Winter 1930-31 and indicate the great amount of industry required to properly dress the bed doll of the period. Complete descriptions have been reproduced including pattern number and price; these patterns are not presently for sale commercially. Fortunate the collector who stumbles across even one of these original patterns in an attic, shop, or auction. The dress, slip, bonnet, and pantalettes patterns were drafted from a doll costume loaned to the author. The Pierrot outfit was designed by the author from a sketch in an old whole-sale catalog.

1776

LEADING FASHIONS FOR FRENCH DOLLS

No. 1738. The stately Elizabethan costume of the doll at center top possesses charms very different from those of her fair companion. The close-fitting bodice and voluminous skirt are made of changeable rose taffeta silk, with front panel collar and cuffs of deep cream lace. The amounts required are 1-1/4 yards of 35" silk for the dress 1-1/2 yards of 7" lace, some insertion, and 12 yards of ruffling. Two more costumes including underwear patterns for all are given. To fit 30" long doll with chest measurement, 10-1/2". Price 35 cents.

No. 1828. Your French doll will be the most charming to grace any boudoir when she appears in one of the fashions from *Godey's Lady Book* — bonnet and all! The details are fully and perfectly worked out to the last tiny velvet bow or the row of miniature buttons. Changeable taffeta or rayon taffeta are suitable materials. The pattern provides for a fitted bust form to be sewn to the doll and gives all directions, stating amounts of material required. Two Godey costumes for 30" doll, including cutting patterns for underwear. Price 35 cents.

No.1765. Black lace over a lustrous gold silk dress and a coquettish black satin hat — Behold! a Spanish lady enters the scene. The deep 13" black lace is skillfully draped over the bodice in mantilla fashion and fully gathered over the skirt. Following the present vogue for things Spanish, your boudoir doll will be very elegant in this costume which is not difficult to make. Patterns and directions for 3 costumes for 30" doll, and underwear included. Price 30 cents.

No. 1776. Imitating the latest pajama fashion worn by her mistress, the boudoir doll at left is seen lounging in smart pajamas of her own, which can be made of flowered silk and trimmed with bands of contrasting silk or velvet, matching the coat. It is surprisingly simple to make. Required material includes: 1 yard for coat and pajama bands, and 1-1/8 yards for pajama and coat bands. Pattern for Negligee suit also included, both to fit 30" doll. Price 30 cents.

Gather to fit armhole

28" Bed Doll

DRESS SLEEVE

Cut Two

Place on Fold

Run elastic thread

Edge with lace

This original dress is of dotted swiss with fine cotton underdress and linings.

28" Bed Doll

To make very full, three-tiered skirt:

28" Bed Doll
TIERED SKIRT — 1st Tier
Cut One at 5" x 56"
Gather to fit lower edge of bodice

28" Bed Doll
TIERED SKIRT — 2nd Tier
Cut One at 5" x 104"
Gather to fit lower edge of next tier

28" Bed Doll
TIERED SKIRT — 3rd Tier
Cut One at 5-1/2" x 136"
Gather to fit lower edge of next tier

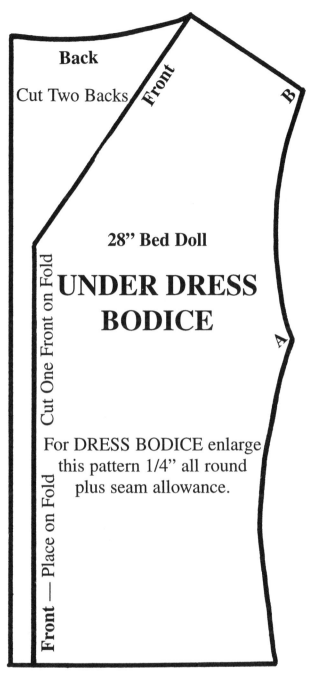

Back

Cut Two Backs

Front

B

Cut One Front on Fold

28" Bed Doll

UNDER DRESS BODICE

Front — Place on Fold

A

For DRESS BODICE enlarge this pattern 1/4" all round plus seam allowance.

Add 1/4" Seam Allowances

28" Bed Doll
UNDER SKIRT
Cut One at 4" x 60"
Gather to fit lower edge of bodice above.

28" Bed Doll
UNDER SKIRT — 2nd Tier
Cut One at 12" x 104"
Gather to fit lower edge of upper tier

28" Bed Doll

o

28" Bed Doll

BONNET BACK

Cut One of Material
Cut One of Lining

x   x

Place on Fold   o

28" Bed Doll

BONNET SIDE

Cut One on Fold of Material
Cut One on Fold of Lining

x

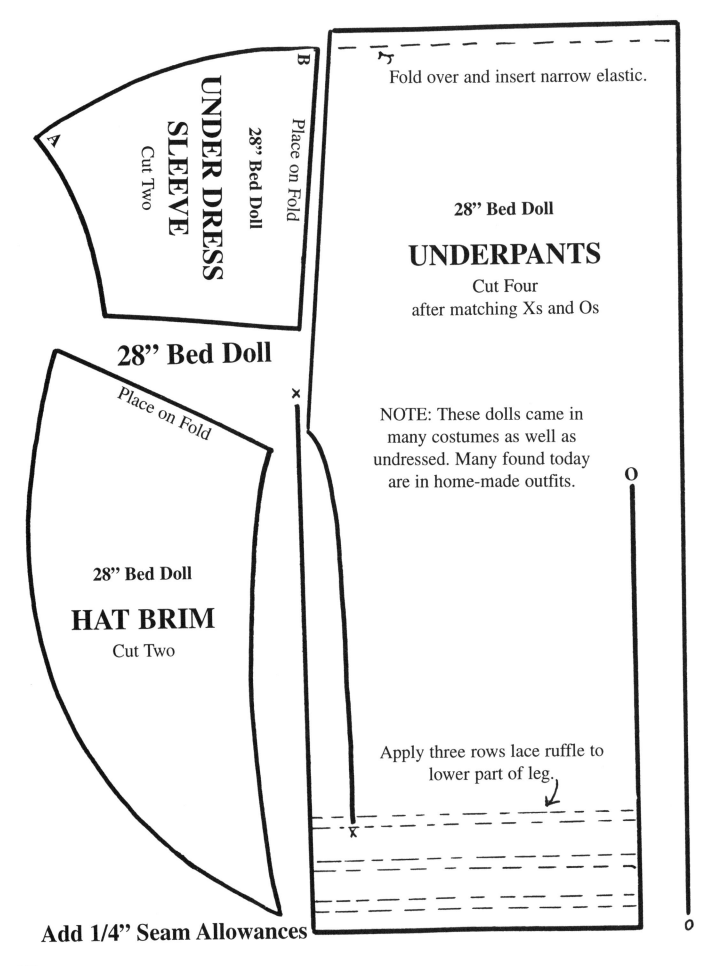

Place on Fold

B

A

**UNDER DRESS
SLEEVE**

28" Bed Doll

Cut Two

28" Bed Doll

Place on Fold

28" Bed Doll

HAT BRIM

Cut Two

Add 1/4" Seam Allowances

Fold over and insert narrow elastic.

28" Bed Doll

UNDERPANTS

Cut Four
after matching Xs and Os

X

NOTE: These dolls came in
many costumes as well as
undressed. Many found today
are in home-made outfits.

O

Apply three rows lace ruffle to
lower part of leg.

X

O

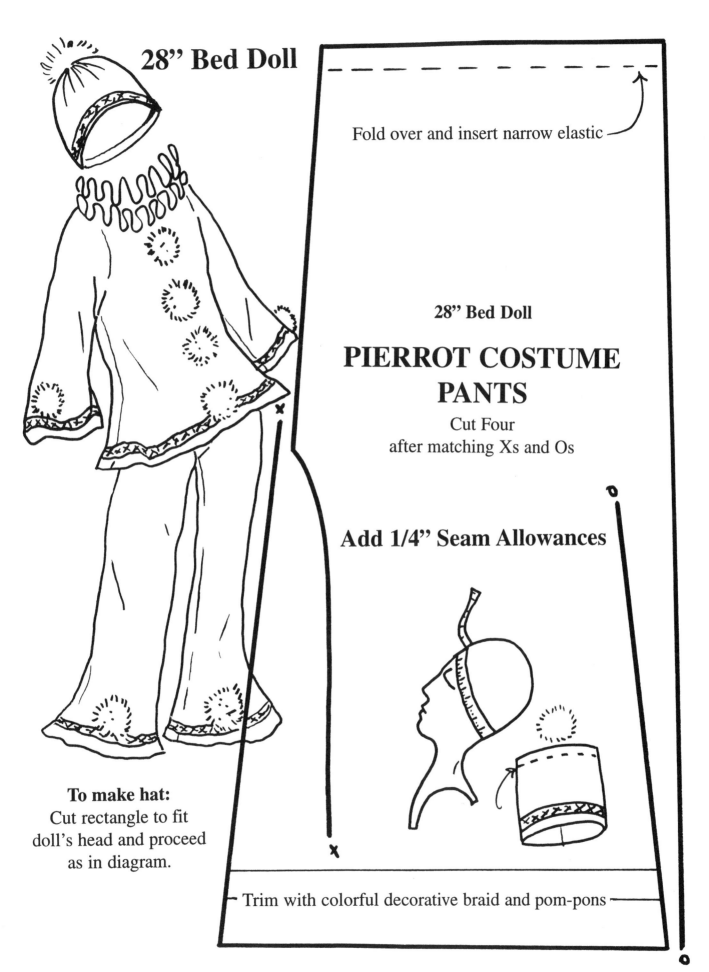

28" Bed Doll

Fold over and insert narrow elastic

28" Bed Doll

PIERROT COSTUME PANTS

Cut Four
after matching Xs and Os

Add 1/4" Seam Allowances

To make hat:
Cut rectangle to fit
doll's head and proceed
as in diagram.

Trim with colorful decorative braid and pom-pons

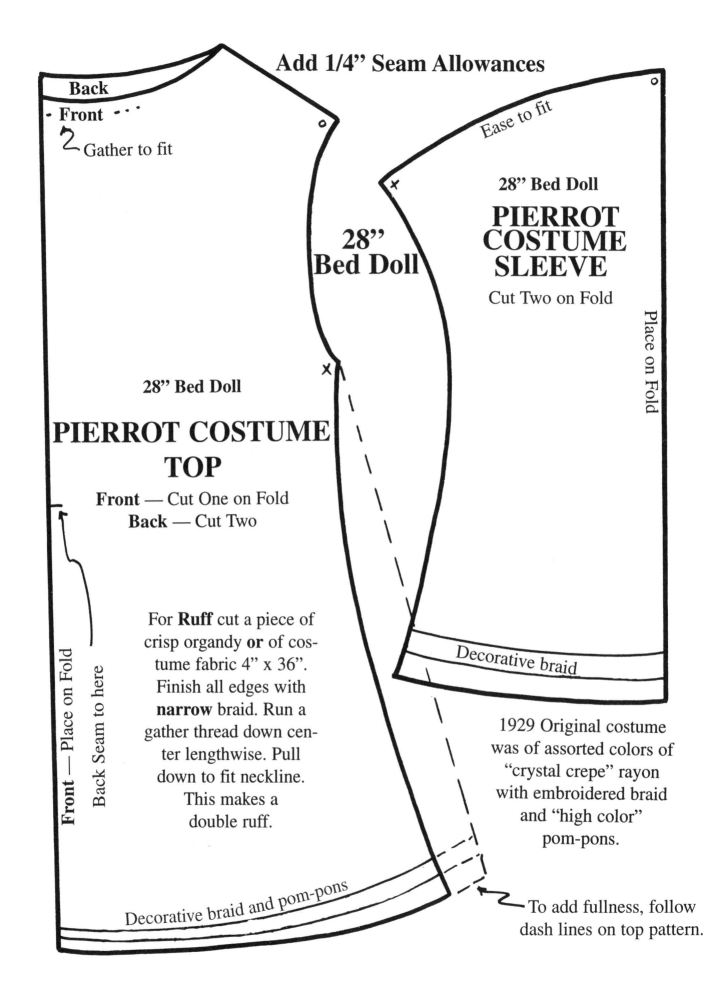

Add 1/4" Seam Allowances

Back

Front · · ·

Gather to fit

28" Bed Doll

28" Bed Doll

PIERROT COSTUME TOP

Front — Cut One on Fold
Back — Cut Two

Front — Place on Fold

Back Seam to here

For **Ruff** cut a piece of crisp organdy **or** of costume fabric 4" x 36". Finish all edges with **narrow** braid. Run a gather thread down center lengthwise. Pull down to fit neckline. This makes a double ruff.

Decorative braid and pom-pons

28" Bed Doll

PIERROT COSTUME SLEEVE

Cut Two on Fold

Ease to fit

Place on Fold

Decorative braid

1929 Original costume was of assorted colors of "crystal crepe" rayon with embroidered braid and "high color" pom-pons.

To add fullness, follow dash lines on top pattern.

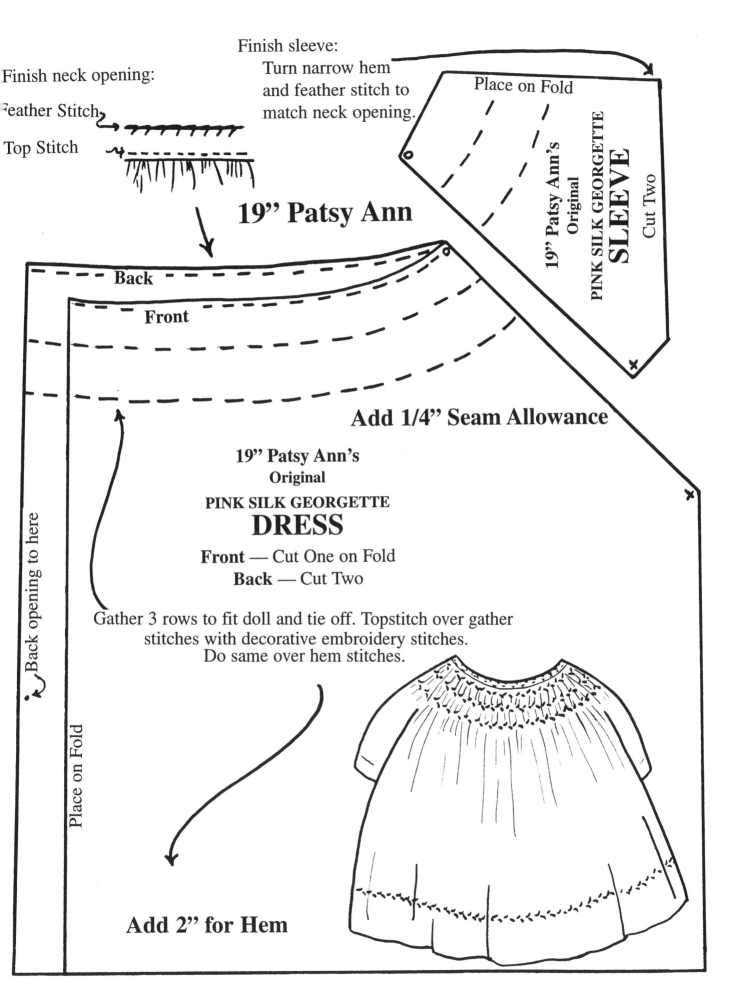

Finish neck opening:

Feather Stitch

Top Stitch

Finish sleeve:
Turn narrow hem
and feather stitch to
match neck opening.

Place on Fold

19" Patsy Ann's
Original
PINK SILK GEORGETTE
SLEEVE
Cut Two

19" Patsy Ann

Back

Front

Add 1/4" Seam Allowance

19" Patsy Ann's
Original
PINK SILK GEORGETTE
DRESS

Front — Cut One on Fold
Back — Cut Two

Gather 3 rows to fit doll and tie off. Topstitch over gather
stitches with decorative embroidery stitches.
Do same over hem stitches.

Back opening to here

Place on Fold

Add 2" for Hem

19" Patsy Ann

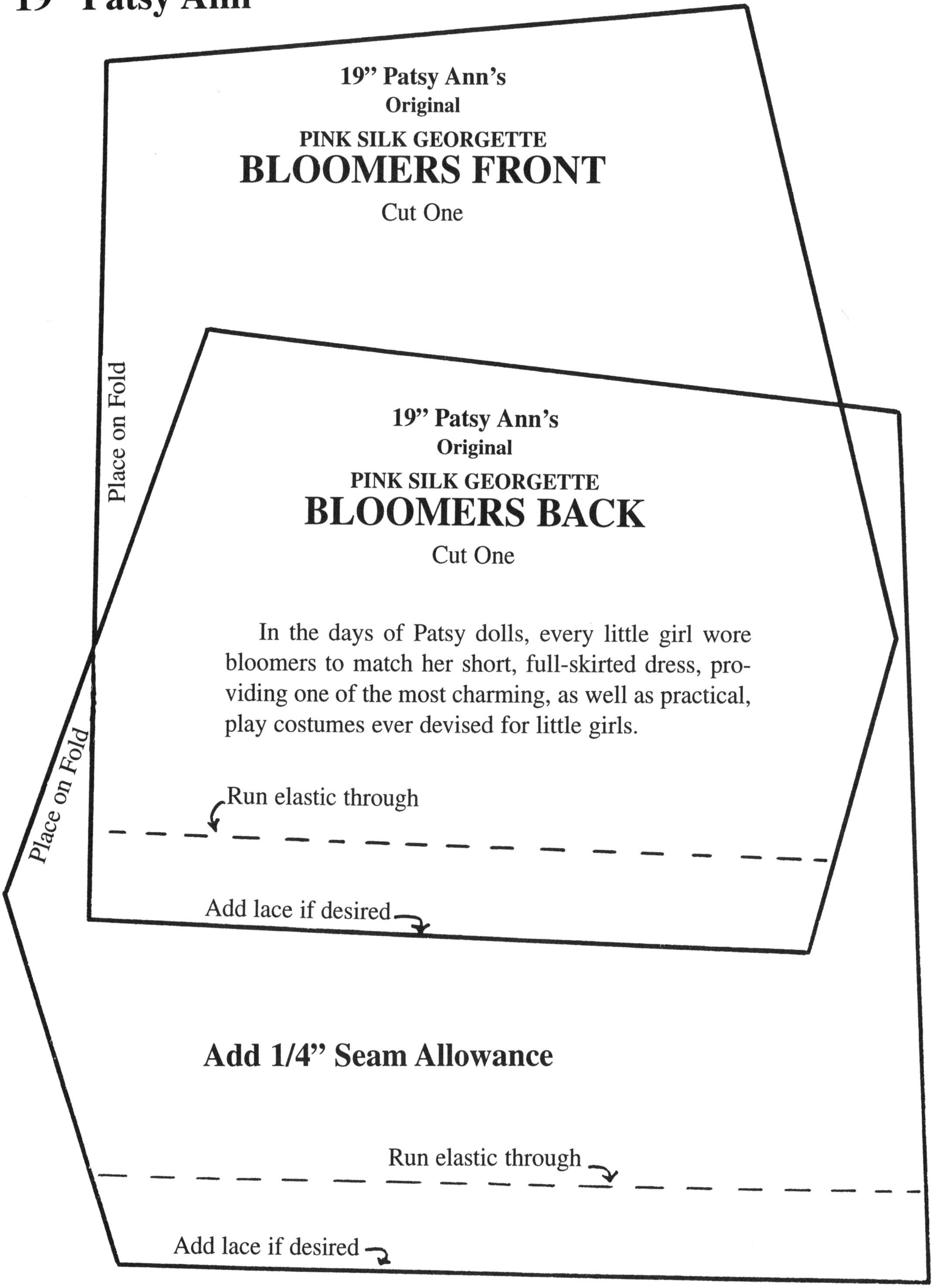

19" Patsy Ann's
Original
PINK SILK GEORGETTE
BLOOMERS FRONT
Cut One

Place on Fold

19" Patsy Ann's
Original
PINK SILK GEORGETTE
BLOOMERS BACK
Cut One

In the days of Patsy dolls, every little girl wore bloomers to match her short, full-skirted dress, providing one of the most charming, as well as practical, play costumes ever devised for little girls.

Place on Fold

Run elastic through

Add lace if desired

Add 1/4" Seam Allowance

Run elastic through

Add lace if desired

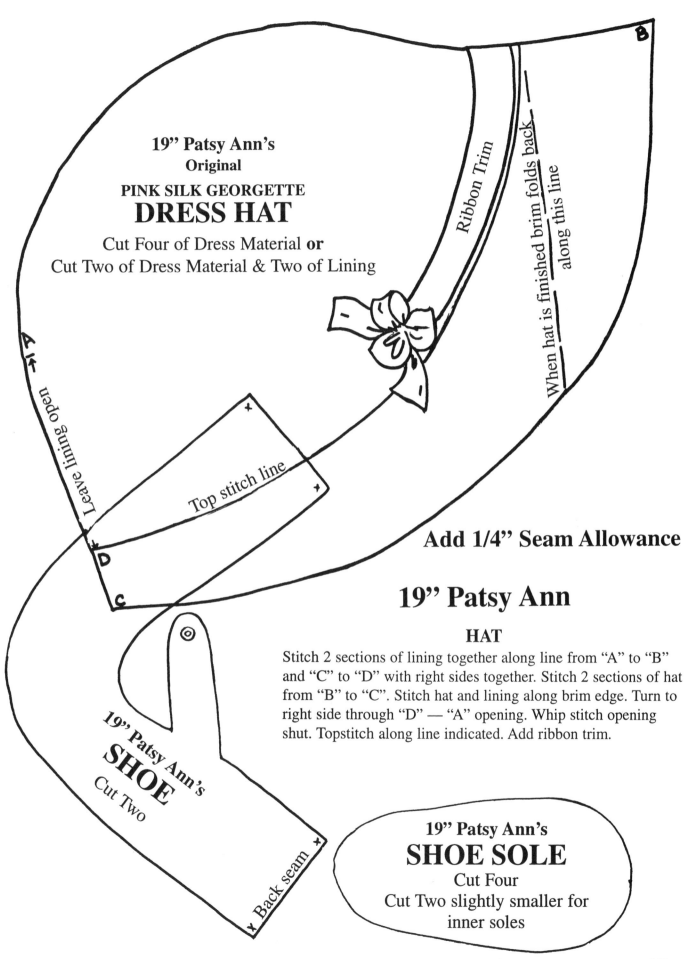

19" Patsy Ann's
Original
PINK SILK GEORGETTE
DRESS HAT

Cut Four of Dress Material **or**
Cut Two of Dress Material & Two of Lining

Ribbon Trim

When hat is finished brim folds back along this line

Leave lining open

Top stitch line

Add 1/4" Seam Allowance

19" Patsy Ann

HAT

Stitch 2 sections of lining together along line from "A" to "B" and "C" to "D" with right sides together. Stitch 2 sections of hat from "B" to "C". Stitch hat and lining along brim edge. Turn to right side through "D" — "A" opening. Whip stitch opening shut. Topstitch along line indicated. Add ribbon trim.

19" Patsy Ann's
SHOE
Cut Two

Back seam

19" Patsy Ann's
SHOE SOLE
Cut Four
Cut Two slightly smaller for
inner soles

111

19" Patsy Ann

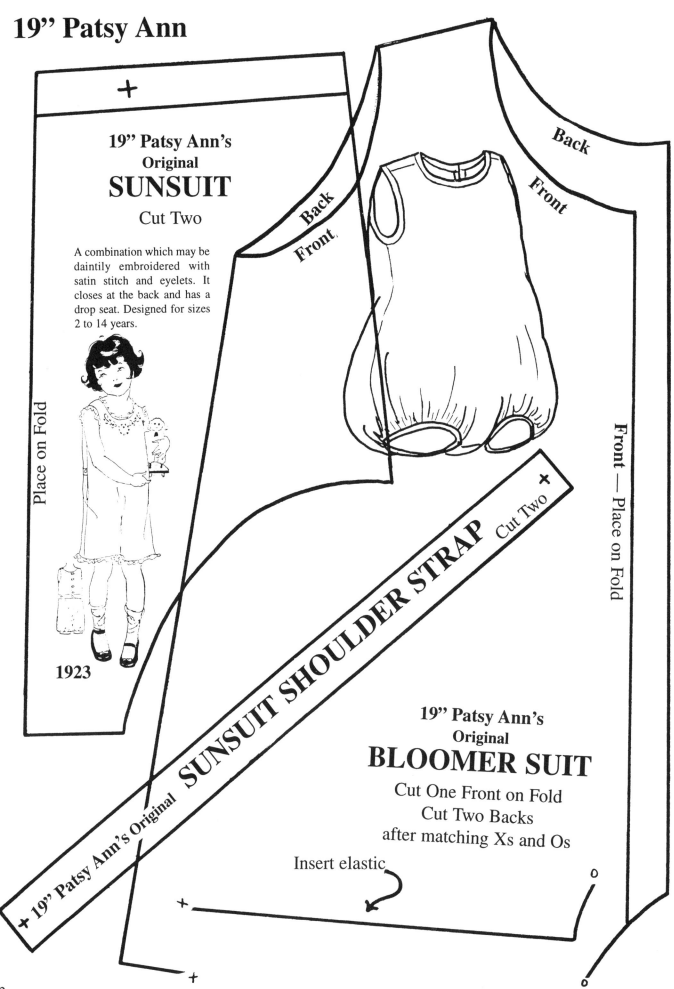

19" Patsy Ann's Original
SUNSUIT
Cut Two

A combination which may be daintily embroidered with satin stitch and eyelets. It closes at the back and has a drop seat. Designed for sizes 2 to 14 years.

Place on Fold

1923

Back
Front

Back
Front

Front

Front — Place on Fold

+ 19" Patsy Ann's Original SUNSUIT SHOULDER STRAP Cut Two

19" Patsy Ann's Original
BLOOMER SUIT
Cut One Front on Fold
Cut Two Backs
after matching Xs and Os

Insert elastic

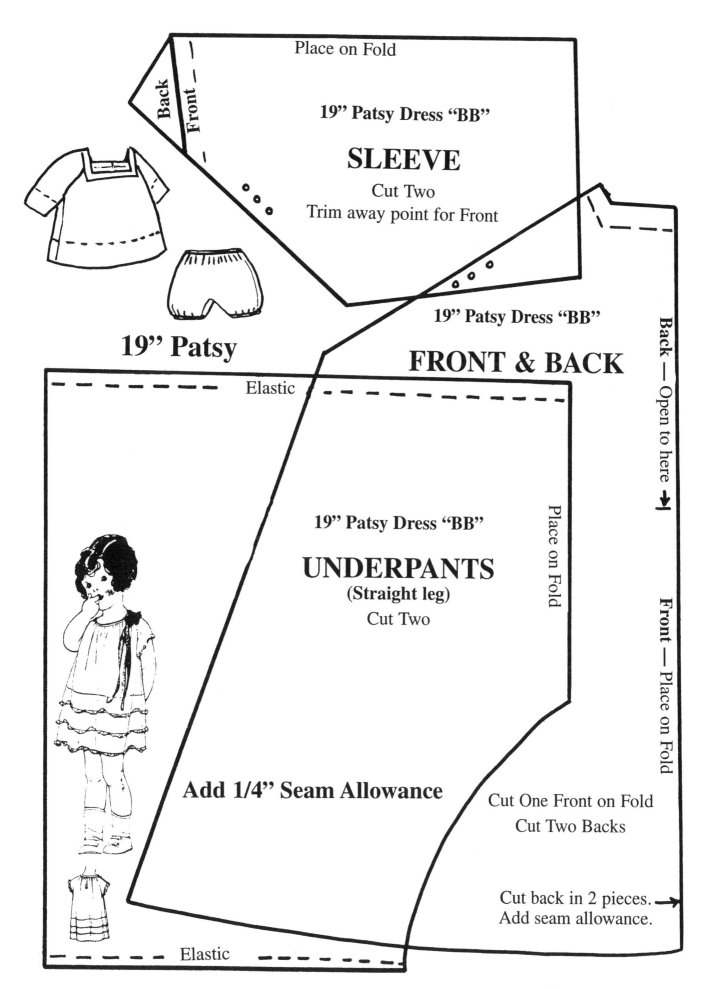

Place on Fold

Back

Front

19" Patsy Dress "BB"

SLEEVE

Cut Two

Trim away point for Front

19" Patsy Dress "BB"

FRONT & BACK

Back — Open to here ➡

Front — Place on Fold

19" Patsy

Elastic

Place on Fold

19" Patsy Dress "BB"

UNDERPANTS

(Straight leg)

Cut Two

Add 1/4" Seam Allowance

Cut One Front on Fold

Cut Two Backs

Cut back in 2 pieces. ➡
Add seam allowance.

Elastic

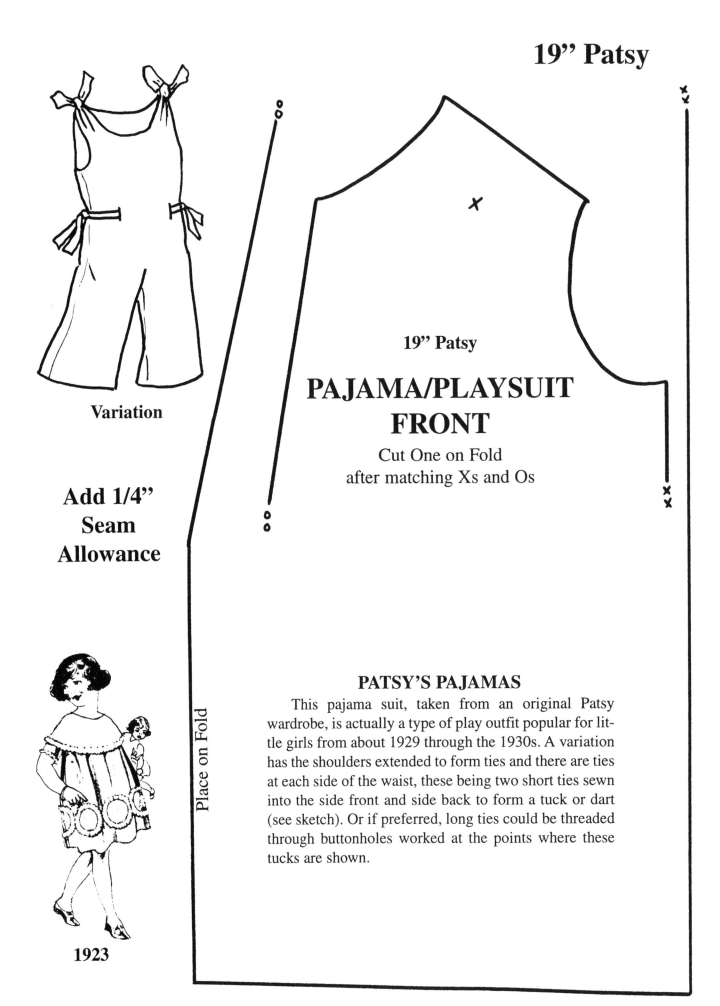

Variation

**Add 1/4"
Seam
Allowance**

1923

Place on Fold

19" Patsy

PAJAMA/PLAYSUIT FRONT

Cut One on Fold
after matching Xs and Os

PATSY'S PAJAMAS

This pajama suit, taken from an original Patsy wardrobe, is actually a type of play outfit popular for little girls from about 1929 through the 1930s. A variation has the shoulders extended to form ties and there are ties at each side of the waist, these being two short ties sewn into the side front and side back to form a tuck or dart (see sketch). Or if preferred, long ties could be threaded through buttonholes worked at the points where these tucks are shown.

19" Patsy

Place on Fold

I

19" Patsy

PAJAMA/PLAYSUIT
BACK

Cut One on Fold
after matching Xs and Os

1923

Add 1/4" Seam Allowance

19" Patsy

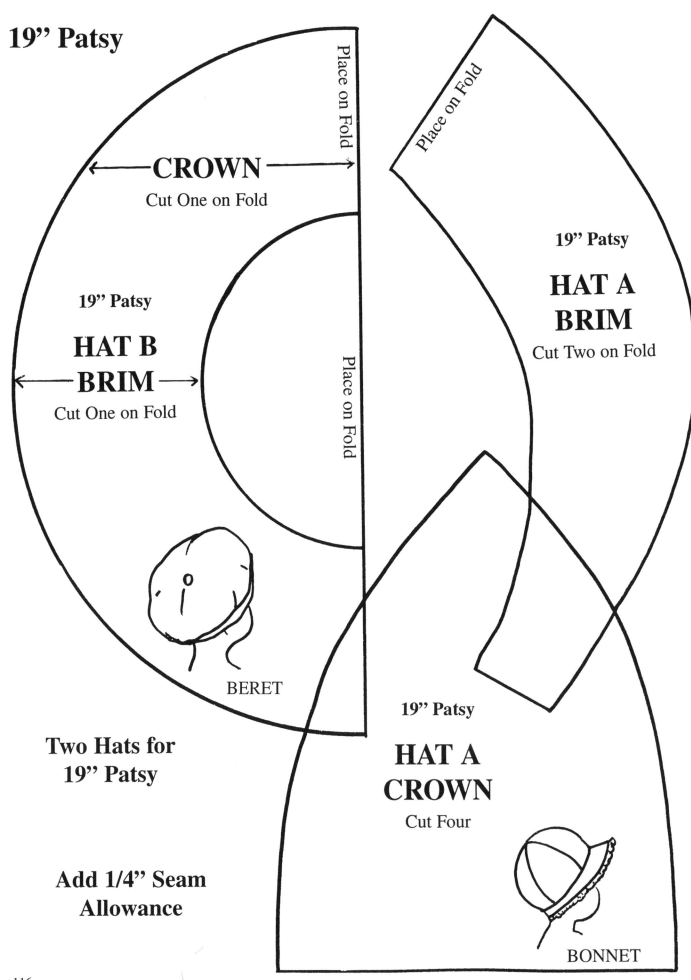

CROWN

Cut One on Fold

Place on Fold

19" Patsy

HAT B BRIM

Cut One on Fold

Place on Fold

Place on Fold

19" Patsy

HAT A BRIM

Cut Two on Fold

BERET

Two Hats for 19" Patsy

Add 1/4" Seam Allowance

19" Patsy

HAT A CROWN

Cut Four

BONNET

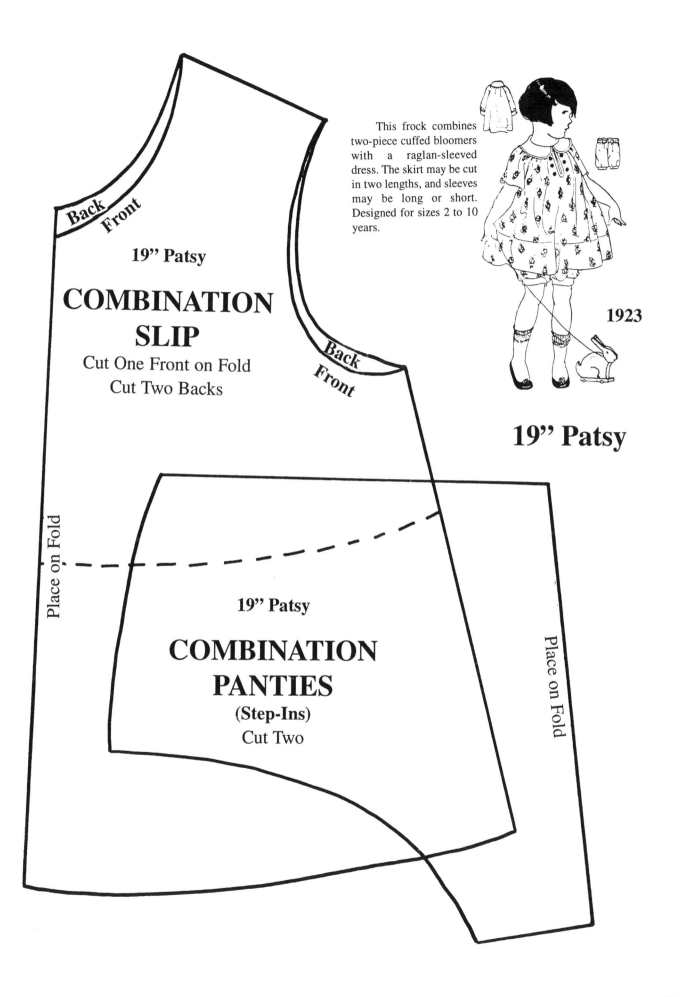

Back **Front**

19" Patsy

COMBINATION SLIP

Cut One Front on Fold
Cut Two Backs

Back **Front**

This frock combines two-piece cuffed bloomers with a raglan-sleeved dress. The skirt may be cut in two lengths, and sleeves may be long or short. Designed for sizes 2 to 10 years.

1923

19" Patsy

Place on Fold

19" Patsy

COMBINATION PANTIES

(Step-Ins)
Cut Two

Place on Fold

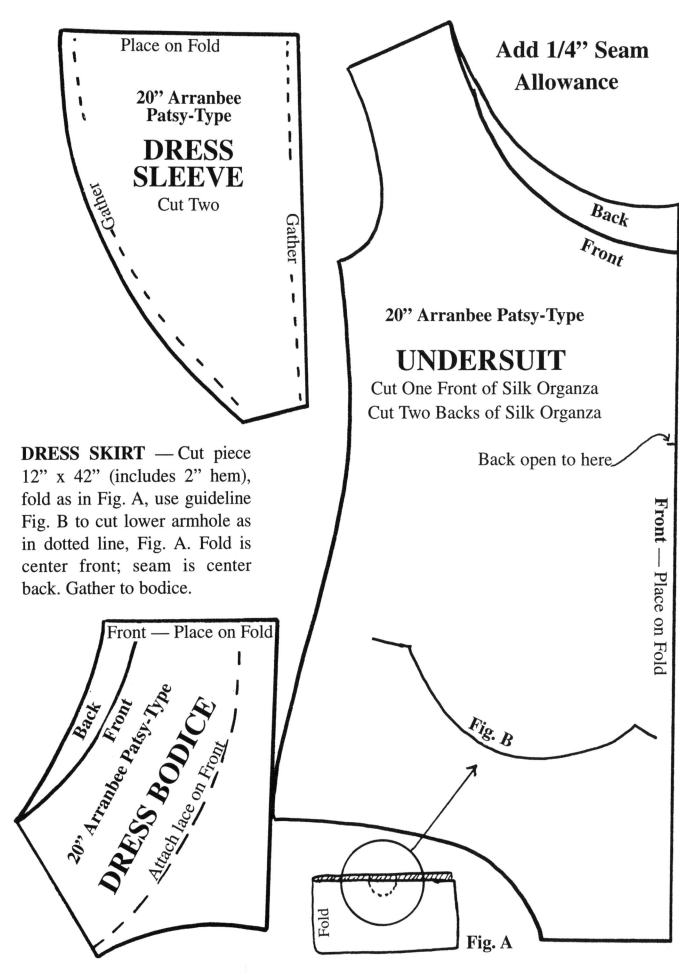

Place on Fold

20" Arranbee Patsy-Type
DRESS SLEEVE
Cut Two

Gather

Gather

Add 1/4" Seam Allowance

Back

Front

20" Arranbee Patsy-Type

UNDERSUIT
Cut One Front of Silk Organza
Cut Two Backs of Silk Organza

Back open to here

Front — Place on Fold

DRESS SKIRT — Cut piece 12" x 42" (includes 2" hem), fold as in Fig. A, use guideline Fig. B to cut lower armhole as in dotted line, Fig. A. Fold is center front; seam is center back. Gather to bodice.

Front — Place on Fold

Back

Front

20" Arranbee Patsy-Type
DRESS BODICE
Attach lace on Front

Fig. B

Fold

Fig. A

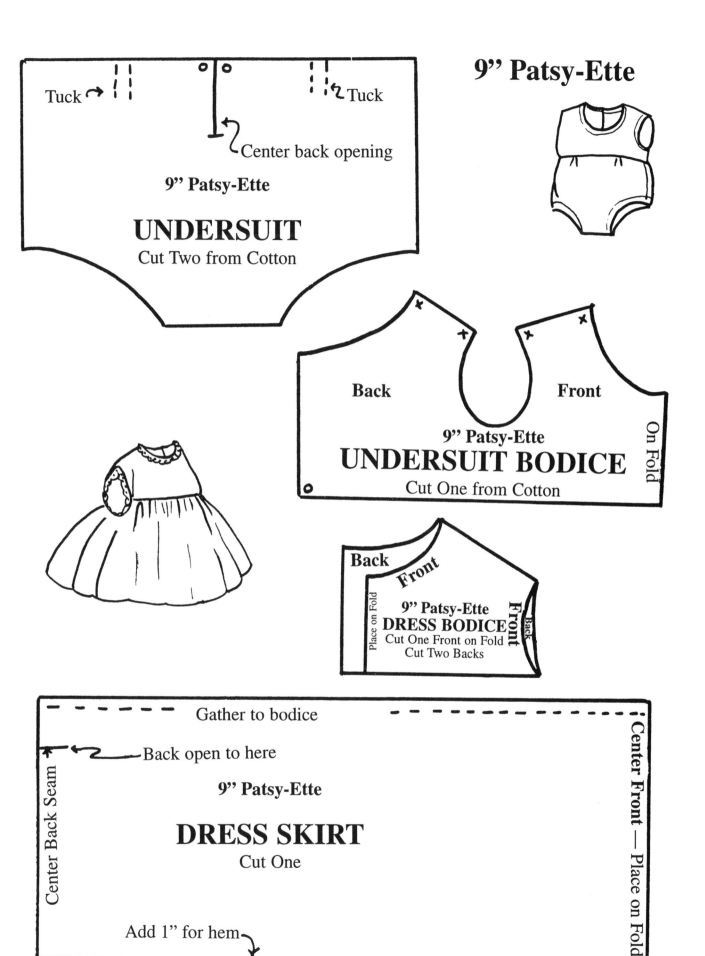

9" Patsy-Ette

Tuck →

Tuck

Center back opening

9" Patsy-Ette

UNDERSUIT
Cut Two from Cotton

Back   Front

9" Patsy-Ette
UNDERSUIT BODICE
Cut One from Cotton

On Fold

Back

Front

Place on Fold

Front

Back

9" Patsy-Ette
DRESS BODICE
Cut One Front on Fold
Cut Two Backs

Gather to bodice

Back open to here

9" Patsy-Ette

DRESS SKIRT
Cut One

Center Back Seam

Center Front — Place on Fold

Add 1" for hem

119

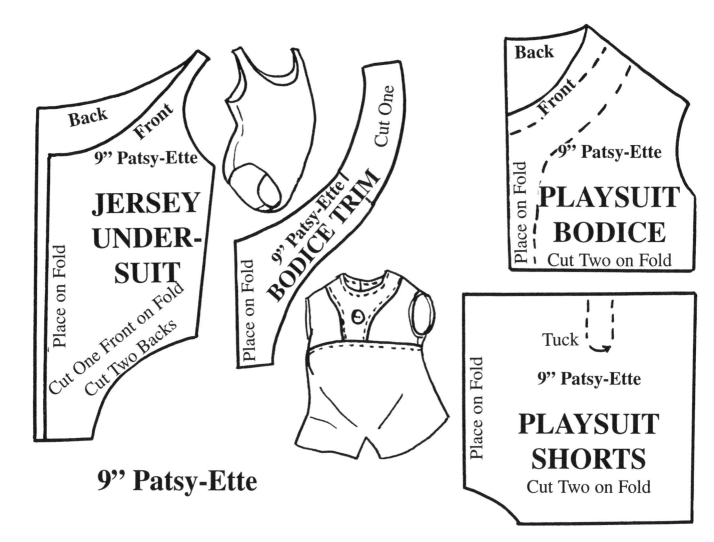

Back

Front

9" Patsy-Ette

JERSEY UNDER-SUIT

Place on Fold

Cut One Front on Fold

Cut Two Backs

9" Patsy-Ette

9" Patsy-Ette **BODICE TRIM**

Cut One

Place on Fold

Back

Front

9" Patsy-Ette

PLAYSUIT BODICE

Place on Fold

Cut Two on Fold

Tuck

9" Patsy-Ette

PLAYSUIT SHORTS

Cut Two on Fold

Place on Fold

9" Patsy-Ette

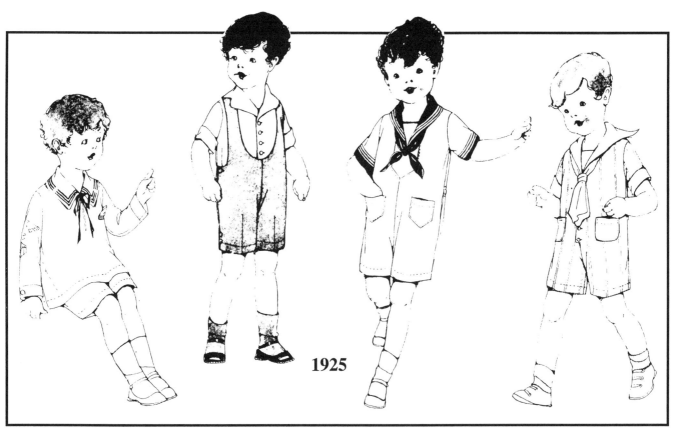

1925

22" E.I. HORSEMAN "BABY DIMPLES"
(ORIGINAL LABELED ENSEMBLE)

This costume is resplendent with lace trimming — lace finishes nearly every available edge — so be lavish with your lace. Slip and dress are of good quality organdy: however, lawn may be substituted for making the slip and panties. Sew and fit underclothes first.

PANTIES

Cut of lawn or other fine cotton. Sew side and crotch seams, turn 1/2" hem at waist and leg openings. Run narrow elastic to fit doll's waist and legs.

DRESS AND SLIP

These are cut from same pattern; cut slip 1" shorter than dress and without sleeves. Cut as shown, sew side seams, attach lace before sewing back seam. Sew only along top edge of lace which may be attached using narrow decorative braid (white). Neckline of dress is finished with lace as are the sleeves.

BONNET

To make bonnet, sew back seam A-A, run gathering thread as indicated, fit to bonnet crown and sew. Stitch lace to bonnet brim and finish edges, then sew brim to bonnet, matching center front dots. Finish face edge of bonnet with lace. Attach ribbon ties.

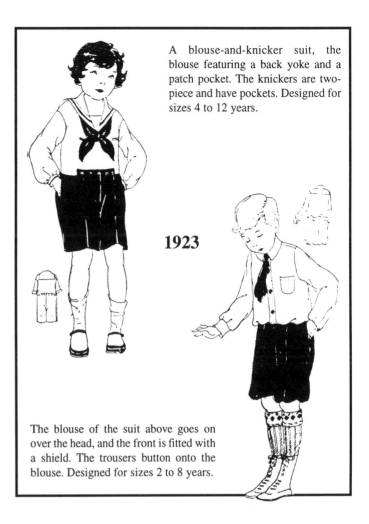

A blouse-and-knicker suit, the blouse featuring a back yoke and a patch pocket. The knickers are two-piece and have pockets. Designed for sizes 4 to 12 years.

1923

The blouse of the suit above goes on over the head, and the front is fitted with a shield. The trousers button onto the blouse. Designed for sizes 2 to 8 years.

The little middy dress below may be made of one or two materials. The gathered and plaited skirt is attached to an underbody, and the separate blouse slips on over the head. Designed for sizes 4 to 14 years.

1923

A comfortable pajama suit for little folks, made with a drop seat. Neck may be finished with a front facing, and with or without collar. Sleeves may be long or short. A handkerchief pocket is also provided for. Designed for sizes 2 to 12 years.

20" E.I. HORSMAN CHILD CA 1920

This original dress was made of red and white checked gingham, trimmed with white bias tape. Underclothes were of white cotton trimmed with cotton lace. Lawn is an excellent cotton for the underclothes since it is both fine-textured and inexpensive. Sew and fit underclothes first.

UNDERSUIT

Assemble undersuit skirt, bodice, and bloomer separately, then sew together, attaching the three into a single unit at the waist. Finish all seams.

DRESS

Cut a piece of dress fabric 6" long and 24" wide (plus seam and hem allowance) for the skirt front of dress. Gather or pleat to front of bodice (original was pleated).

Make two belts from pieces of dress fabric 8" long and 2" wide. Seam and turn, topstitch. Baste one belt to each side back at X on underarm seam.

Seam back and front sections together at shoulder and side seams. Set in sleeves.

Work buttonhole on end of one belt and sew button to end of remaining belt.

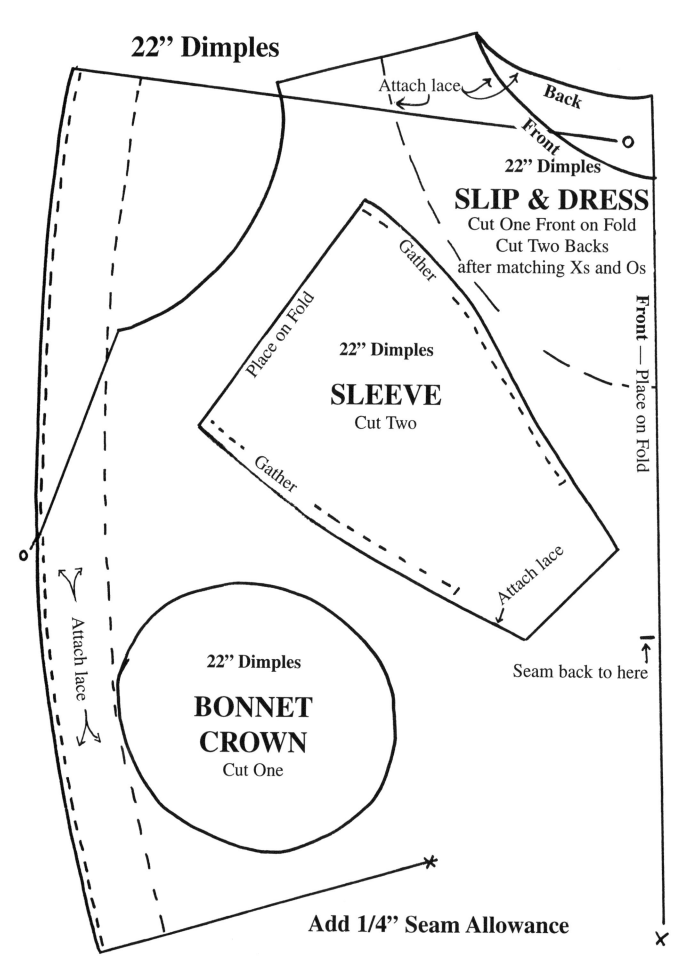

22" Dimples

Attach lace

Back

Front

o

22" Dimples

SLIP & DRESS
Cut One Front on Fold
Cut Two Backs
after matching Xs and Os

Gather

Place on Fold

Front — Place on Fold

22" Dimples

SLEEVE
Cut Two

Gather

Attach lace

Seam back to here

Place on Fold

o

Attach lace

22" Dimples

BONNET
CROWN
Cut One

✱

Add 1/4" Seam Allowance

✕

22" Dimples

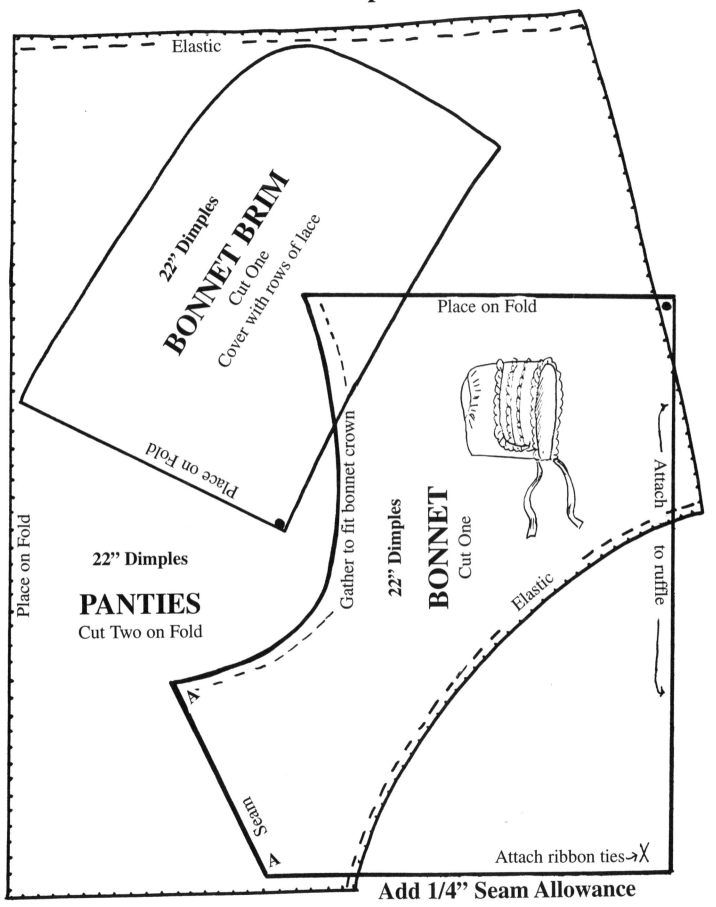

Elastic

22" Dimples

BONNET BRIM

Cut One

Cover with rows of lace

Place on Fold

Place on Fold

Place on Fold

22" Dimples

PANTIES

Cut Two on Fold

Gather to fit bonnet crown

22" Dimples

BONNET

Cut One

Elastic

Attach to ruffle

A

Seam

A

Attach ribbon ties→X

Add 1/4" Seam Allowance

20" Horsman Child

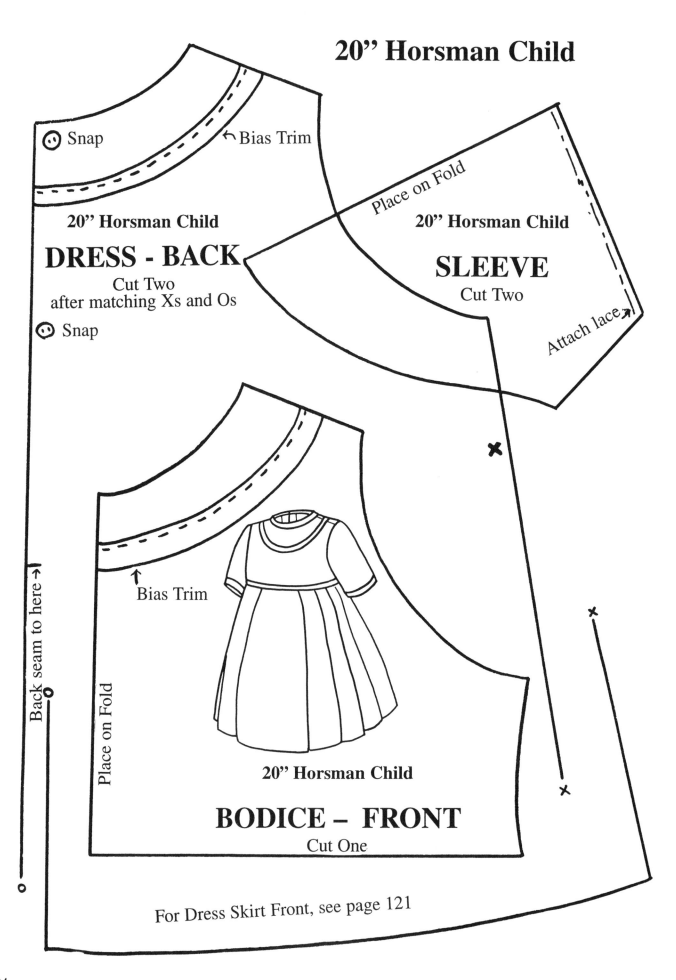

⊙ Snap ← Bias Trim

20" Horsman Child

DRESS - BACK
Cut Two
after matching Xs and Os

⊙ Snap

Place on Fold

20" Horsman Child

SLEEVE
Cut Two

Attach lace ↗

Back seam to here →

Place on Fold

← Bias Trim

↑ Bias Trim

Place on Fold

20" Horsman Child

BODICE – FRONT
Cut One

For Dress Skirt Front, see page 121

124

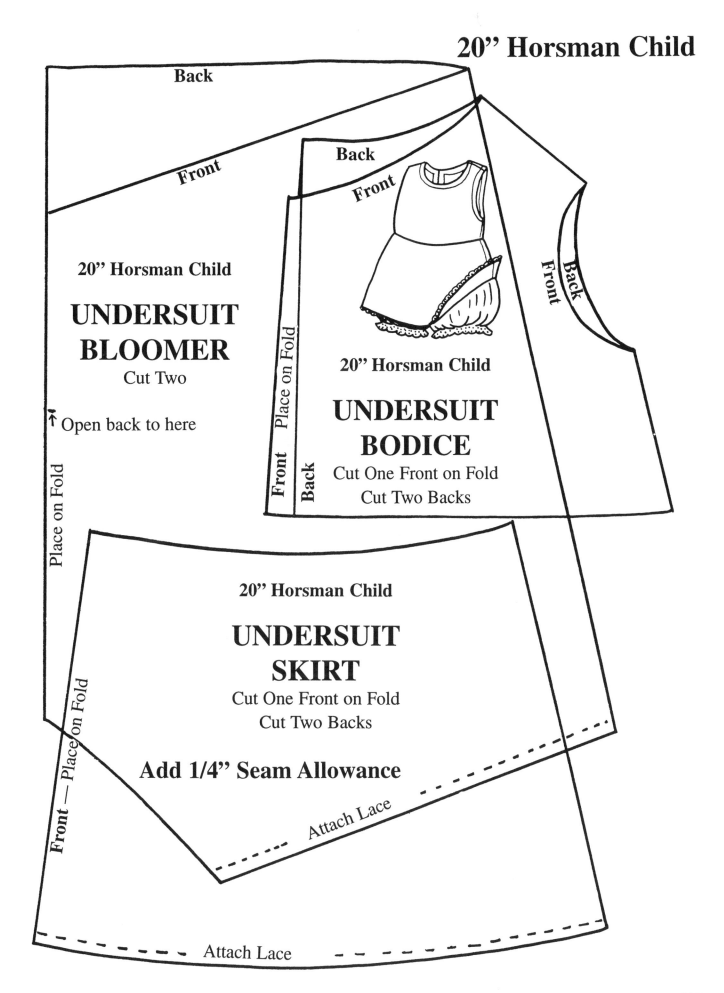

Back

Front

20" Horsman Child

UNDERSUIT BLOOMER

Cut Two

↑ Open back to here

Place on Fold

Back

Front

Front — Place on Fold

Back

Front

Back

Front

Place on Fold

20" Horsman Child

UNDERSUIT BODICE

Cut One Front on Fold

Cut Two Backs

20" Horsman Child

UNDERSUIT SKIRT

Cut One Front on Fold

Cut Two Backs

Add 1/4" Seam Allowance

Front — Place on Fold

Attach Lace

Attach Lace

1925

Chapter 10

THE 1930S

Silky, slinky pajamas with coats of the same fabric were considered quite chic in 1931. Baby dolls wore moccasin-style shoes of white leather in 1932. Ladies' fashions featured *Glamorous Hollywood Stars* in catalogs of 1933 and 1934. Such stars as Claudette Colbert in *Death Takes a Holiday*, Marlene Dietrich in *Song of Songs*, and Sylvia Sidney in *World's Fair Favorites* were posed to display the fashions to advantage. Hollywood was quoted as recommending: *"suit the women with mannish flannels"*.

That same year girls' dresses had puff sleeves and boleros. The fabrics were rayon and cotton blends, percale, organdy, wool jersey, and wool and silk blends. Bows trimmed collars and cuffs. Hair was bobbed and sometimes slightly marcelled or Patsy-styled, only fluffier. Cover-all style playsuits were recommended for girls.

Underwear included bloomers, vests, slips, and "French combinations" of rayon or cotton. Little boys wore knickers, Corduroy Cossack suits, short, banded jackets and trousers, and aviator-style suits.

In ladies' fashions many separate collars were shown in white silk, organdy, and lace. Scarves and belts were recommended to "perk up that old dress-this is 1933!" Children's coats reflected adult fashions with double breasted closings, aviator-style collars, raccoon collars, or fur fabric trim. Small girls wore double-breasted, semi-fitted coats with matching tams and fitted leggings with side zipper. Chinchilla cloth was often the choice for both adults and children. *"Autographed fashions"* were the vogue in 1934 and featured *Fay May, Frances Dee, and Loretta Young*.

This decade saw a decided change in women's clothing. In 1933 McCall's recommended decorative embroidery on graceful, fluid sleeves. By the end of the decade, shoulders had widened almost without exception to the padded, mannish appearance which was to become a trend lasting into the 1940s.

1930

Good Count Fast Color Broadcloth

Broadcloth and Linene

Suggested 25¢ to 29¢ Retailers
BROADCLOTH AND LINENE
— ALL COLORS FAST

1933

Broadcloth

"Mickey
Mouse"
Fidelity Rib

Children's
Anklets

Long Pants Suits

128

1937

1936

Cable Stitching

India Prints

Saw-tooth trim

Plaiting

Applique

1937

EXCLUSIVE shops give proof that trimmings are increasing in importance both for apparel and for home furnishings, and it seems that every kind of fabric is being decorated. Light-weight woolens, firm cottons, and linens are smart for short-sleeved, flare-skirted frocks. On these, cable stitching is used as an effective trimming.

Sometimes a bias tubing of the fabric is used and cable stitched in place with embroidery threads in two or three colors. Some of the peasant skirts have three rows of fabric tubing caught down with cable stitches. We see this trim on many sturdy frocks and on beach clothes.

Some good dresses show the tubing covered with the same stitching to make a cord for the waistline. Again, a cord is used for the trim for the neck and the sleeves, and the cord is caught in place with fine hand-stitches.

The very popular saw-tooth trimming of piqué, of linen braid, of bias binding, or of the fabric itself, is ideal because it launders readily. The smartest kind is easy to make with a machine-craft guide. The saw-tooth trimming is made by winding the fabric diagonally on the guide, stitching two rows through the center one-eighth inch apart, and cutting between the rows and in that way obtaining two lengths of trimming.

Turbans, scarfs, and blouses of Paisley prints continue everywhere. Many of these are made of medium-sized or large handkerchiefs. Paisley blouses are decidedly smart for beach or sports wear, particularly with plain skirts or with slacks.

Embroidery

Stitching

Printed Tops

Shirring

1939

1939

1938

1939

1938

1938

1938

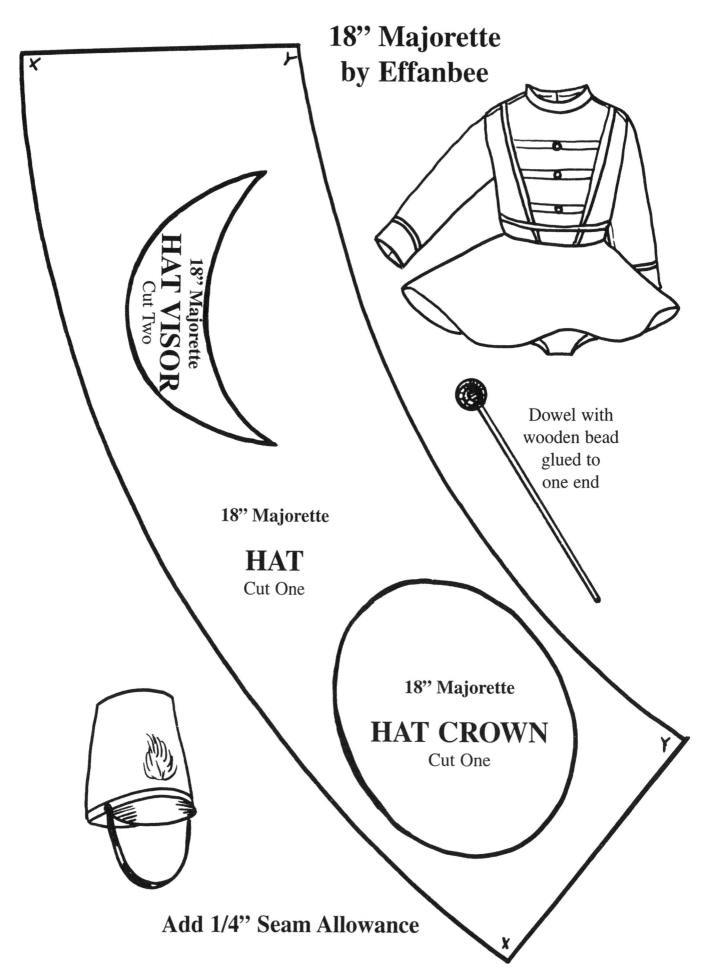

18" Majorette
by Effanbee

18" Majorette
HAT VISOR
Cut Two

18" Majorette

HAT
Cut One

Dowel with wooden bead glued to one end

18" Majorette

HAT CROWN
Cut One

Add 1/4" Seam Allowance

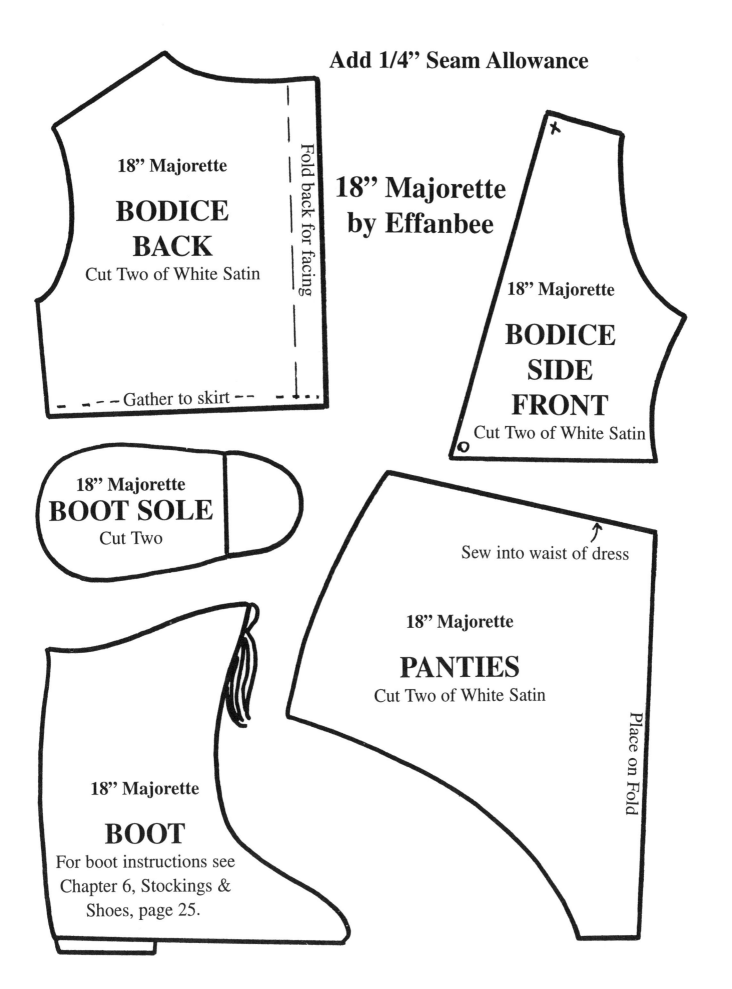

Add 1/4" Seam Allowance

18" Majorette
BODICE BACK
Cut Two of White Satin

Fold back for facing

Gather to skirt

18" Majorette by Effanbee

18" Majorette
BODICE SIDE FRONT
Cut Two of White Satin

18" Majorette
BOOT SOLE
Cut Two

Sew into waist of dress

18" Majorette
PANTIES
Cut Two of White Satin

Place on Fold

18" Majorette
BOOT
For boot instructions see Chapter 6, Stockings & Shoes, page 25.

133

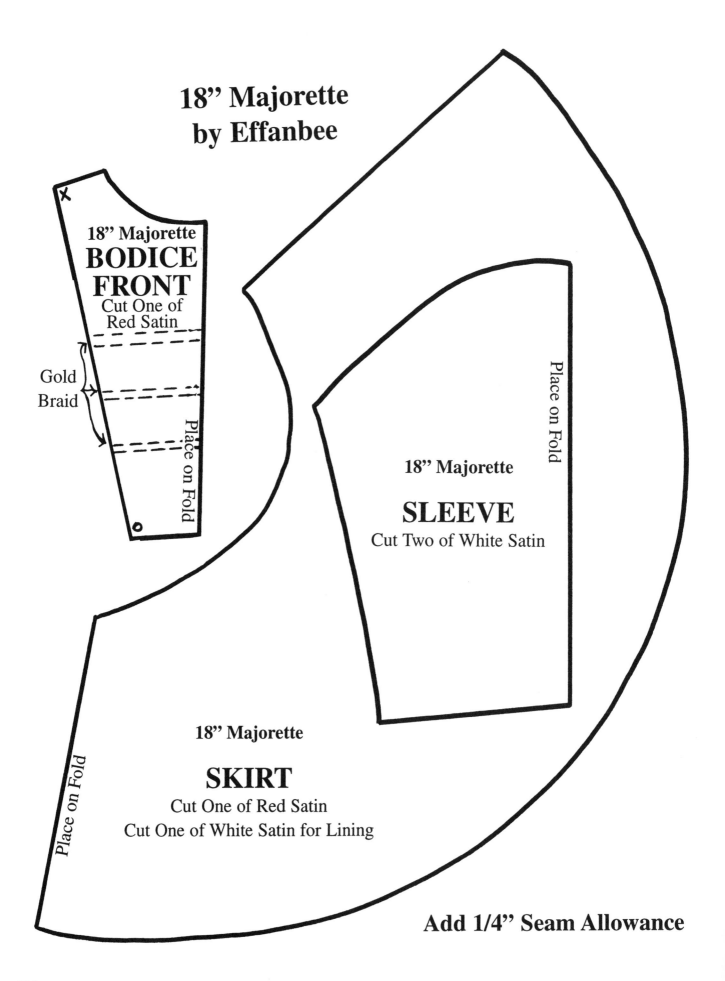

18" Majorette
by Effanbee

18" Majorette
BODICE
FRONT
Cut One of
Red Satin

Gold
Braid

Place on Fold

18" Majorette

SLEEVE
Cut Two of White Satin

Place on Fold

18" Majorette

SKIRT
Cut One of Red Satin
Cut One of White Satin for Lining

Place on Fold

Add 1/4" Seam Allowance

21" Deanna Durbin

For skirt of dress cut rectangle 11-1/2" x 52" and gather to bodice.

Extend to 10-1/2"

21" Deanna Durbin

HALF SLIP
Cut Four

Extend to 10-1/2"

1937

21" Deanna Durbin

Place on Fold

DRESS BODICE FRONT
Cut One

Add 1/4" Seam Allowance

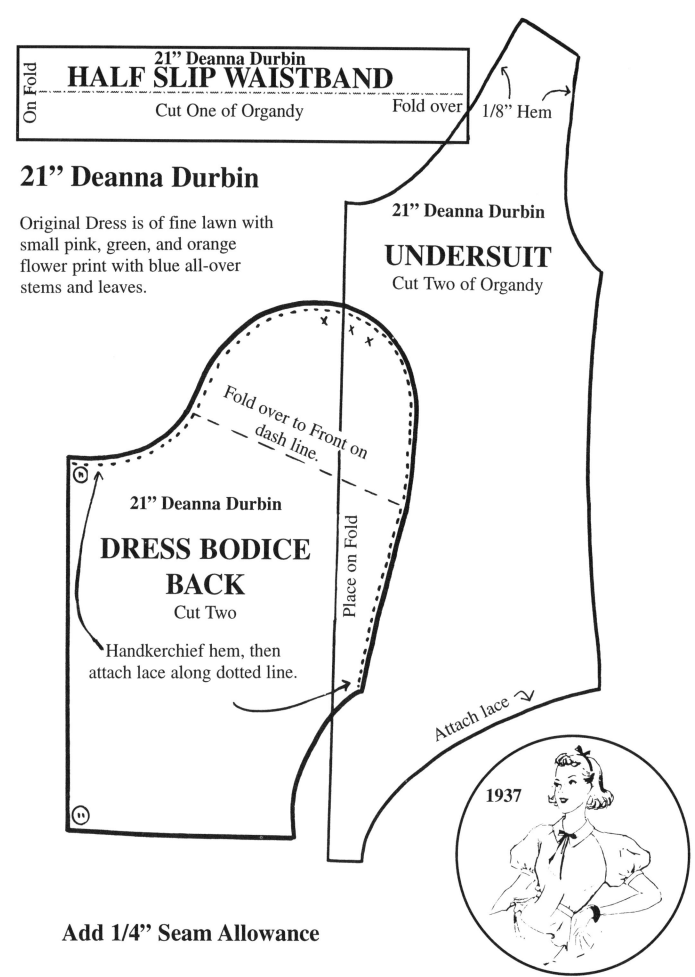

21" Deanna Durbin
HALF SLIP WAISTBAND
On Fold

Cut One of Organdy   Fold over   1/8" Hem

21" Deanna Durbin

Original Dress is of fine lawn with small pink, green, and orange flower print with blue all-over stems and leaves.

21" Deanna Durbin

UNDERSUIT
Cut Two of Organdy

Fold over to Front on dash line.

21" Deanna Durbin

DRESS BODICE BACK
Cut Two

Handkerchief hem, then attach lace along dotted line.

Place on Fold

Attach lace

1937

Add 1/4" Seam Allowance

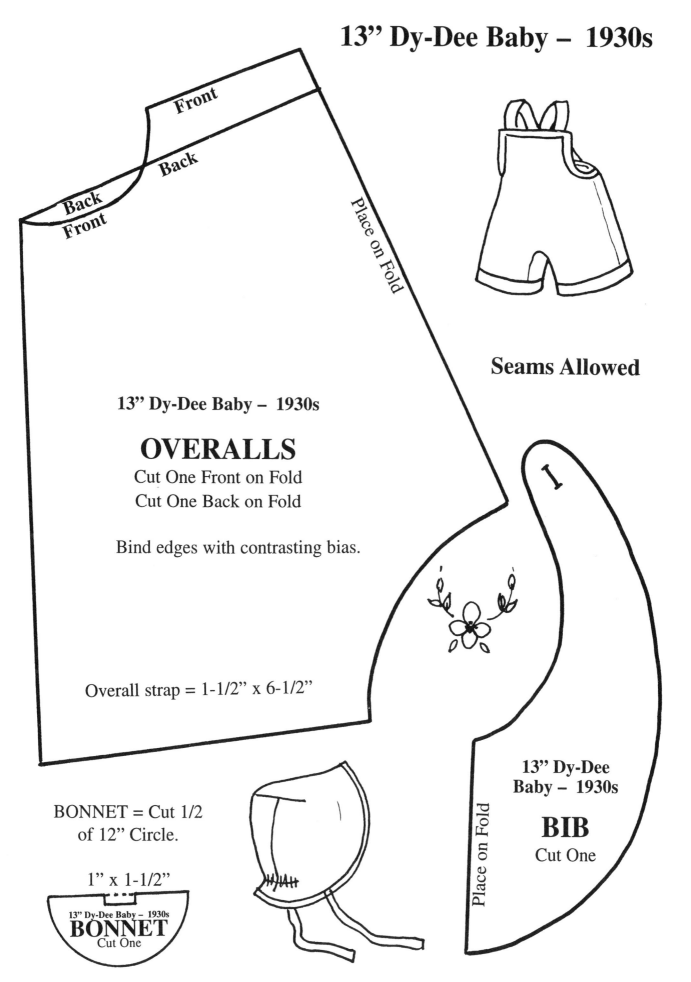

Front

Back

Back

Front

Place on Fold

Seams Allowed

13" Dy-Dee Baby – 1930s

OVERALLS

Cut One Front on Fold

Cut One Back on Fold

Bind edges with contrasting bias.

Overall strap = 1-1/2" x 6-1/2"

BONNET = Cut 1/2
of 12" Circle.

1" x 1-1/2"

13" Dy-Dee Baby – 1930s
BONNET
Cut One

13" Dy-Dee
Baby – 1930s

BIB

Cut One

Place on Fold

1936

18" JUDY GARLAND (IDEAL)

Original costume worn by the actress as Dorothy in the movie, *The Wizard of Oz*: blue and white checked rayon with white organdy bodice trimmed with tiny blue ric-rac and organdy underclothes.

BODICE — Cut entire bodice of white organdy, then cut lower (shaded) area of pattern from checked material. Bands on bodice are cut from checked material on bias. Back is finished same as front. Collar is 1/2" ruffle or organdy edged with ric-rac and finished off around neck with another row of ric-rac.

SKIRT — Cut three strips of checked fabric as follows:

a) One piece 2-3/4" by 30" on straight

b) One piece 1-1/4" by 30" on bias

c) One piece 2-1/2" by 30" on straight

Sew together with bias strip (b) between strips (a) and (c). Turn (c) up 1" for hem and finish. Set aside.

Make organdy petticoat of strip of fabric 3-1/2" by 24", edge one long edge with lace, baste other long edge to upper edge of (a) on skirt unit.

Gather as one to fit bodice and seam to bodice. Seam up back to within 2" of waist seam.

SHOES — See Chapter 6 STOCKINGS AND SHOES.

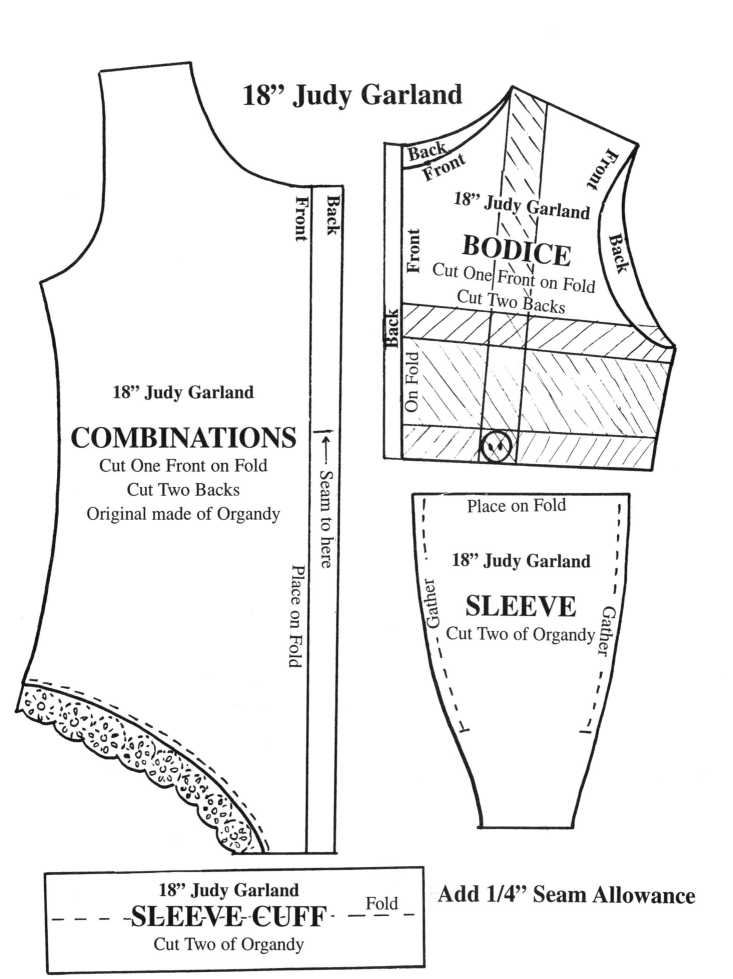

18" Judy Garland

18" Judy Garland

COMBINATIONS

Cut One Front on Fold

Cut Two Backs

Original made of Organdy

Front | Back

Seam to here

Place on Fold

Back / Front

Front

18" Judy Garland

BODICE

Cut One Front on Fold

Cut Two Backs

Front | Back

Back

On Fold

Place on Fold

18" Judy Garland

SLEEVE

Cut Two of Organdy

Gather | Gather

18" Judy Garland

SLEEVE CUFF

Cut Two of Organdy

Fold

Add 1/4" Seam Allowance

24" Composition
Girl Doll — 1930s

Back

Front

Front — Place on Fold

24" Composition
Girl Doll – 1930s

BODICE
Cut One Front on Fold
Cut Two Backs

Add 1/4" Seam Allowance

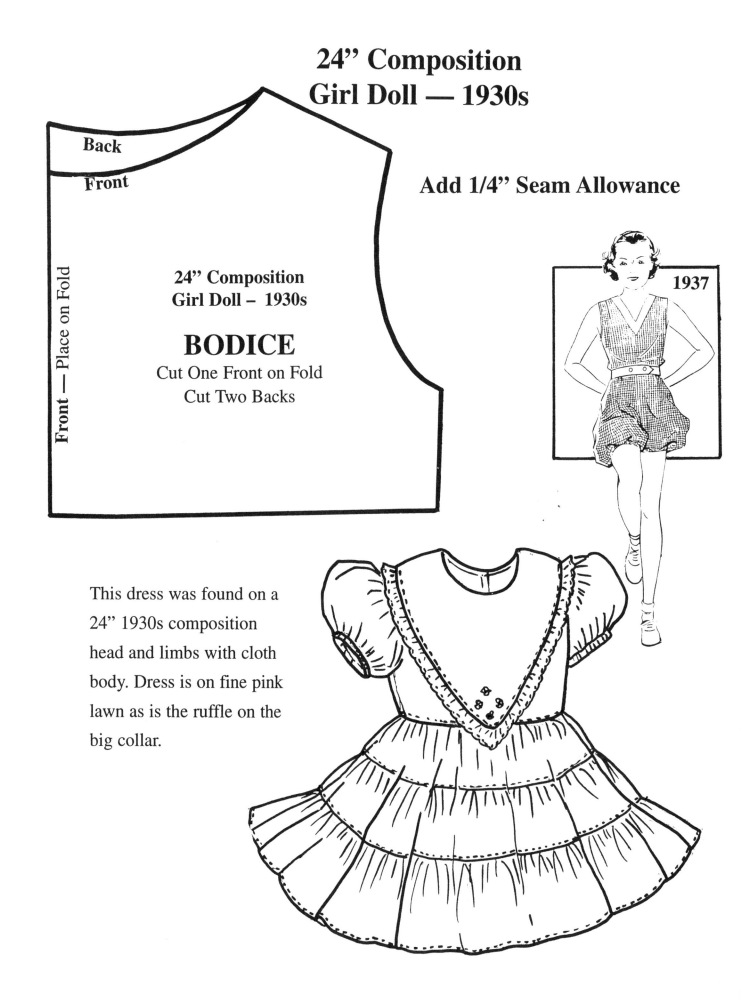

1937

This dress was found on a 24" 1930s composition head and limbs with cloth body. Dress is on fine pink lawn as is the ruffle on the big collar.

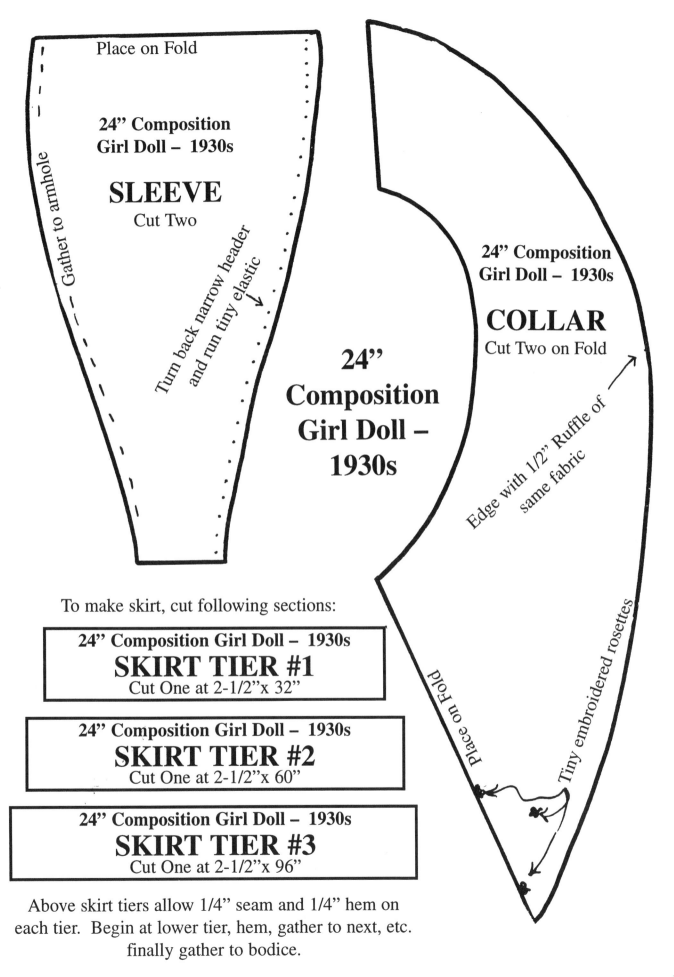

Place on Fold

Gather to armhole

**24" Composition
Girl Doll – 1930s**

SLEEVE
Cut Two

Turn back narrow header and run tiny elastic

**24"
Composition
Girl Doll –
1930s**

**24" Composition
Girl Doll – 1930s**

COLLAR
Cut Two on Fold

Edge with 1/2" Ruffle of same fabric

Place on Fold

Tiny embroidered rosettes

To make skirt, cut following sections:

24" Composition Girl Doll – 1930s
SKIRT TIER #1
Cut One at 2-1/2"x 32"

24" Composition Girl Doll – 1930s
SKIRT TIER #2
Cut One at 2-1/2"x 60"

24" Composition Girl Doll – 1930s
SKIRT TIER #3
Cut One at 2-1/2"x 96"

Above skirt tiers allow 1/4" seam and 1/4" hem on
each tier. Begin at lower tier, hem, gather to next, etc.
finally gather to bodice.

**18" Shirley Temple
Doll Outfits**

18" Shirley Temple
Doll Outfits

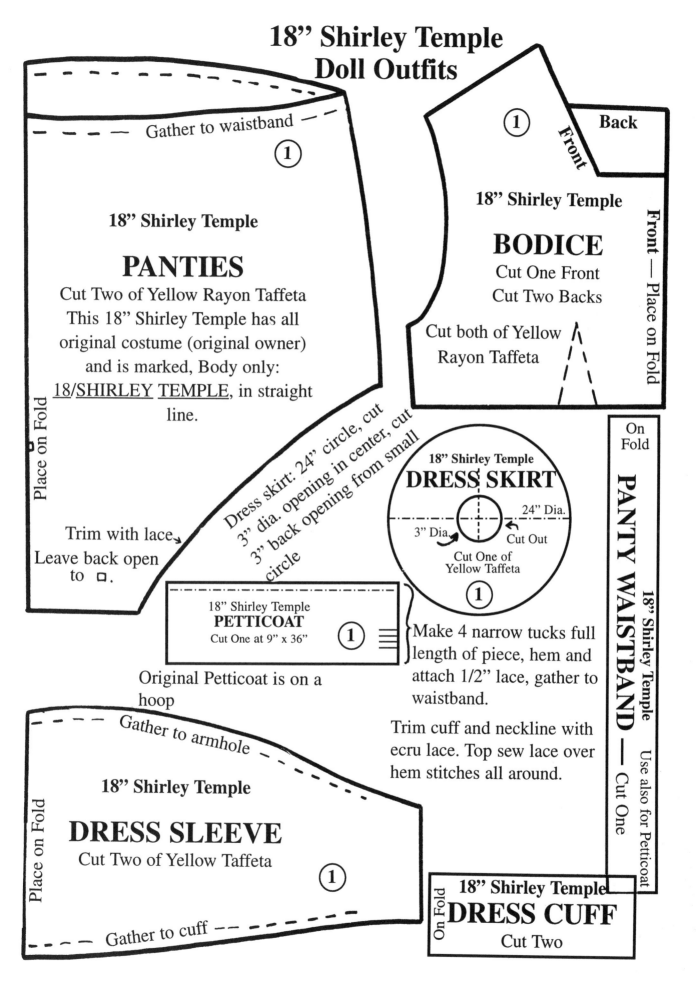

Gather to waistband ①

18" Shirley Temple

PANTIES

Cut Two of Yellow Rayon Taffeta
This 18" Shirley Temple has all
original costume (original owner)
and is marked, Body only:
<u>18/SHIRLEY</u> <u>TEMPLE</u>, in straight
line.

Place on Fold

Trim with lace
Leave back open
to ▫.

Dress skirt: 24" circle, cut
3" dia. opening in center, cut
3" back opening from small
circle

① ①

18" Shirley Temple

BODICE

Cut One Front
Cut Two Backs

Cut both of Yellow
Rayon Taffeta

Back

Front

Front — Place on Fold

18" Shirley Temple
DRESS SKIRT

24" Dia.

3" Dia.

Cut Out

Cut One of
Yellow Taffeta

①

On
Fold

PANTY WAISTBAND — Cut One

18" Shirley Temple

Use also for Petticoat

18" Shirley Temple
PETTICOAT
Cut One at 9" x 36"

①

Original Petticoat is on a
hoop

Make 4 narrow tucks full
length of piece, hem and
attach 1/2" lace, gather to
waistband.

Trim cuff and neckline with
ecru lace. Top sew lace over
hem stitches all around.

Gather to armhole

18" Shirley Temple

DRESS SLEEVE

Cut Two of Yellow Taffeta

Place on Fold

① ①

Gather to cuff

On Fold

18" Shirley Temple
DRESS CUFF
Cut Two

18" Shirley Temple
Doll Outfits

Back

Front

Place on Fold

Bias Trim

18" Shirley Temple
BODICE
Cut One Front on Fold
Cut Two Backs

②

Gather

18" Shirley Temple
SLEEVE
②

Place on Fold

Gather

18" Shirley Temple Original Dress
Skirt of Dress:

Cut rectangle 5-1/2" x 30", cut scallops along one long side using profile below. Bind scallop edge with very narrow bias in same color as dots on dress fabric. Using same narrow bias, stitch 2 rows of trim one inch apart and one inch from hem following scallop pattern.

Make petticoat of white organdy piece 4-1/2" x 24". Hem, then gather skirt and petticoat as one and attach to bodice.

This Shirley wears an undergarment identical to that worn by Judy Garland, shown.

Add 1/4" Seam Allowance

Profile of scallops

②

18" Shirley Temple Doll Outfits

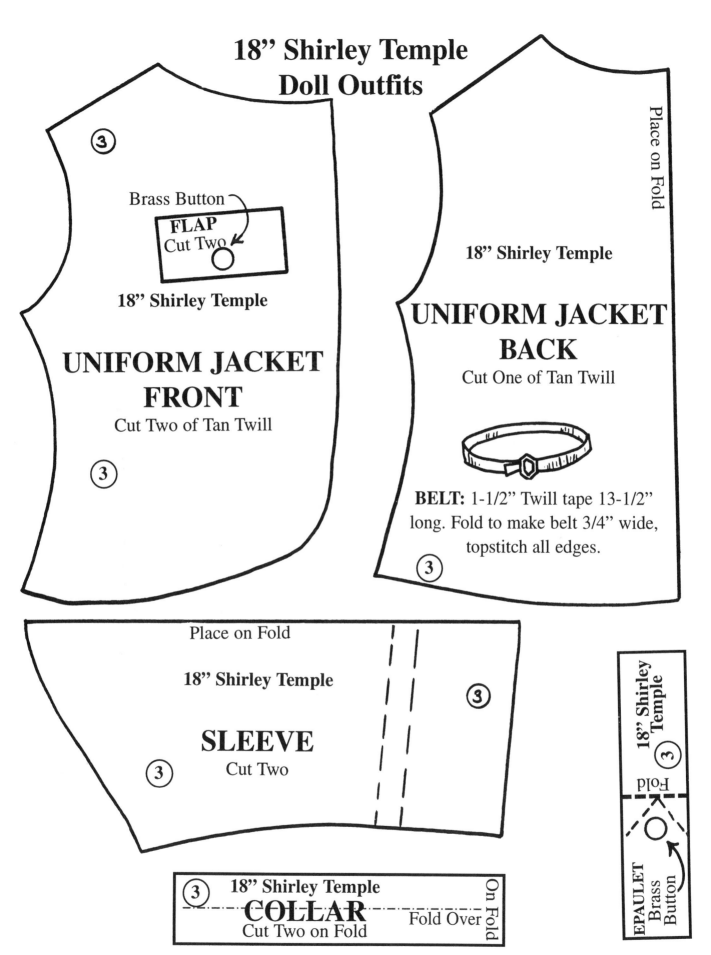

Brass Button

FLAP
Cut Two

18" Shirley Temple

UNIFORM JACKET FRONT

Cut Two of Tan Twill

18" Shirley Temple

UNIFORM JACKET BACK

Cut One of Tan Twill

Place on Fold

BELT: 1-1/2" Twill tape 13-1/2" long. Fold to make belt 3/4" wide, topstitch all edges.

Place on Fold

18" Shirley Temple

SLEEVE

Cut Two

18" Shirley Temple
COLLAR
Cut Two on Fold

Fold Over

On Fold

18" Shirley Temple

Fold

EPAULET
Brass Button

Add 1/4" Seam Allowance

145

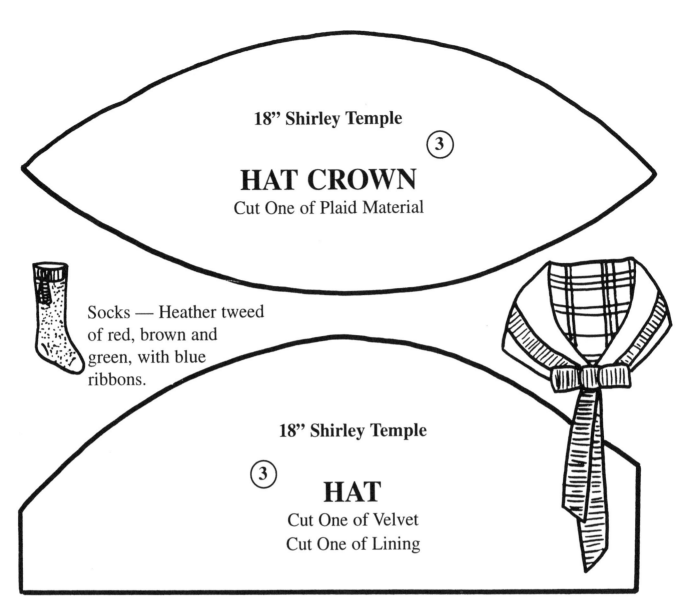

18" Shirley Temple

③

HAT CROWN
Cut One of Plaid Material

Socks — Heather tweed of red, brown and green, with blue ribbons.

18" Shirley Temple

③

HAT
Cut One of Velvet
Cut One of Lining

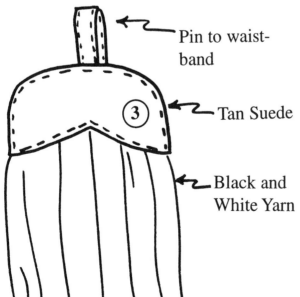

← Pin to waist-band

③ ← Tan Suede

← Black and White Yarn

To make kilt:
Cut rectangle 5-1/2" x 24" plus hem and seam allowance. Pleat evenly to waistband.

Waistband of skirt (kilt):

18" Shirley Temple Doll Outfits

18" Shirley Temple
KILT WAISTBAND ③
Cut One at 1" x 8"

Add 1/4" Seam Allowance

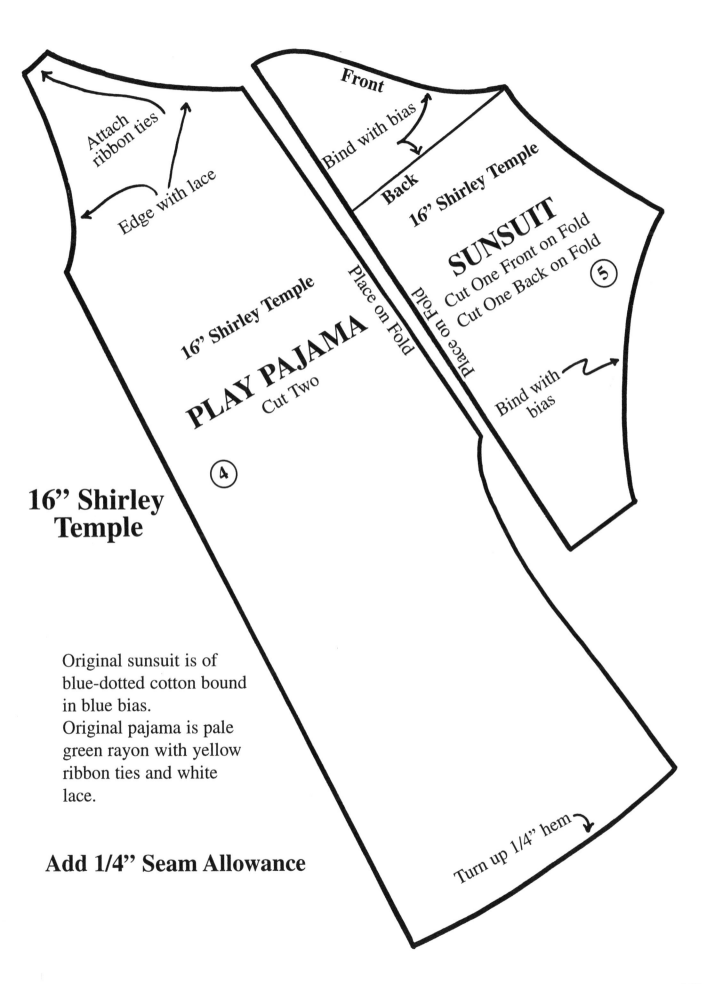

Attach ribbon ties

Edge with lace

Front

Bind with bias

Back

16" Shirley Temple

PLAY PAJAMA

Cut Two

④

Place on Fold

16" Shirley Temple

SUNSUIT

Cut One Front on Fold
Cut One Back on Fold

⑤

Place on Fold

Bind with bias

**16" Shirley
Temple**

Original sunsuit is of
blue-dotted cotton bound
in blue bias.
Original pajama is pale
green rayon with yellow
ribbon ties and white
lace.

Turn up 1/4" hem

Add 1/4" Seam Allowance

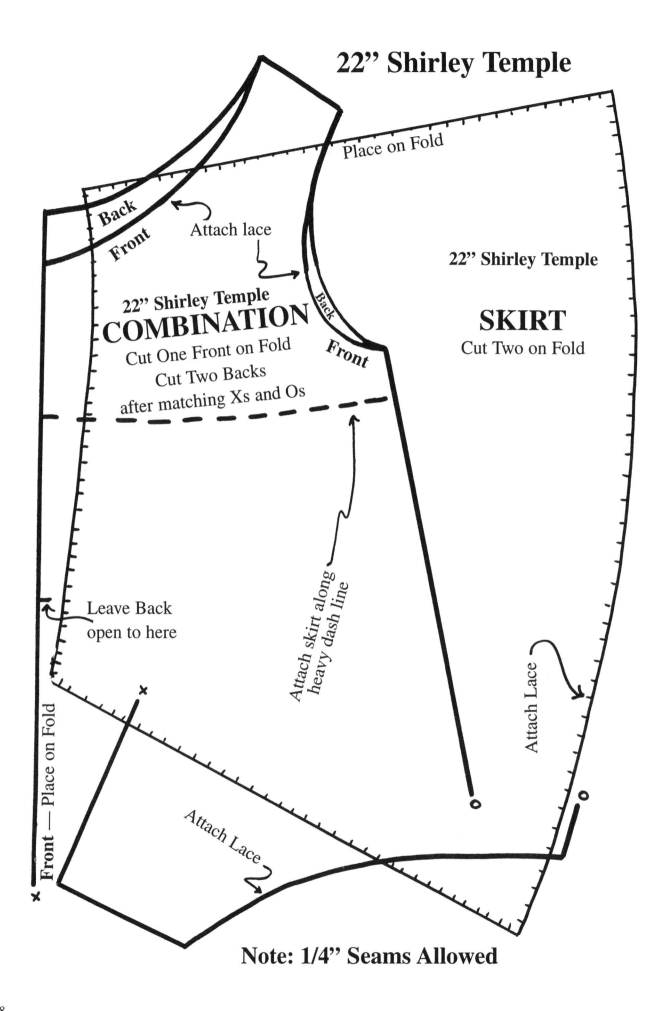

22" Shirley Temple

Place on Fold

Back

Front

Attach lace

22" Shirley Temple

Back

Front

22" Shirley Temple
COMBINATION
Cut One Front on Fold
Cut Two Backs
after matching Xs and Os

22" Shirley Temple

SKIRT
Cut Two on Fold

Leave Back
open to here

Attach skirt along
heavy dash line

Front — Place on Fold

Attach Lace

Attach Lace

Attach Lace

Note: 1/4" Seams Allowed

22" Shirley Temple

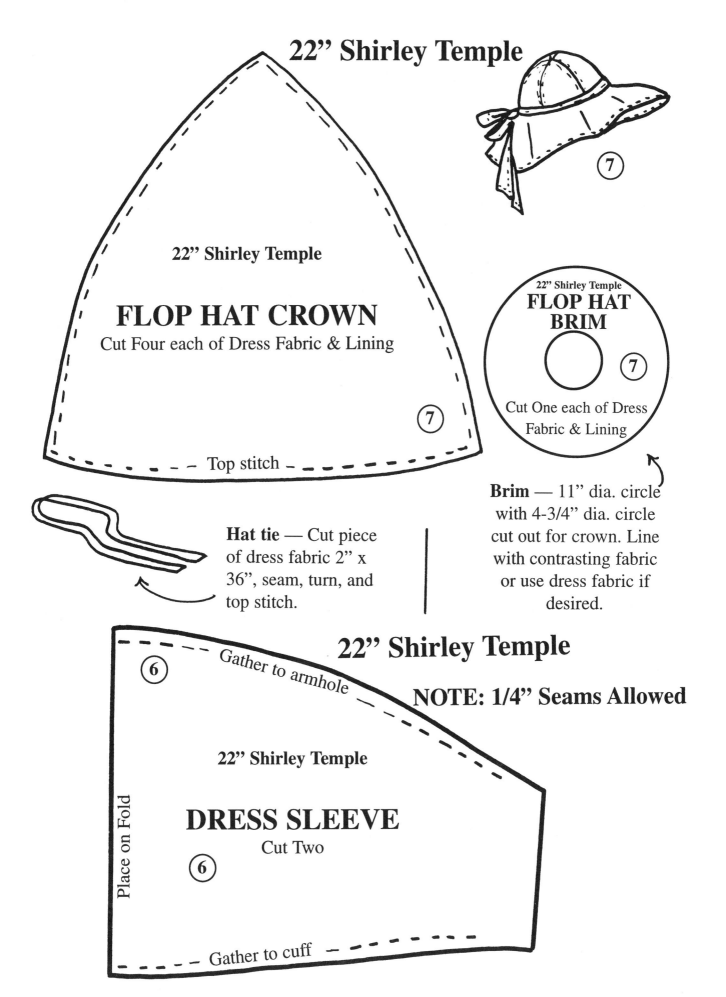

22" Shirley Temple

FLOP HAT CROWN
Cut Four each of Dress Fabric & Lining

⑦

- Top stitch -

22" Shirley Temple
FLOP HAT BRIM
Cut One each of Dress Fabric & Lining

⑦

Hat tie — Cut piece of dress fabric 2" x 36", seam, turn, and top stitch.

Brim — 11" dia. circle with 4-3/4" dia. circle cut out for crown. Line with contrasting fabric or use dress fabric if desired.

22" Shirley Temple

⑥   Gather to armhole

NOTE: 1/4" Seams Allowed

22" Shirley Temple

Place on Fold

DRESS SLEEVE
Cut Two

⑥

Gather to cuff

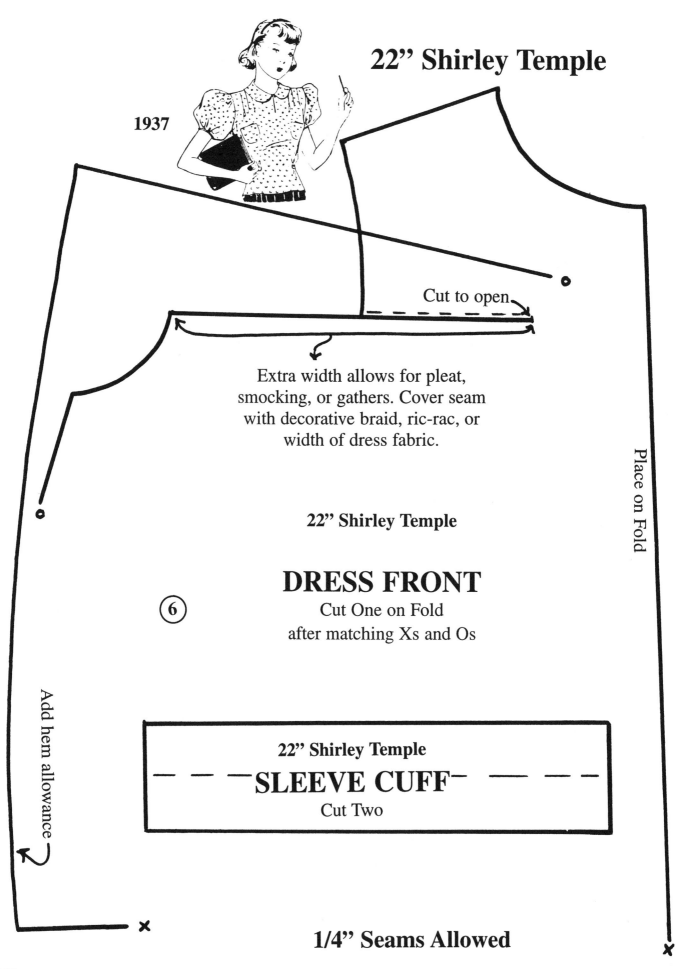

22" Shirley Temple

1937

Cut to open

Extra width allows for pleat, smocking, or gathers. Cover seam with decorative braid, ric-rac, or width of dress fabric.

22" Shirley Temple

DRESS FRONT

Cut One on Fold
after matching Xs and Os

(6)

Place on Fold

Add hem allowance

22" Shirley Temple

SLEEVE CUFF

Cut Two

1/4" Seams Allowed

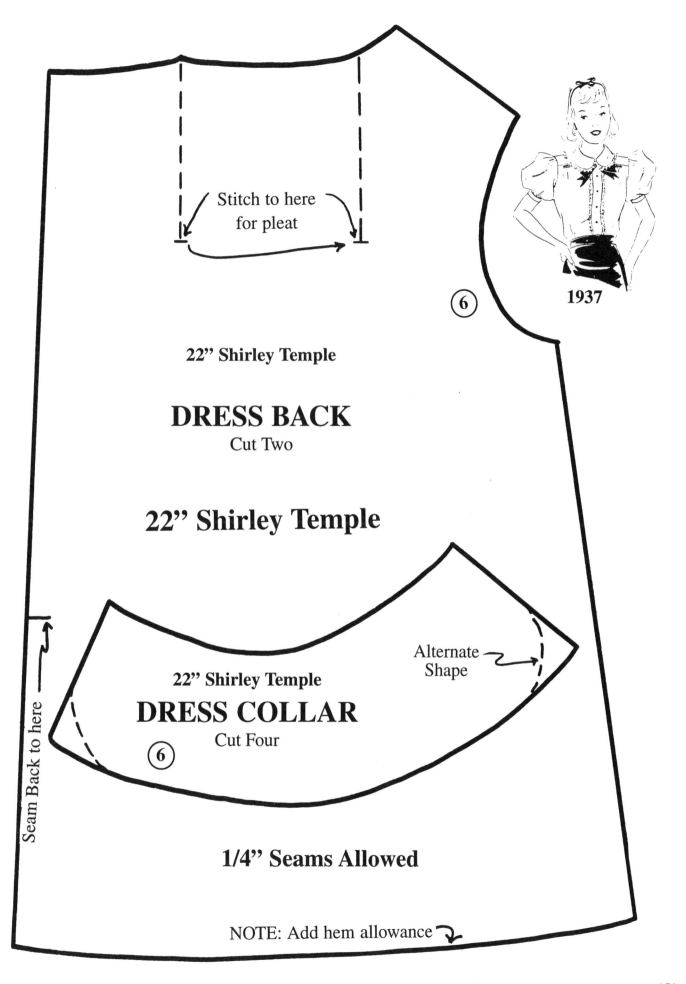

Stitch to here
for pleat

⑥

1937

22" Shirley Temple

DRESS BACK
Cut Two

22" Shirley Temple

Alternate
Shape

22" Shirley Temple

DRESS COLLAR
Cut Four

⑥

Seam Back to here

1/4" Seams Allowed

NOTE: Add hem allowance ↘

19" EMELIE DIONNE BY MADAME ALEXANDER

Tiny lavendar flowers and leaves, narrow lace and soft white cotton make up this original Dionne costume by Madame Alexander. Fit and sew undergarments first; fit dress over completed underwear on doll.

COMBINATIONS

Cut from lawn or other fine white cotton. Cut a rectangle 20" long and 5" wide (plus hem and seam allowances) for skirt of this combination panty-slip. Hem and attach 3/8" lace on one long side, gather remaining long side and fit to undersuit along broken line on pattern.

DRESS

For skirt front cut a rectangle of dress fabric 20" long and 5-1/2" wide (plus hem and seam allowances). Gather and fit to bodice on one long side. Seam bodice-skirt unit to dress back at shoulder, insert sleeves and stitch side seams, continuing through sleeve underarm seam. Finish neck opening with tiny ric-rac; sew narrow insertion lace around waist over seam; insert narrow black satin ribbon and tie bow in front.

BONNET

Seam bonnet together at back seam, sew side A to bonnet crown. Seam two pieces of bonnet brim, right sides together, turn and attach to side B of bonnet. Finish edges and attach black satin ribbon ties.

SHOES

For Emelie's shoes, see Chapter 6 STOCKINGS AND SHOES.

19" Emelie Dionne

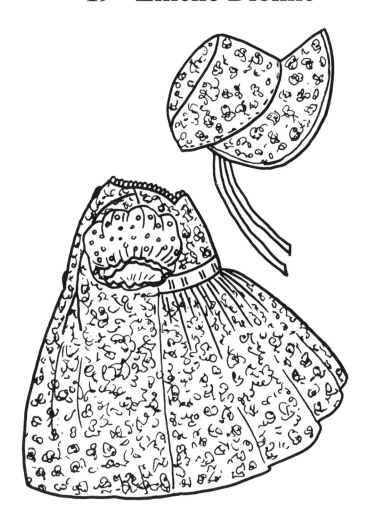

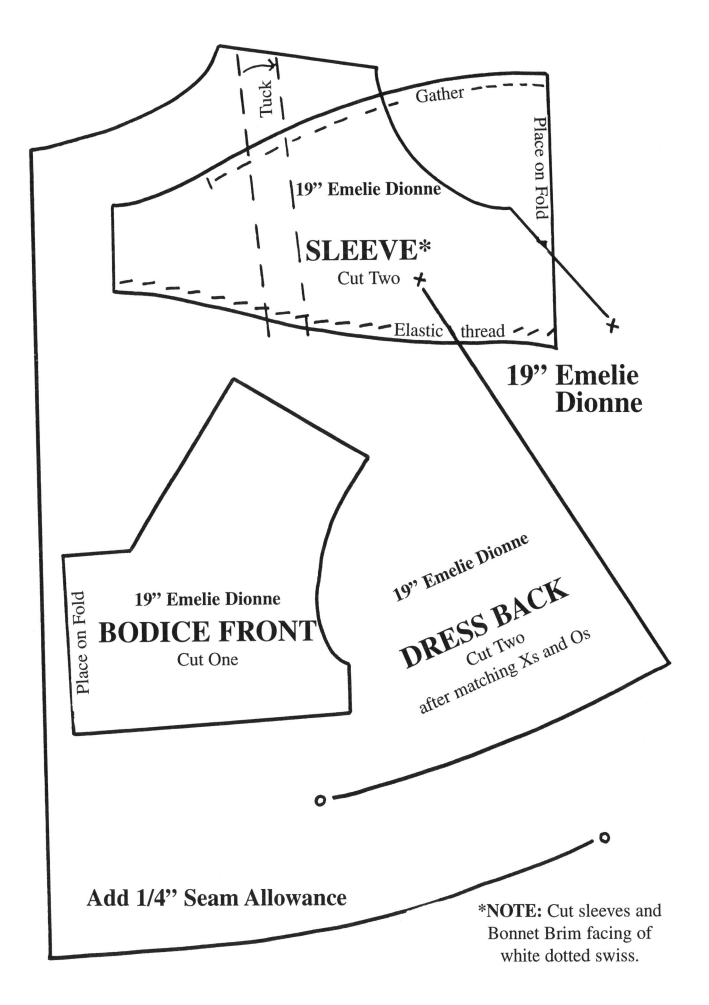

Tuck

Gather

Place on Fold

19" Emelie Dionne

SLEEVE*

Cut Two

Elastic thread

19" Emelie Dionne

19" Emelie Dionne

Place on Fold

19" Emelie Dionne
BODICE FRONT
Cut One

19" Emelie Dionne

DRESS BACK

Cut Two

after matching Xs and Os

Add 1/4" Seam Allowance

*NOTE: Cut sleeves and
Bonnet Brim facing of
white dotted swiss.

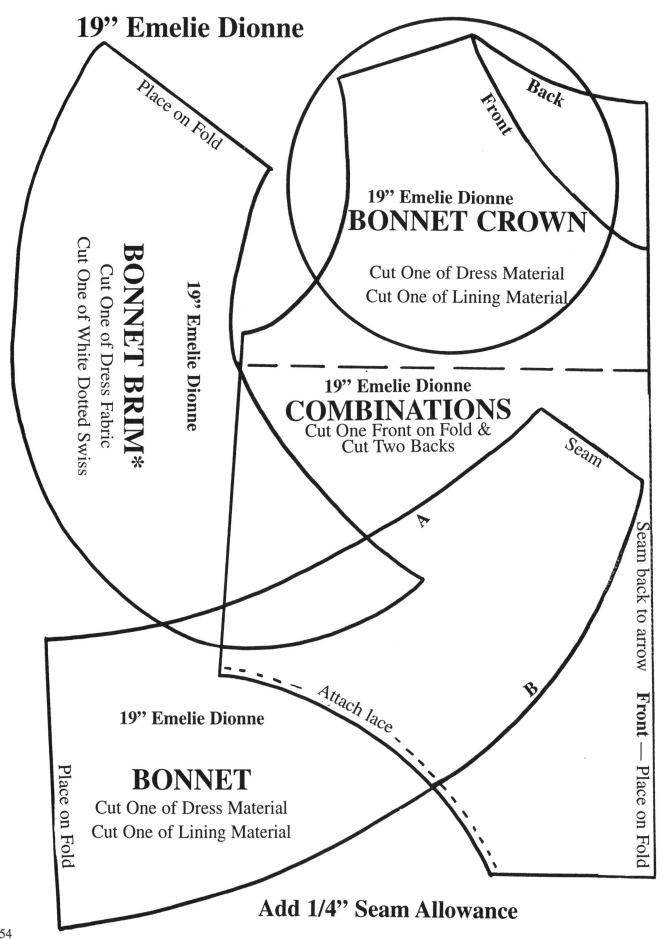

19" Emelie Dionne

Place on Fold

Front

Back

19" Emelie Dionne
BONNET CROWN

Cut One of Dress Material

Cut One of Lining Material

BONNET BRIM*
Cut One of Dress Fabric
Cut One of White Dotted Swiss

19" Emelie Dionne

19" Emelie Dionne
COMBINATIONS
Cut One Front on Fold &
Cut Two Backs

Seam

A

Seam back to arrow

Front — Place on Fold

B

Attach lace

19" Emelie Dionne

BONNET
Cut One of Dress Material
Cut One of Lining Material

Place on Fold

Add 1/4" Seam Allowance

154

Chapter 11

THE 1940s

Styles for women and girls were still soft and feminine in 1940, with large puffed sleeves and wide skirts. With the advent of World War II, the sleeves and shoulders took on a grim, mannish appearance and skirts narrowed into more conservative lines. Work clothes for women gave designers the challenge of providing attractive fashions for all the "Rosie Riveters" and "Victory Gardeners" who rushed into jobs formerly held by men.

Dirndl skirts and peasant blouses were a must in every wardrobe of 1942. More and more slacks for girls and women were shown in 1943. These were of woven plaids, rayons, spun rayon, and in the lighter fabrics, linen weave rayon, and striped seersucker. One piece sleepers called Dr. Dentons, were a must for the young set. Jumpers for little girls had circular skirts, dresses were along *Princess* lines. 1943 School clothes included long, long sweaters in sets with plaid skirts in coordinated colors. Skirts had four, six, or eight gores, or were pleated all around. Jodphurs were a classic for small girls and boys.

Tailored, two-piece suits with fitted jackets and four-gored "swing" skirts in woven plaids and herringbone tweeds for young girls were shown in 1943. Dresses that year were two-piece, tailored with short sleeves and six-gore skirts in striped cotton, chambray, striped chambray, and checked seersucker. Tailored sportswear consisted of wide-legged slacks suits and overalls for victory farmers. The 1944 pinafore had wide shoulder ruffles although the skirts were not so full as in pre-war years.

Later styles of the decade are illustrated with patterns and sketches.

MOTHER-AND-DAUGHTER FASHIONS. In the 1850's, there was a great vogue for mothers and daughters to dress exactly alike. That fashion has been bobbing up for recognition every season for several years. Now it is important in all types of merchandise, especially in cotton frocks and smocks, aprons, and housecoats. We show you some of the smartest of such fashions because early in the year is the time to make wash frocks for spring and summer — to have time to make them nicely — to do nice finishing, make nice buttonholes, and have such ready for wear when the crocuses come.

GINGHAM FROCKS. Short sleeves, bias-cut waists, and peasant skirts, finished with Peter Pan collars and center-front buttons or slide-fasteners, are a popular type of gingham dress. The brighter the plaid, the smarter the frock.

DENIM OR BROADCLOTH SMOCKS. Long sleeves and roomy pockets are an essential part of the new smocks. All have wide hems and ample fabric throughout. The length of the new smocks varies from the top of the hip to the bottom of the skirt. Many have large pearl buttons and bound buttonholes for fastening. Grand for maternity wear.

WAISTLINE APRONS. Something new in aprons! The fitted waistline, gathered skirts, halter neck, and wide rick-rack trimming make aprons gay — without disturbing their functional quality. Blue with red stripes and white rick-rack, or red and white stripes with blue rick-rack make a patriotic affair of these aprons — popular with mothers and daughters the country across.

1940

1940

PINAFORES. The movie version of *The Wizard of Oz* may be responsible for the new vogue for pinafores. They are young and smart and practical. Many women make a little chemise dress; the skirt of which serves as a slip, and then the pinafore for wear over this. Notice the (surplice) back which laps, and strings that come around and tie at the center-front. Pinafore opens out, making the ironing easy.

PRINCESS FROCKS. Make these for dress-up of fine wool, silk, rayon, or cotton, or make them for home wear. The dresses shown are of a rayon print in brightest color, with velvet bows for accent. Use slide-fasteners at the center-front to make them easy to get in and out of.

HOUSECOATS. Make them of velveteen, corduroy, flannel, seersucker, or unbleached muslin, but style them smartly. Put "dash" in the silhouette, and "umph" in the trimming, and the fabric can be inexpensive because the smartness will balance the result for you.

BRAID,BRAID, AND *MORE* BRAID. Perhaps it is the military influence, perhaps it is the acceptance of decoration — anyway, braid is everywhere. Middy and soutache braids are the most popular. Some is put in with beads to simulate necklaces; some straight; some in designs; others to form a fringe. Anyway, use braid with beads or without to decorate a new frock, or to revive an old one. Fashion likes it and so will you.

1943

5376

5377

5373

5325

5360

5361

5347

SCHOOL Days

1943

5342

5341

5349

5315

5316

The brisk boxy coat with velvet collar is as mannish as Dad's, with its fly pleat closing. No. 5315.

The double-breasted coat, cut nice and boxy, is for Brother. He has a velvet collar, too. No. 5316.

The shorts button to the shirt in this two-piece suit. Everything is very correct here. No. 5325.

The feminine half of the brother-and-sister set, above center, buttons all the way down. No. 5341.

Scalloped edging outlines the tucks on Brother's suit. His pants button to his blouse. No. 5342.

The grey flannel school suit is pretty snappy! And done in the very best tailored tradition. No. 5347.

The green coat is beautifully fitted with princess seams at back. The best one for best. No. 5349.

A red jacket, suspender skirt, and a crisp blouse for the smaller half of this sister pair. No. 5360.

The same three-piece suit for Big Sister, with important pleats in the bias plaid skirt. No. 5361.

The best of all school dresses is the jumper in pinafore style with its own beige blouse. No. 5373.

The sailor dress buttons all the way down. She will love the white buttons and the braid. No. 5376.

Last but not least, a blue shirt frock made just like Mother's shown on a preceding page. No. 5377.

The illustrations on these two pages are taken from McCall pattern listings of 1943, and give a good resume of the styles of the war years.

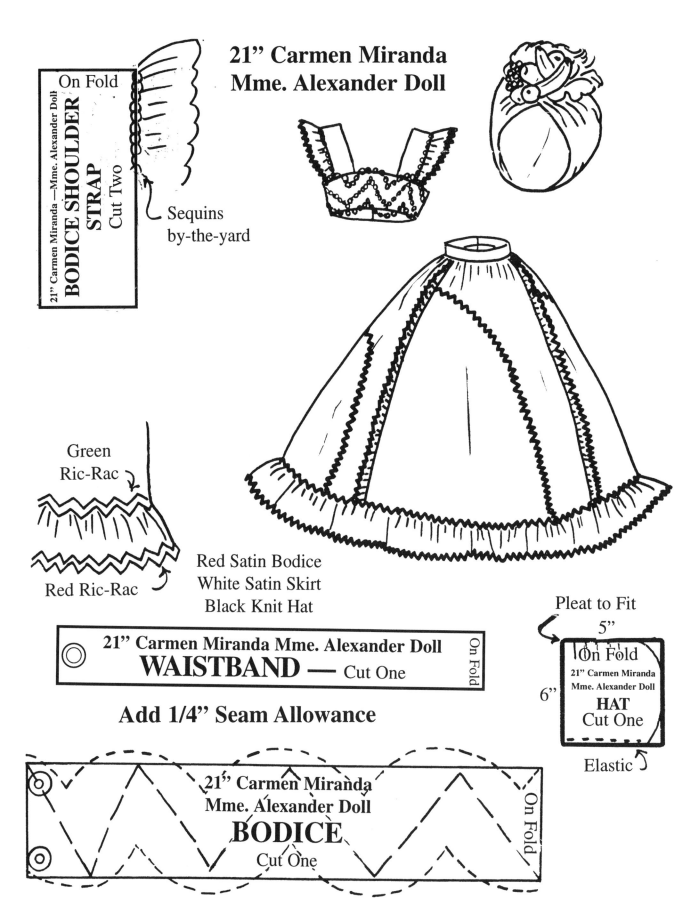

21" Carmen Miranda
Mme. Alexander Doll

On Fold

21" Carmen Miranda —Mme. Alexander Doll
BODICE SHOULDER STRAP
Cut Two

Sequins by-the-yard

Green Ric-Rac

Red Ric-Rac

Red Satin Bodice
White Satin Skirt
Black Knit Hat

21" Carmen Miranda Mme. Alexander Doll
WAISTBAND — Cut One
On Fold

Add 1/4" Seam Allowance

Pleat to Fit
5"
On Fold
6"
21" Carmen Miranda
Mme. Alexander Doll
HAT
Cut One
Elastic

21" Carmen Miranda
Mme. Alexander Doll
BODICE
Cut One
On Fold

Attach sequins-by-the-yard following dotted and dashed lines on pattern.

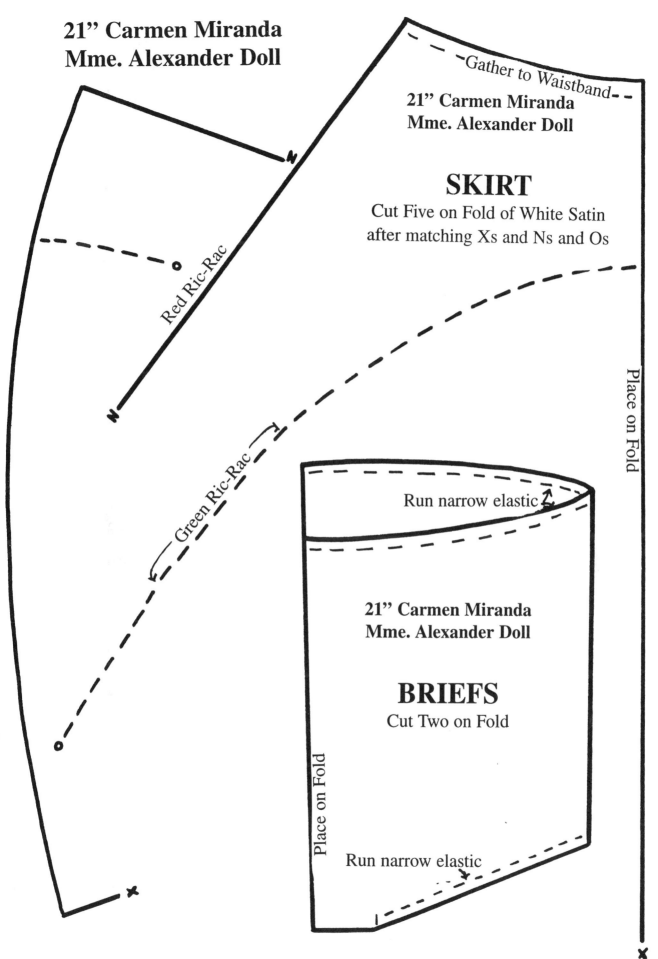

**21" Carmen Miranda
Mme. Alexander Doll**

Gather to Waistband

**21" Carmen Miranda
Mme. Alexander Doll**

SKIRT
Cut Five on Fold of White Satin
after matching Xs and Ns and Os

Red Ric-Rac

Green Ric-Rac

Place on Fold

Run narrow elastic

**21" Carmen Miranda
Mme. Alexander Doll**

BRIEFS
Cut Two on Fold

Place on Fold

Run narrow elastic

Add 1/4" Seam Allowance

SKI COSTUME
14" SONJA HENIE

Pale beige, fine-wale corduroy fashions this original ski costume. The hood was edged about the face with white fur, probably rabbit. This material may be purchased in larger fabric shops in a narrow strip sold by the yard. The ski-pants bodice is of plain tan cotton.

SKI PANTS — Sew inside leg seam between O's and turn one leg to right side. Insert this leg inside the other, right sides together, matching seams, and sew crotch seam, leaving opening in back from waist to X.

SKIS — Skis may be made of thin balsa wood strips, following pattern and contour sketch, or by laminating three thicknesses of cardboard and shaping as glue dries. Paint and glue on black elastic straps.

SKI POLES — Insert 7-1/2" pieces of dowel into cardboard circles, paint, add black elastic wrist straps.

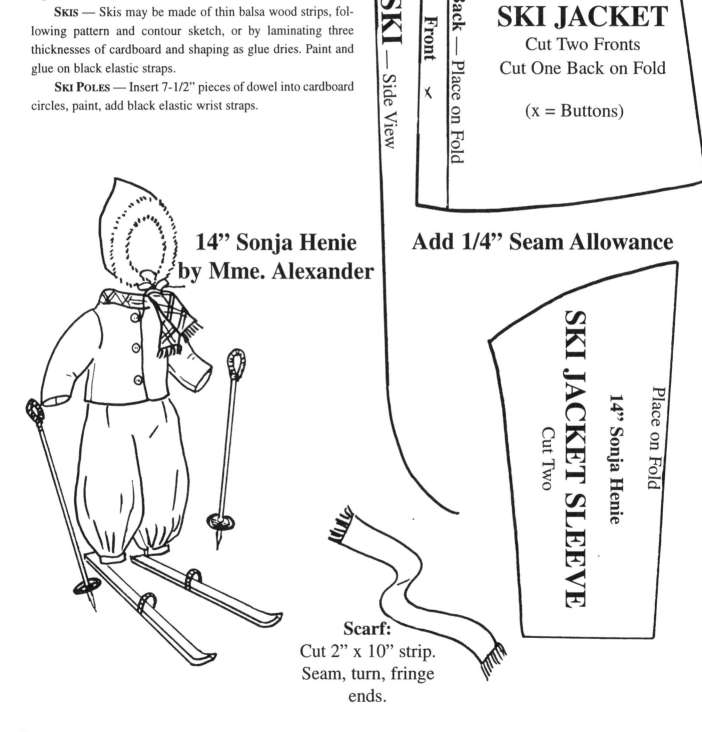

SKI — Side View

SKI JACKET
14" Sonja Henie

Cut Two Fronts
Cut One Back on Fold

(x = Buttons)

Back — Place on Fold

Back   Front

Add 1/4" Seam Allowance

14" Sonja Henie
by Mme. Alexander

SKI JACKET SLEEVE
14" Sonja Henie
Cut Two

Place on Fold

Scarf:
Cut 2" x 10" strip.
Seam, turn, fringe
ends.

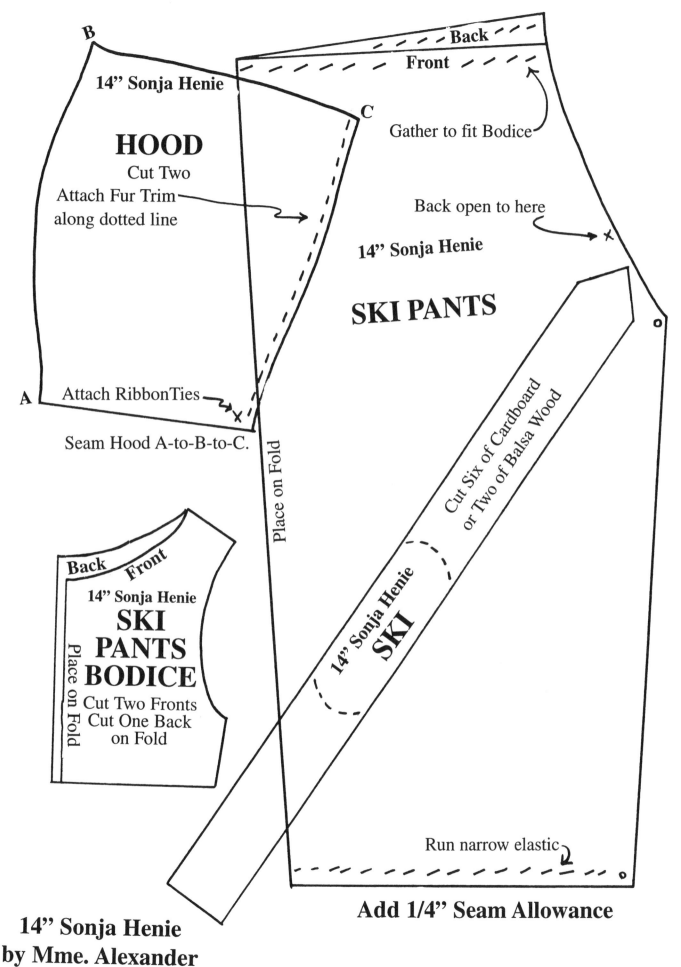

B

14" Sonja Henie

HOOD
Cut Two
Attach Fur Trim
along dotted line

A   Attach RibbonTies

Seam Hood A-to-B-to-C.

C

Back

Front

Gather to fit Bodice

Back open to here

14" Sonja Henie

SKI PANTS

Place on Fold

Cut Six of Cardboard
or Two of Balsa Wood

14" Sonja Henie
SKI

Back   Front

14" Sonja Henie
SKI
PANTS
BODICE
Cut Two Fronts
Cut One Back
on Fold

Place on Fold

Run narrow elastic

Add 1/4" Seam Allowance

14" Sonja Henie
by Mme. Alexander

14" Sonja Henie
by Mme. Alexander

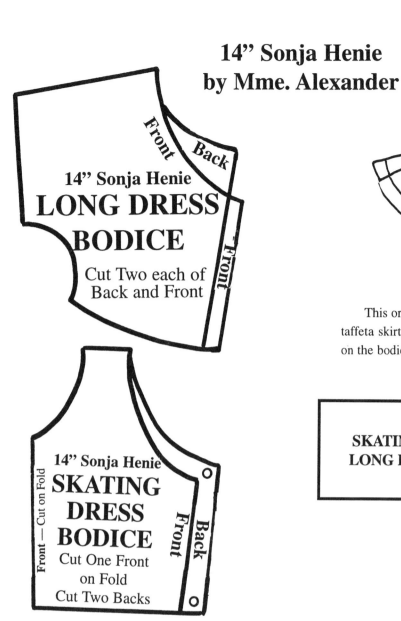

Front **Back**

14" Sonja Henie
LONG DRESS BODICE
Cut Two each of Back and Front

Front

14" Sonja Henie
SKATING DRESS BODICE
Cut One Front on Fold
Cut Two Backs

Front — Cut on Fold

Back **Front**

Add 1/4" Seam Allowance

Gather with elastic

14" Sonja Henie

SATIN PANTIES
Cut Two on Fold

Place on Fold

These are not shaped — only finished then caught with a stitch at the center for a crotch.

SKATING COSTUME 14" SONJA HENIE

This original skating costume is of pale pink satin, with a taffeta skirt trimmed with 1" band of satin and a satin flower on the bodice.

14" Sonja Henie
SKATING DRESS SKIRT — 3" x 26"
LONG DRESS SKIRT — 6-1/4"" x 30"
Cut One

LONG DRESS 14" SONJA HENIE

Dress is of pale blue silk crepe with ecru lace overskirt. Bodice is covered with ecru lace net, trimmed with narrow lace.

18" Sonja Henie

18" Sonja Henie

SKATING STAR COSTUME BODICE

Cut One Front
Cut Two Backs

Front — Place on Fold

Facing

Add 1/4" Seam Allowance

Elastic stitching

Place on Fold

18" Sonja Henie

SAKTING STAR COSTUME SLEEVE

Cut Two

18" SONJA HENIE SKATING STAR COSTUME

HAT — Cardboard circle 3-1/2" in diameter for crown, sides 1" cardboard, glued together with tabs. Cover entirely with rabbit fur or fake fur.

MUFF — Piece of fabric 3" x 5", folded over and stitched; this also is covered with fur. Wrist strap gold elastic.

BELT — Piece of dress fabric 9" long x 1", folded over with gold decorative braid topstitched the length, finished off with gold bow, could be piece of jewelry or child's hair barrette.

NECK RUFF — This is separate from dress: Piece of rabbit fur 7" long, tied with gold elastic.

DRESS — White taffeta, trimmed about the skirt with rabbit fur. Skirt is 10" diameter circle, with waist circle cut out. Bottom of skirt is folded to right side and glued, then rabbit fur strip is glued over that, giving finished underside to hem. Glue often darkens fabric; therefore you may wish to stitch this hem and catchstitch the fur to hem.

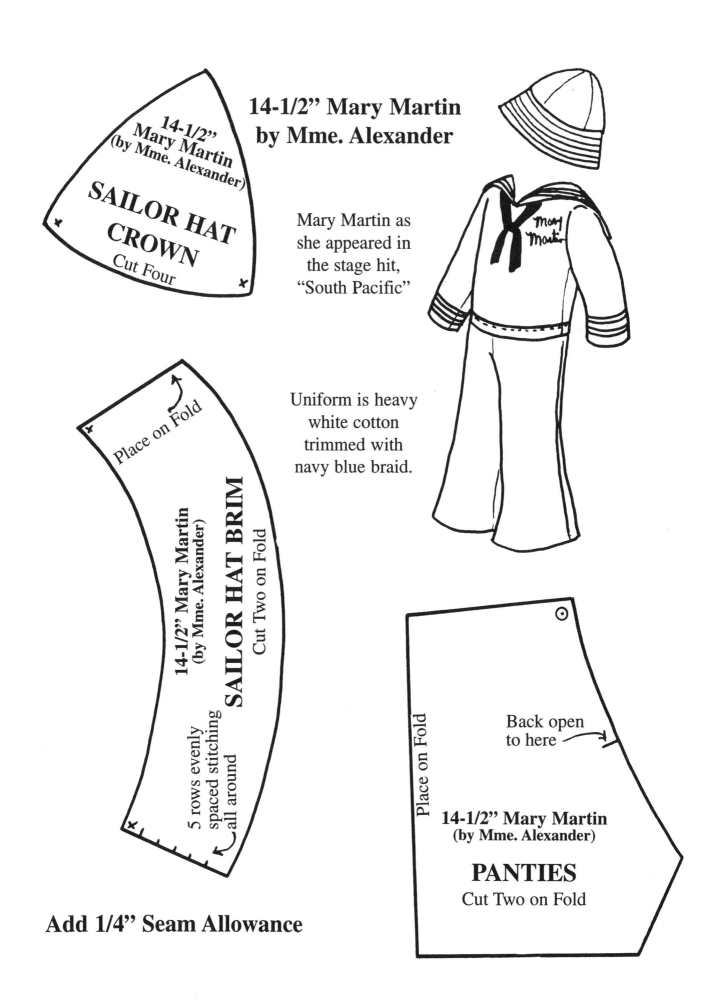

14-1/2"
Mary Martin
(by Mme. Alexander)
SAILOR HAT
CROWN
Cut Four

14-1/2" Mary Martin
by Mme. Alexander

Mary Martin as she appeared in the stage hit, "South Pacific"

Uniform is heavy white cotton trimmed with navy blue braid.

Place on Fold

14-1/2" Mary Martin
(by Mme. Alexander)
SAILOR HAT BRIM
Cut Two on Fold

5 rows evenly spaced stitching all around

Add 1/4" Seam Allowance

Place on Fold

Back open to here

14-1/2" Mary Martin
(by Mme. Alexander)

PANTIES
Cut Two on Fold

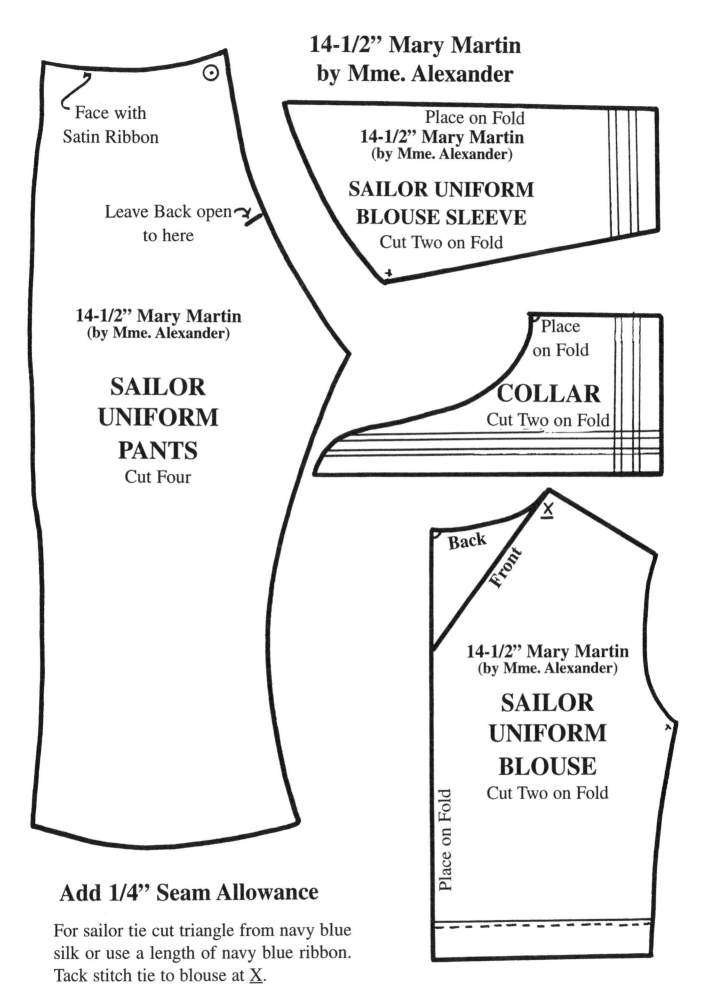

14-1/2" Mary Martin
by Mme. Alexander

Face with
Satin Ribbon

Leave Back open
to here

14-1/2" Mary Martin
(by Mme. Alexander)

SAILOR
UNIFORM
PANTS
Cut Four

Place on Fold
14-1/2" Mary Martin
(by Mme. Alexander)

SAILOR UNIFORM
BLOUSE SLEEVE
Cut Two on Fold

Place
on Fold

COLLAR
Cut Two on Fold

Back

Front

X

14-1/2" Mary Martin
(by Mme. Alexander)

SAILOR
UNIFORM
BLOUSE
Cut Two on Fold

Place on Fold

Add 1/4" Seam Allowance

For sailor tie cut triangle from navy blue
silk or use a length of navy blue ribbon.
Tack stitch tie to blouse at X.

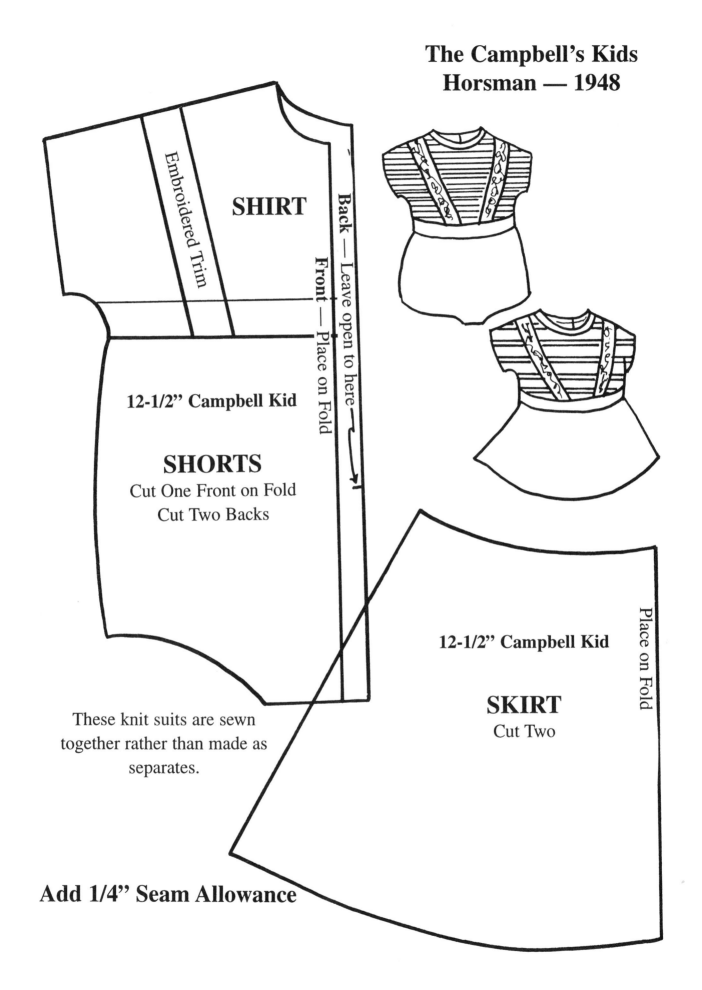

The Campbell's Kids
Horsman — 1948

SHIRT

Embroidered Trim

Back — Leave open to here →

Front — Place on Fold

12-1/2" Campbell Kid

SHORTS
Cut One Front on Fold
Cut Two Backs

12-1/2" Campbell Kid

SKIRT
Cut Two

Place on Fold

These knit suits are sewn
together rather than made as
separates.

Add 1/4" Seam Allowance

①

②

Back

12-3/4" Mannequin "Just like those in the store windows of the 1940s and early 1950s."

③

③

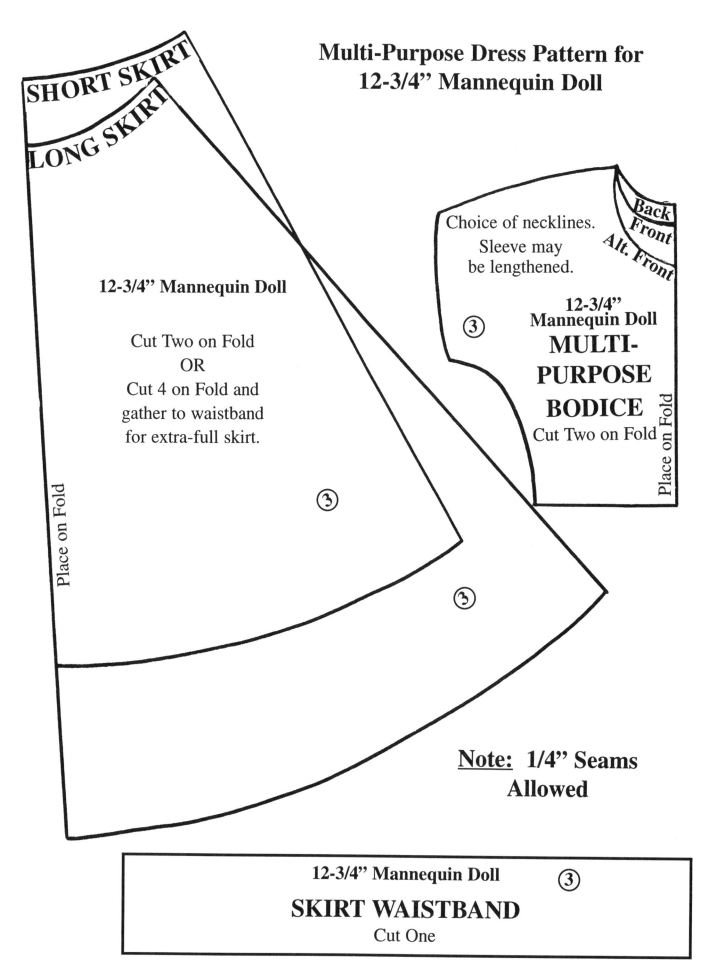

Multi-Purpose Dress Pattern for 12-3/4" Mannequin Doll

SHORT SKIRT

LONG SKIRT

12-3/4" Mannequin Doll

Cut Two on Fold
OR
Cut 4 on Fold and
gather to waistband
for extra-full skirt.

Place on Fold

③

③

Choice of necklines.
Sleeve may
be lengthened.

Back
Front
Alt. Front

③

**12-3/4"
Mannequin Doll
MULTI-
PURPOSE
BODICE**
Cut Two on Fold

Place on Fold

Note: 1/4" Seams
Allowed

12-3/4" Mannequin Doll   ③

SKIRT WAISTBAND
Cut One

Multi-Purpose Dress Pattern for 12-3/4" Mannequin Doll

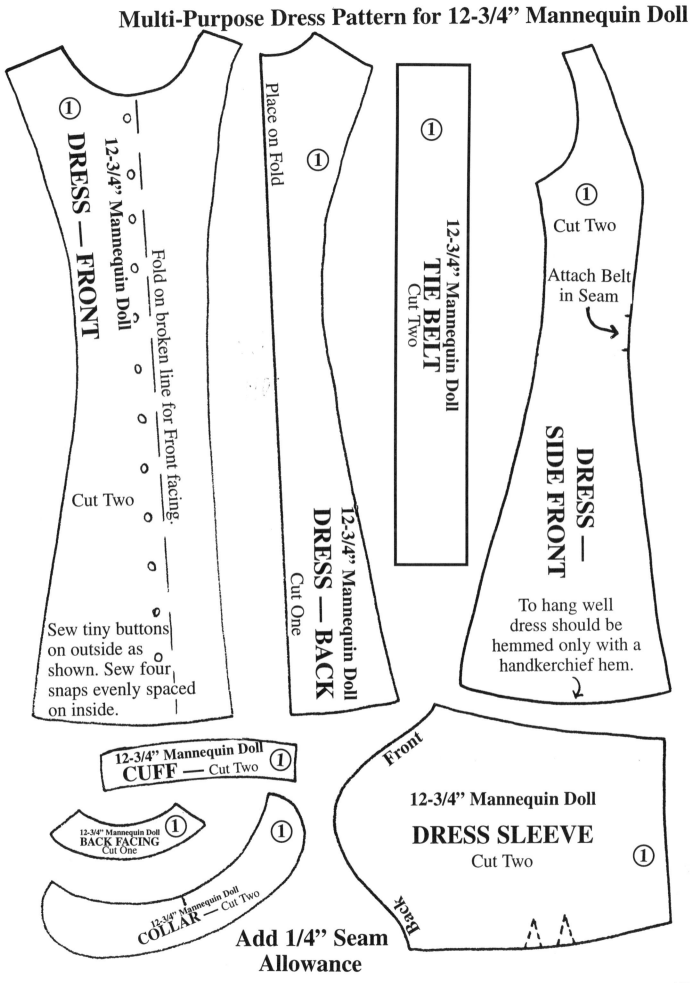

1

12-3/4" Mannequin Doll

DRESS — FRONT

Fold on broken line for Front facing.

Cut Two

Sew tiny buttons on outside as shown. Sew four snaps evenly spaced on inside.

Place on Fold

1

12-3/4" Mannequin Doll
DRESS — BACK
Cut One

1

12-3/4" Mannequin Doll
TIE BELT
Cut Two

1

Cut Two

Attach Belt in Seam

DRESS — SIDE FRONT

To hang well dress should be hemmed only with a handkerchief hem.

12-3/4" Mannequin Doll ①
CUFF — Cut Two

12-3/4" Mannequin Doll ①
BACK FACING
Cut One

12-3/4" Mannequin Doll ①
COLLAR — Cut Two

Front

12-3/4" Mannequin Doll

DRESS SLEEVE

Cut Two

1

Back

Add 1/4" Seam Allowance

Multi-Purpose Dress Pattern for 12-3/4" Mannequin Doll

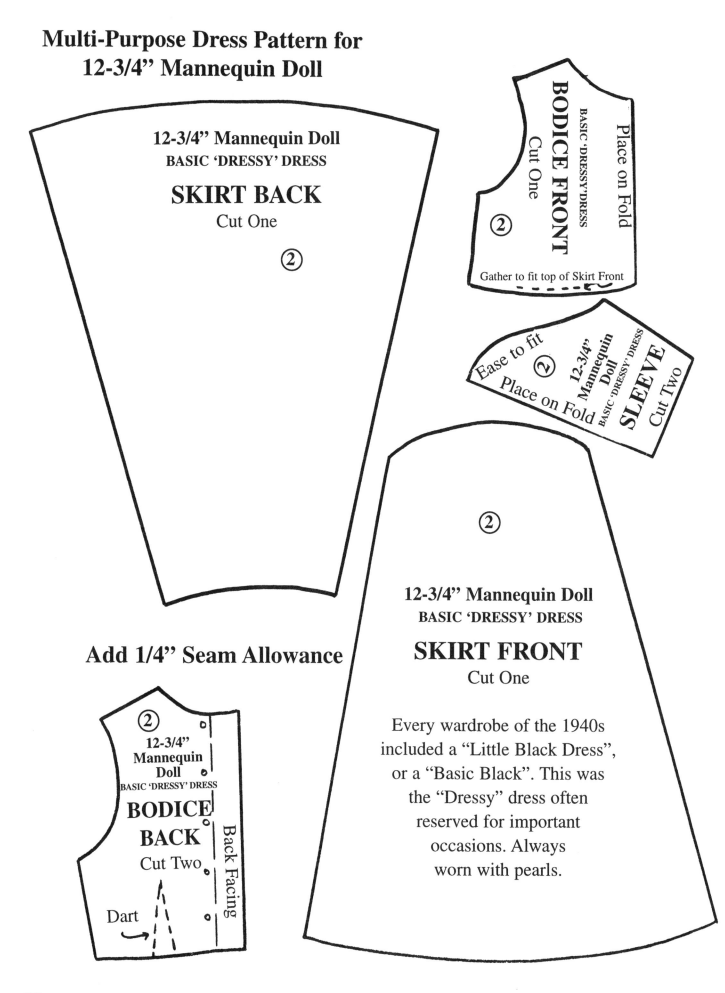

12-3/4" Mannequin Doll
BASIC 'DRESSY' DRESS

SKIRT BACK
Cut One

②

12-3/4" Mannequin Doll
BASIC 'DRESSY' DRESS
BODICE FRONT
Cut One
Place on Fold
②
Gather to fit top of Skirt Front

Ease to fit
②
Place on Fold
12-3/4" Mannequin Doll
BASIC 'DRESSY' DRESS
SLEEVE
Cut Two

Add 1/4" Seam Allowance

②
12-3/4" Mannequin Doll
BASIC 'DRESSY' DRESS
BODICE BACK
Cut Two
Back Facing
Dart

②
12-3/4" Mannequin Doll
BASIC 'DRESSY' DRESS

SKIRT FRONT
Cut One

Every wardrobe of the 1940s included a "Little Black Dress", or a "Basic Black". This was the "Dressy" dress often reserved for important occasions. Always worn with pearls.

Chapter 12

THE 1950s

Embossed cottons, polished cottons, wool jersey, cottons with gold metallic overprint, and corduroy were a few of the varied fabrics of the '50s. Man-made fibers were becoming more available and blends of cotton/wool were being created. Skirts were long and hair was short. The Italian cut, a short, curly, little-boy hair-do could easily be styled to an individual's face and figure. The effect was that of a pyramid, with a tiny head and flared skirt.

The full, full skirts were held triumphantly bouffant with the aid of at least two petticoats. A new material, nylon, furnished excellent net petticoats which remained stiff and bouncy through countless washings.

Raglan sleeves, batwing sleeves, big collars on blouses, and wide waistbands were all marks of the 1950s. Suits often had boxy jackets and straight skirts. These were buttoned high to a stand-up collar.

In the doll world, several fashionable misses were introduced, including *Toni, Betsy McCall, Terri Lee, Miss Revlon, Cissy*, and *Sweet Sue*. It is these charming style setters who will review for us the fashions of the 1950s since their wardrobes were so extensive as to include nearly every whim and nuance of the elusive thing called style.

On the following three pages are reprints from a booklet packed with a *Toni* doll, showing the various outfits available for *Betsy McCall* and *Toni*. These are the American Character versions of the two dolls; there are also Ideal *Toni* and *Betsy McCall* dolls. Style numbers and prices of the costumes appear with each outfit; a lucky find in old store stock may yield several of these fashions. These clothes are ca. 1959-1960.

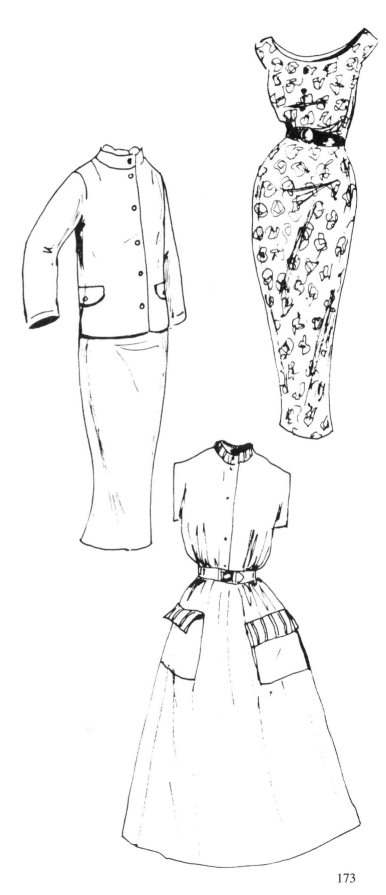

HERE ARE YOUR EXTRA OUTFITS FOR THE 8-1/2" BETSY McCALL DOLL

B100 — Doll dressed in a chemise, shoes, and socks
$2.25

B29
April Showers
$1.50

B49
Riding Habit
$1.50

B39
Ballerina
$1.50

B19
Schoolgirl
$1.50

HERE ARE YOUR EXTRA OUTFITS FOR THE 8-1/2" BETSY McCALL DOLL

B79
Coat and Hat
$2.00

B129
Sugar & Spice
$3.00

B99
Sunday Best
$2.50

B69
On the Ice
$2.00

HERE ARE YOUR EXTRA OUTFITS FOR THE 8-1/2" BETSY McCALL DOLL

B119
Bride
$3.00

B109
Town and Country
$2.50

B89
Sweet Dreams
$2.50

B59
Holiday
$2.00

HERE ARE YOUR EXTRA OUTFITS FOR THE 10-1/2" TONI DOLL

A95
Coat and Hat
$2.50

A98
Bon Soir
$3.00

A96
Shopping Time
$2.50

A911
Bride
$4.00

HERE ARE YOUR EXTRA OUTFITS FOR THE 10-1/2" TONI DOLL

A99
Suburbanite
$3.00

A97
High Society
$2.50

A912
American Beauty
$4.00

A910
Sunday Best
$3.00

These illustrations are from a booklet packed with a *Betsy McCall* doll.

HERE ARE YOUR EXTRA OUTFITS FOR THE 10-1/2" TONI DOLL

A300
$2.98

A92
Brunch Time
$2.00

A93
Tea Time
$2.00

A91
Collegiate
$2.00

A94
At the Beach
$2.00

**TONI with Toni Playwave
Set dressed in Brassalette
and High Heel Shoes**

BETSY McCALL DOLL 14" TALL COMPLETE WITH COSTUME

#914
Doll in Chemise with Trunk and
Three Outfits
$12.98

#414
Holiday
$8.98

#614
Bride
$9.98

#214
School days
$7.98

TONI DOLL 20" TALL COMPLETE WITH COSTUME AND TONI PLAYWAVE SET

She walks, wears high
heels, has wavy hair
and rolls her eyes.

#204
Bride
$17.98

#201
Sunday Best
$12.98

#203
American Beauty
$17.98

BETSY McCALL DOLL 20" TALL COMPLETE WITH COSTUME

#220
Sunday Best
$11.98

#320
Ensemble
$12.98

#520
Sugar & Spice
$12.98

16" Terri Lee

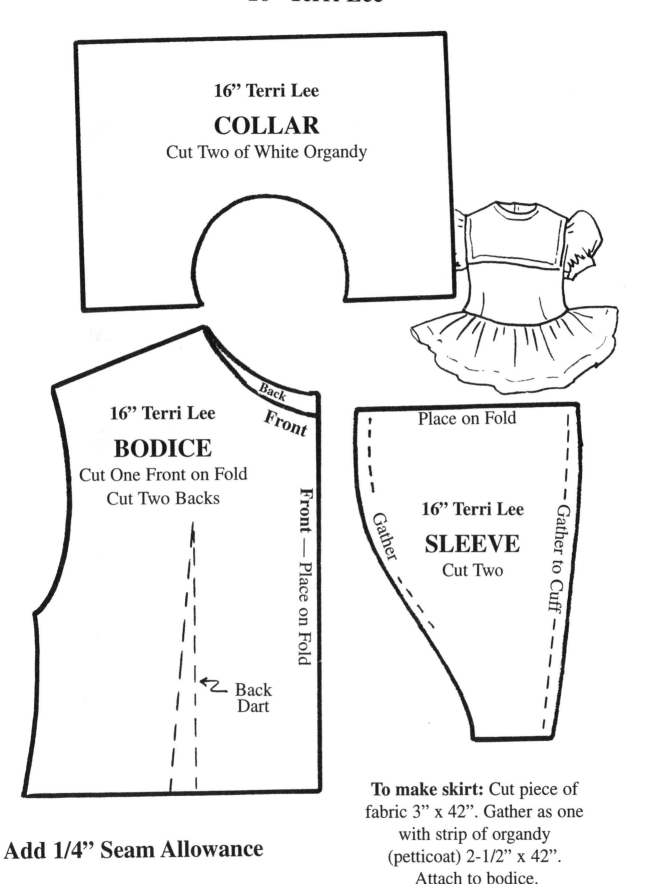

16" Terri Lee

COLLAR
Cut Two of White Organdy

16" Terri Lee

BODICE
Cut One Front on Fold
Cut Two Backs

Back

Front

Front — Place on Fold

Back Dart

Place on Fold

Gather

16" Terri Lee

SLEEVE
Cut Two

Gather to Cuff

Add 1/4" Seam Allowance

To make skirt: Cut piece of fabric 3" x 42". Gather as one with strip of organdy (petticoat) 2-1/2" x 42". Attach to bodice.

16" Terri Lee & Jerri Lee
Play Togs

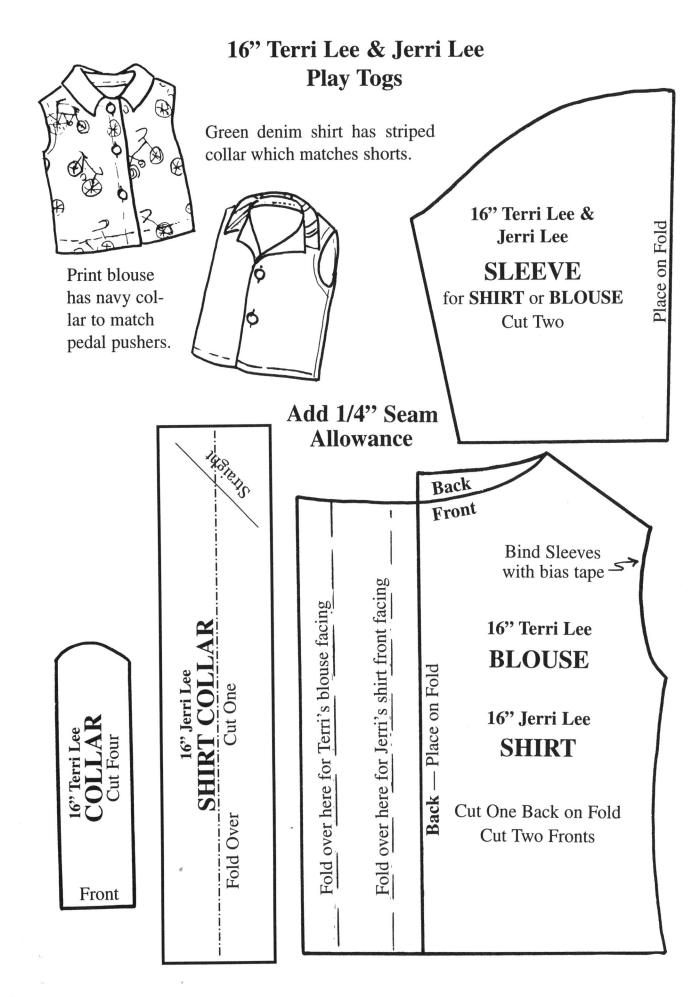

Green denim shirt has striped collar which matches shorts.

Print blouse has navy collar to match pedal pushers.

16" Terri Lee & Jerri Lee

SLEEVE for **SHIRT** or **BLOUSE** Cut Two

Place on Fold

Add 1/4" Seam Allowance

16" Terri Lee COLLAR Cut Four

Front

Straight

16" Jerri Lee SHIRT COLLAR Cut One

Fold Over

Fold over here for Terri's blouse facing

Fold over here for Jerri's shirt front facing

Back — Place on Fold

Back

Front

Bind Sleeves with bias tape

16" Terri Lee BLOUSE

16" Jerri Lee SHIRT

Cut One Back on Fold
Cut Two Fronts

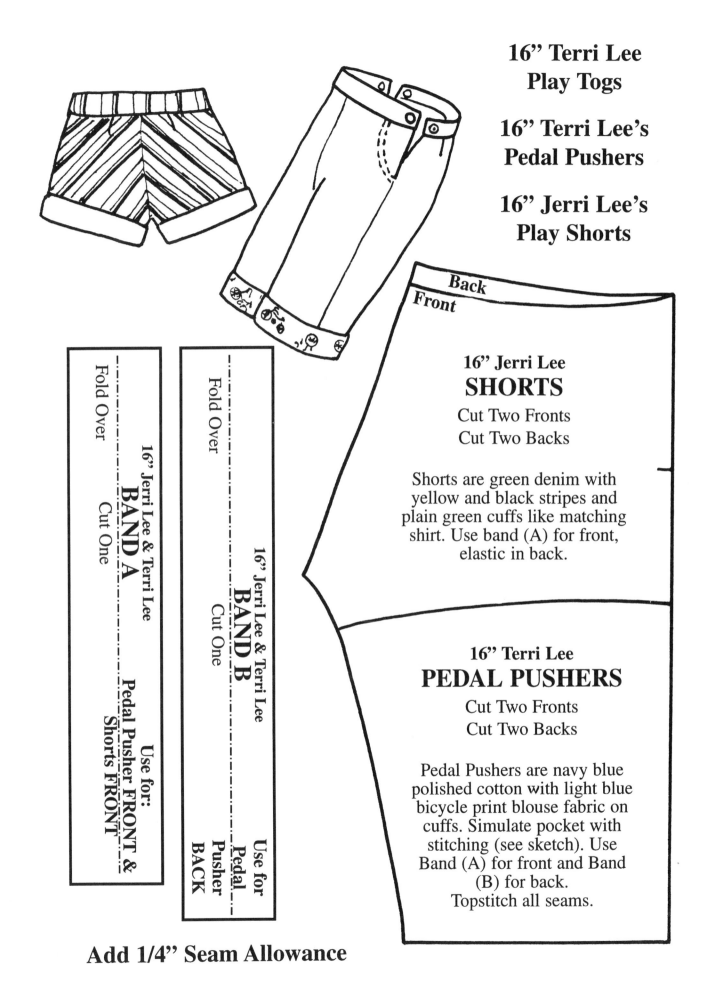

16" Terri Lee Play Togs

16" Terri Lee's Pedal Pushers

16" Jerri Lee's Play Shorts

Back
Front

16" Jerri Lee
SHORTS

Cut Two Fronts
Cut Two Backs

Shorts are green denim with yellow and black stripes and plain green cuffs like matching shirt. Use band (A) for front, elastic in back.

16" Terri Lee
PEDAL PUSHERS

Cut Two Fronts
Cut Two Backs

Pedal Pushers are navy blue polished cotton with light blue bicycle print blouse fabric on cuffs. Simulate pocket with stitching (see sketch). Use Band (A) for front and Band (B) for back.
Topstitch all seams.

Fold Over

16" Jerri Lee & Terri Lee
BAND A
Cut One

Use for:
Pedal Pusher FRONT & Shorts FRONT

Fold Over

16" Jerri Lee & Terri Lee
BAND B
Cut One

Use for
Pedal Pusher BACK

Add 1/4" Seam Allowance

179

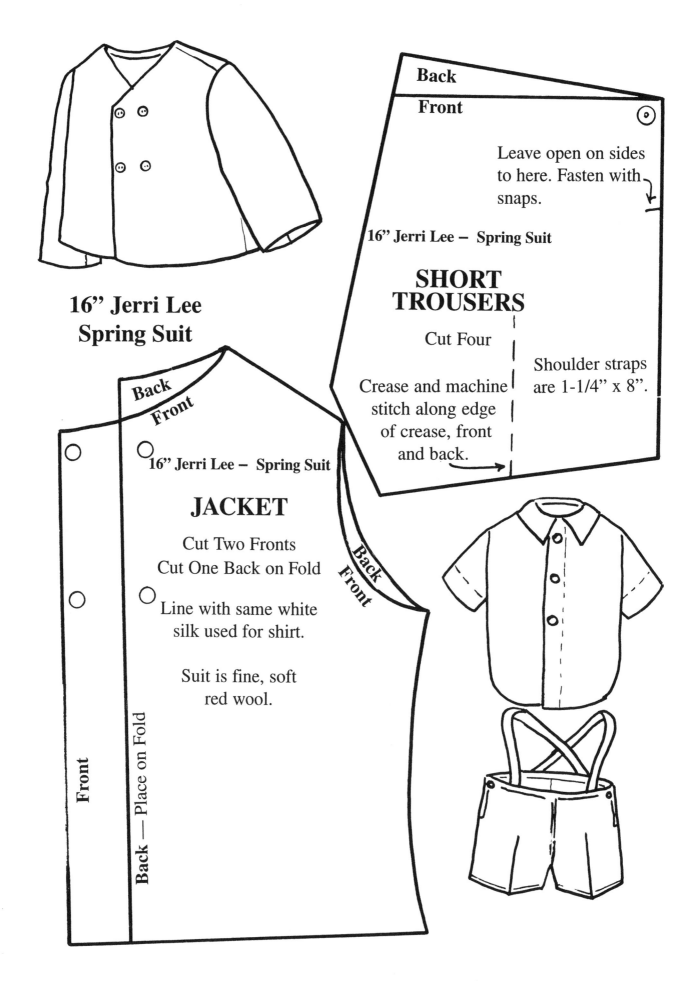

**16" Jerri Lee
Spring Suit**

Back

Front

⊙

Leave open on sides to here. Fasten with snaps.

16" Jerri Lee — Spring Suit

SHORT TROUSERS

Cut Four

Crease and machine stitch along edge of crease, front and back.

Shoulder straps are 1-1/4" x 8".

Back

Front

16" Jerri Lee — Spring Suit

JACKET

Cut Two Fronts
Cut One Back on Fold

Line with same white silk used for shirt.

Suit is fine, soft red wool.

Back

Front

Front

Back — Place on Fold

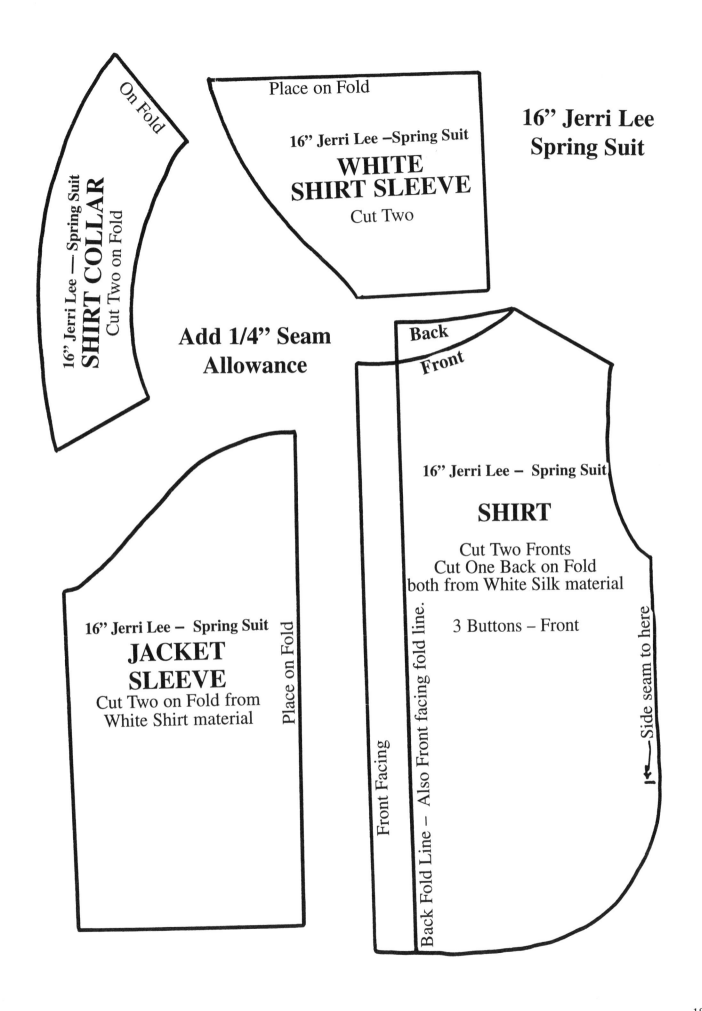

On Fold

16" Jerri Lee — Spring Suit
SHIRT COLLAR
Cut Two on Fold

Place on Fold

16" Jerri Lee –Spring Suit
WHITE
SHIRT SLEEVE
Cut Two

16" Jerri Lee
Spring Suit

Add 1/4" Seam
Allowance

16" Jerri Lee — Spring Suit
JACKET
SLEEVE
Cut Two on Fold from
White Shirt material

Place on Fold

Back

Front

16" Jerri Lee — Spring Suit

SHIRT

Cut Two Fronts
Cut One Back on Fold
both from White Silk material

3 Buttons – Front

Front Facing

Back Fold Line – Also Front facing fold line.

Side seam to here

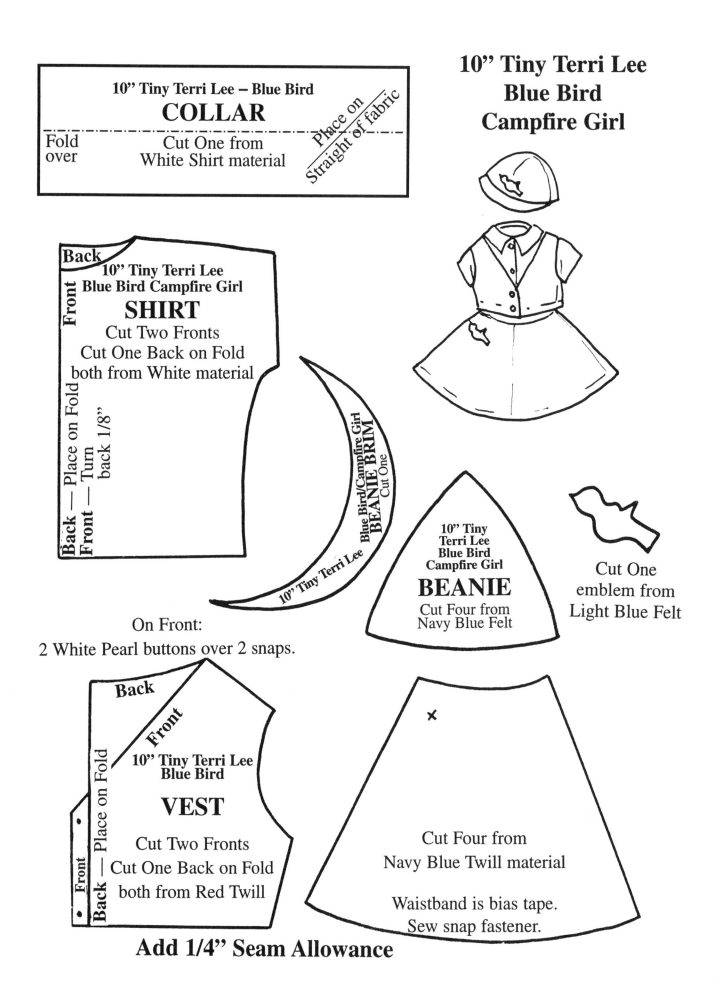

10" Tiny Terri Lee – Blue Bird
COLLAR

Fold over

Cut One from
White Shirt material

Place on Straight of fabric

10" Tiny Terri Lee
Blue Bird
Campfire Girl

Back

Front

10" Tiny Terri Lee
Blue Bird Campfire Girl
SHIRT
Cut Two Fronts
Cut One Back on Fold
both from White material

Back — Place on Fold
Front — Turn back 1/8"

10" Tiny Terri Lee
Blue Bird/Campfire Girl
BEANIE BRIM
Cut One

10" Tiny
Terri Lee
Blue Bird
Campfire Girl
BEANIE
Cut Four from
Navy Blue Felt

Cut One
emblem from
Light Blue Felt

On Front:
2 White Pearl buttons over 2 snaps.

Back

Front

10" Tiny Terri Lee
Blue Bird
VEST
Cut Two Fronts
Cut One Back on Fold
both from Red Twill

Back — Place on Fold

Front

Cut Four from
Navy Blue Twill material

Waistband is bias tape.
Sew snap fastener.

Add 1/4" Seam Allowance

16" Terri Lee Girl Scout

Place on Fold

16" Terri Lee
Girl Scout Uniform

SLEEVE
Cut Two

16" Terri Lee
Girl Scout Uniform

SKIRT BACK

Cut One

16" Terri Lee
Girl Scout Uniform

SKIRT FRONT

Cut Two

Fold over for Front Facing

Add 1/4" Seam Allowance

16" Terri Lee Girl Scout

16"
Terri Lee
Girl Scout
Uniform

**SKIRT
SIDE
BACK**

Cut Two

16"
Terri Lee
Girl Scout
Uniform

**SKIRT
SIDE
FRONT**

Cut Two

To make beret, cut
4-1/2" circle of dark
green felt, hem. Run
elastic around to gather.
Cut trefoil of yellow felt.

4-1/2"

Add 1/4" Seam Allowance

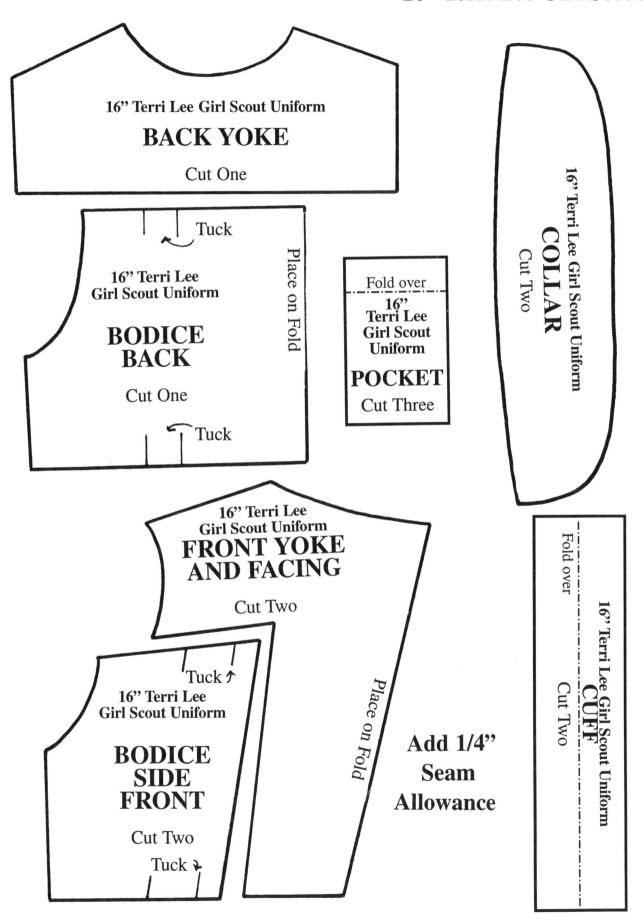

16" Terri Lee Girl Scout

16" Terri Lee Girl Scout Uniform
BACK YOKE
Cut One

16" Terri Lee
Girl Scout Uniform
BODICE BACK
Cut One

Tuck

Tuck

Place on Fold

Fold over
16" Terri Lee Girl Scout Uniform
POCKET
Cut Three

16" Terri Lee Girl Scout Uniform
COLLAR
Cut Two

16" Terri Lee
Girl Scout Uniform
FRONT YOKE AND FACING
Cut Two

Place on Fold

16" Terri Lee
Girl Scout Uniform
BODICE SIDE FRONT
Cut Two
Tuck

Tuck

Add 1/4" Seam Allowance

Fold over
16" Terri Lee Girl Scout Uniform
CUFF
Cut Two

185

16" Terri Lee

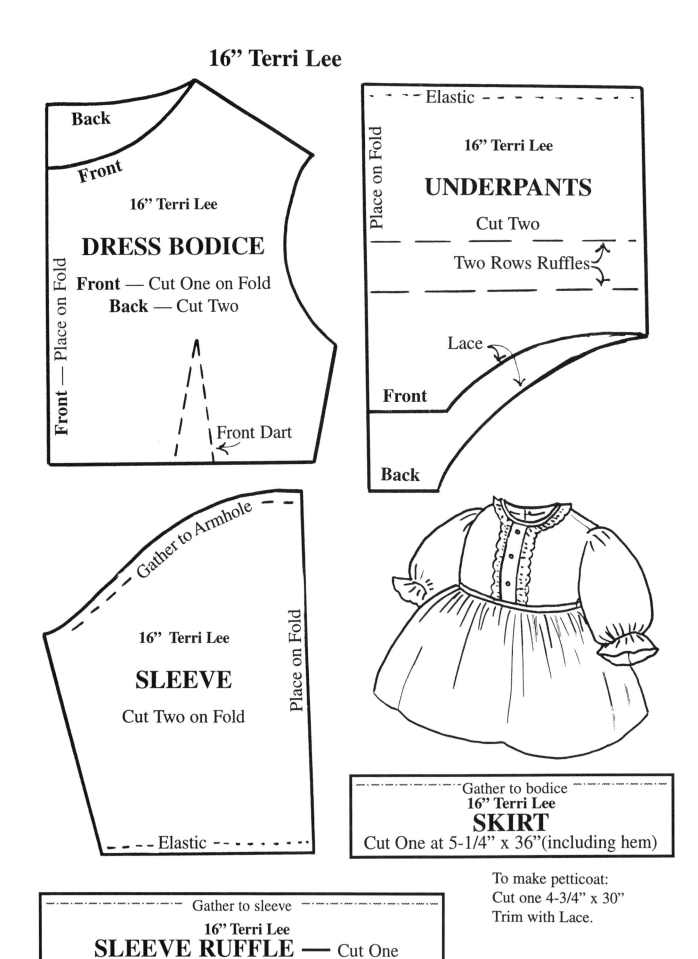

Back

Front

16" Terri Lee

DRESS BODICE

Front — Cut One on Fold
Back — Cut Two

Front — Place on Fold

Front Dart

Place on Fold

Elastic

16" Terri Lee

UNDERPANTS

Cut Two

Two Rows Ruffles

Lace

Front

Back

Gather to Armhole

16" Terri Lee

SLEEVE

Cut Two on Fold

Place on Fold

Elastic

Gather to bodice
16" Terri Lee
SKIRT
Cut One at 5-1/4" x 36"(including hem)

To make petticoat:
Cut one 4-3/4" x 30"
Trim with Lace.

Gather to sleeve
16" Terri Lee
SLEEVE RUFFLE — Cut One

Add 1/4" Seam Allowance

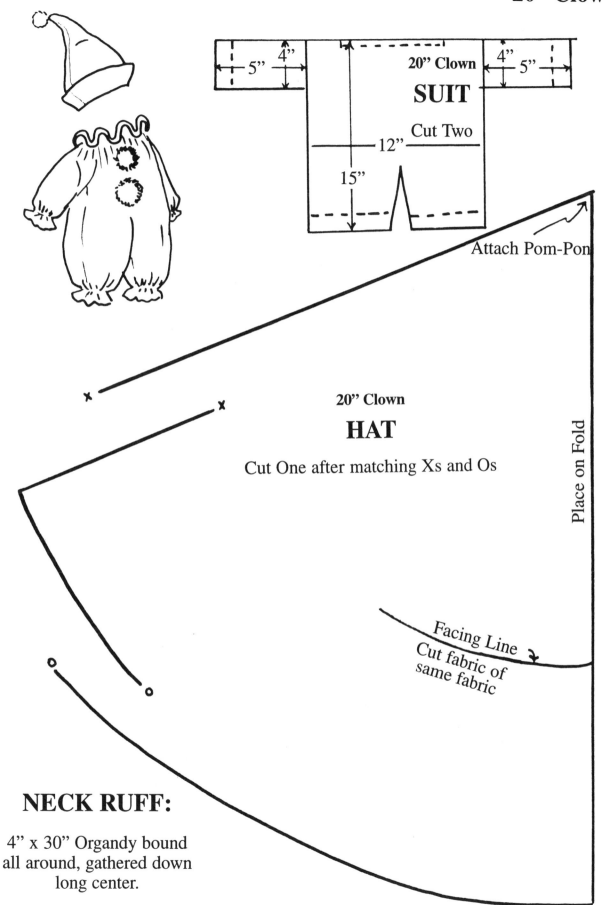

20" Clown

SUIT

Cut Two

5"   4"

4"   5"

12"

15"

Attach Pom-Pon

20" Clown

HAT

Cut One after matching Xs and Os

Place on Fold

Facing Line
Cut fabric of
same fabric

x
x

o
o

NECK RUFF:

4" x 30" Organdy bound
all around, gathered down
long center.

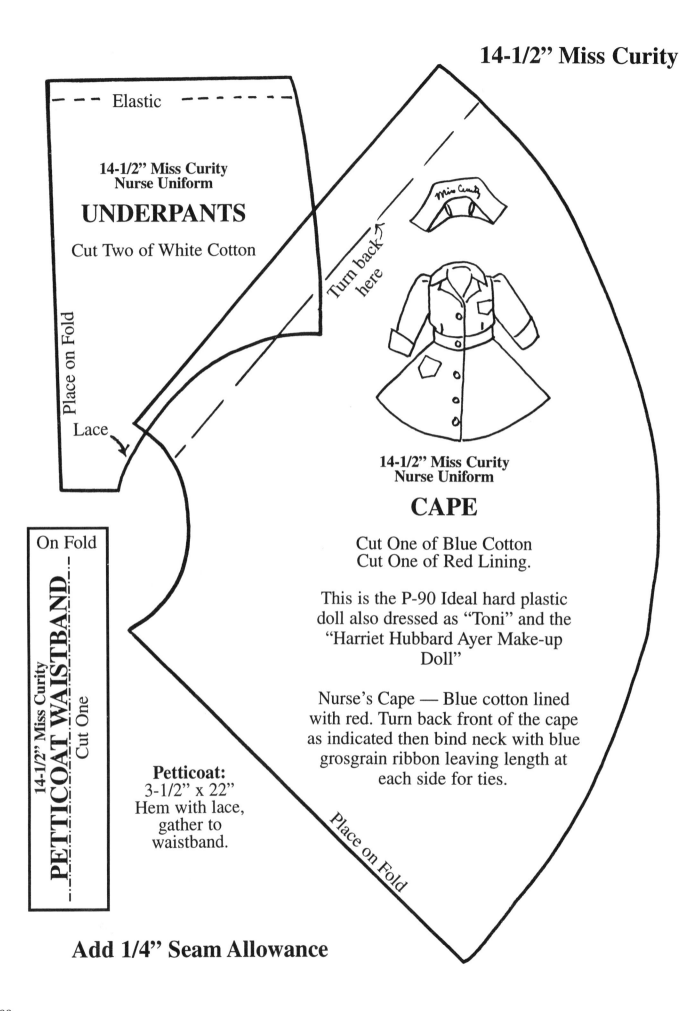

Elastic

14-1/2" Miss Curity
Nurse Uniform

UNDERPANTS

Cut Two of White Cotton

Place on Fold

Lace

Turn back here

14-1/2" Miss Curity
Nurse Uniform

CAPE

Cut One of Blue Cotton
Cut One of Red Lining.

This is the P-90 Ideal hard plastic doll also dressed as "Toni" and the "Harriet Hubbard Ayer Make-up Doll"

Nurse's Cape — Blue cotton lined with red. Turn back front of the cape as indicated then bind neck with blue grosgrain ribbon leaving length at each side for ties.

On Fold

14-1/2" Miss Curity
PETTICOAT WAISTBAND
Cut One

Petticoat:
3-1/2" x 22"
Hem with lace,
gather to
waistband.

Place on Fold

Add 1/4" Seam Allowance

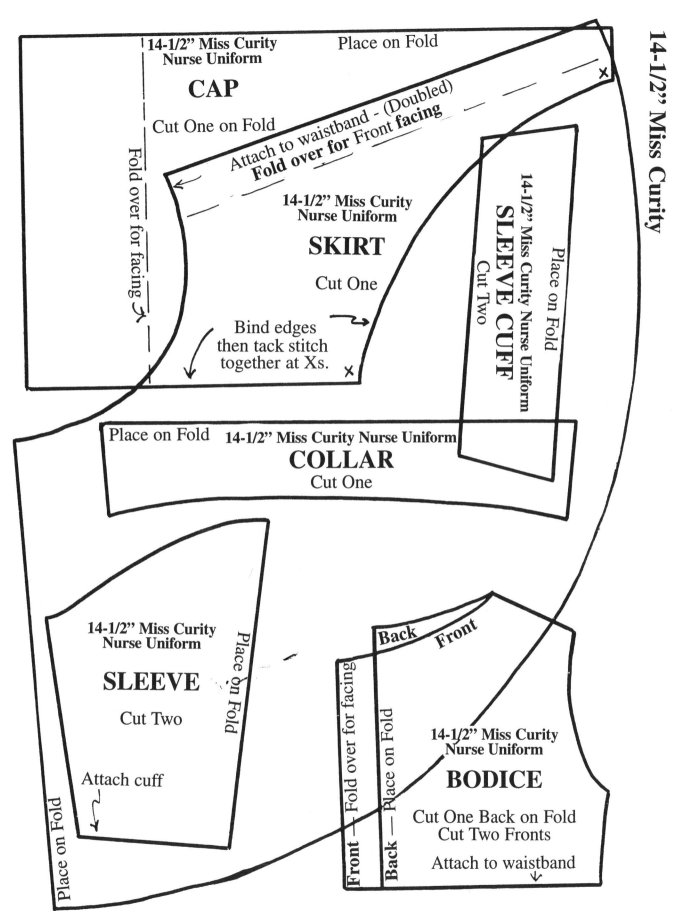

14-1/2" Miss Curity Nurse Uniform

CAP

Cut One on Fold

Fold over for facing

Place on Fold

Attach to waistband - (Doubled)
Fold over for Front **facing**

14-1/2" Miss Curity Nurse Uniform

SKIRT

Cut One

Bind edges then tack stitch together at Xs.

14-1/2" Miss Curity Nurse Uniform

SLEEVE CUFF
Cut Two

Place on Fold

14-1/2" Miss Curity

Place on Fold   **14-1/2" Miss Curity Nurse Uniform**

COLLAR

Cut One

14-1/2" Miss Curity Nurse Uniform

SLEEVE

Cut Two

Attach cuff

Place on Fold

Place on Fold

Back   **Front**

Front — Fold over for facing

Back — Place on Fold

14-1/2" Miss Curity Nurse Uniform

BODICE

Cut One Back on Fold
Cut Two Fronts

Attach to waistband

For **Waistband** — Double a piece of fabric 1-1/2" x 8-1/2", stitch to skirt, then top stitch to Bodice.

Add 1/4" Seam Allowance

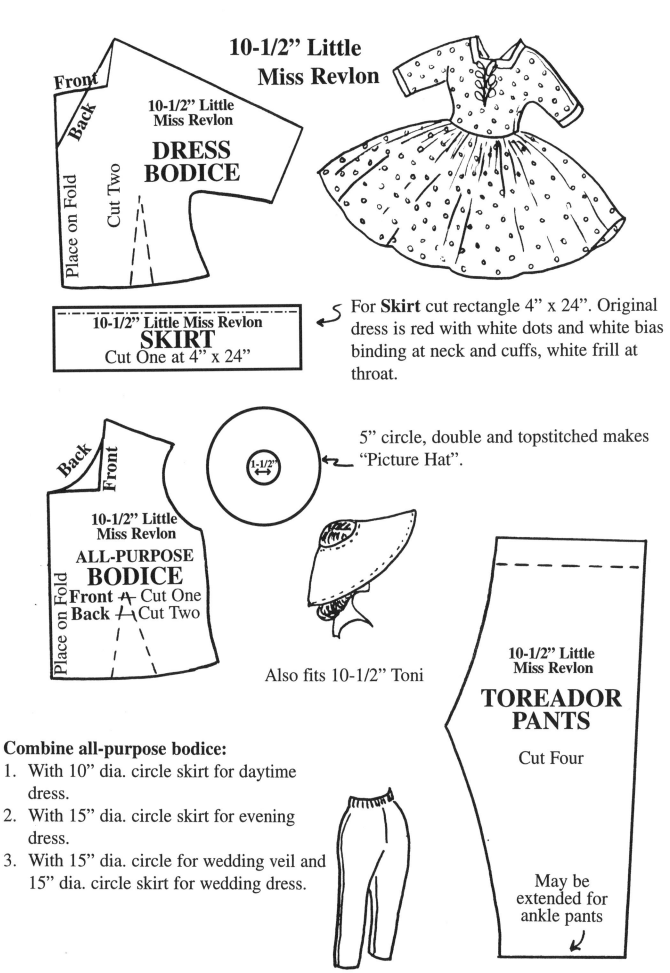

10-1/2" Little Miss Revlon

Front

Back

10-1/2" Little Miss Revlon

DRESS BODICE

Cut Two

Place on Fold

10-1/2" Little Miss Revlon

SKIRT

Cut One at 4" x 24"

For **Skirt** cut rectangle 4" x 24". Original dress is red with white dots and white bias binding at neck and cuffs, white frill at throat.

Back

Front

10-1/2" Little Miss Revlon

ALL-PURPOSE BODICE

Front ⊬ Cut One
Back ⊢ Cut Two

Place on Fold

1-1/2"

5" circle, double and topstitched makes "Picture Hat".

Also fits 10-1/2" Toni

10-1/2" Little Miss Revlon

TOREADOR PANTS

Cut Four

May be extended for ankle pants

Combine all-purpose bodice:

1. With 10" dia. circle skirt for daytime dress.
2. With 15" dia. circle skirt for evening dress.
3. With 15" dia. circle for wedding veil and 15" dia. circle skirt for wedding dress.

Add 1/4" Seam Allowance

190

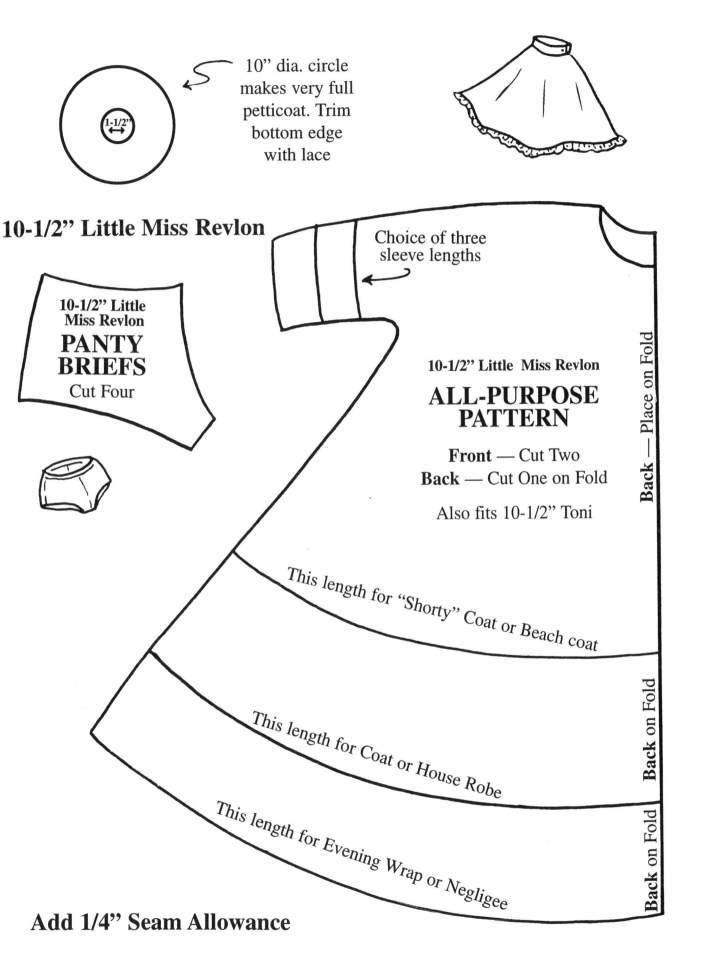

10" dia. circle makes very full petticoat. Trim bottom edge with lace

10-1/2" Little Miss Revlon

1-1/2"

10-1/2" Little Miss Revlon
PANTY BRIEFS
Cut Four

Choice of three sleeve lengths

10-1/2" Little Miss Revlon

ALL-PURPOSE PATTERN

Front — Cut Two
Back — Cut One on Fold

Also fits 10-1/2" Toni

Back — Place on Fold

This length for "Shorty" Coat or Beach coat

This length for Coat or House Robe

Back on Fold

This length for Evening Wrap or Negligee

Back on Fold

Add 1/4" Seam Allowance

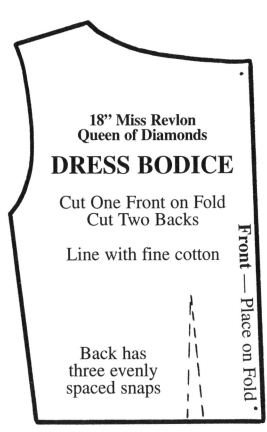

**18" Miss Revlon
Queen of Diamonds**

DRESS BODICE

Cut One Front on Fold
Cut Two Backs

Line with fine cotton

Back has
three evenly
spaced snaps

Front — Place on Fold

18" Miss Revlon Queen of Diamonds
SLEEVE BAND
Cut Two

On Fold

18" Miss Revlon
"Queen of Diamonds"

Red velveteen dress with pink rayon sash and "boat" neckline.

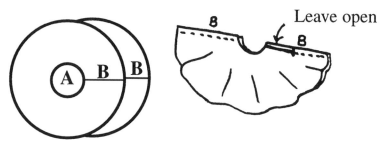

Leave open

To make skirt of dress: Cut 2 circles 13" dia. Cut out circle 1-1/2" dia. from center of each (A). Cut along line (B). Stitch the two 13" dia. circles together along lines (B), leaving one open 1-1/2". Attach to lined bodice.

Jewelry, nylon stockings with seams, and high heeled plastic sandals complete the outfit.

Add 1/4" Seam Allowance

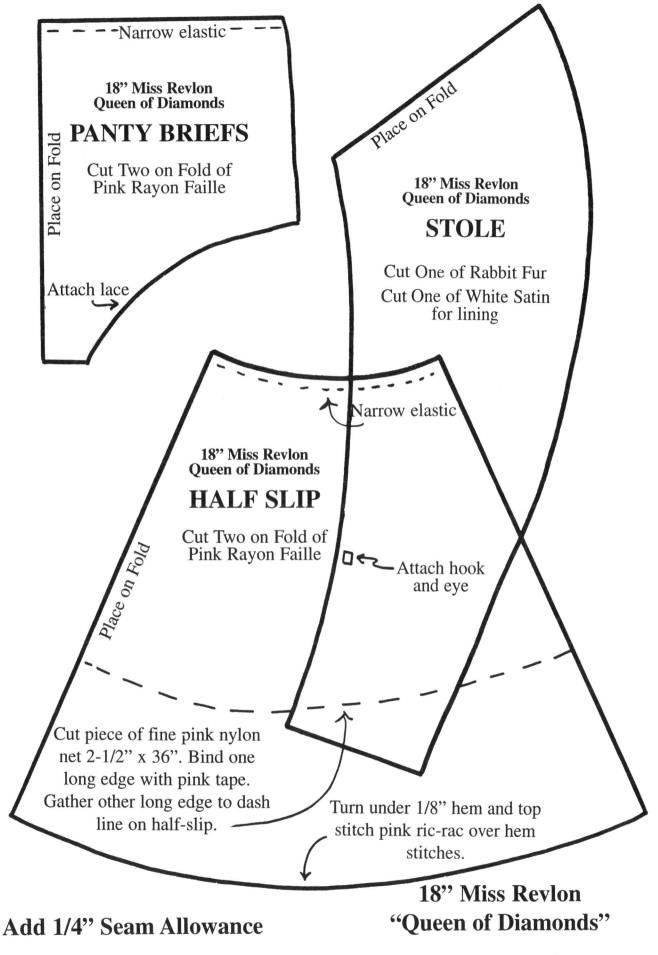

Narrow elastic

**18" Miss Revlon
Queen of Diamonds**

PANTY BRIEFS

Cut Two on Fold of
Pink Rayon Faille

Place on Fold

Attach lace

Place on Fold

**18" Miss Revlon
Queen of Diamonds**

STOLE

Cut One of Rabbit Fur

Cut One of White Satin
for lining

Narrow elastic

**18" Miss Revlon
Queen of Diamonds**

HALF SLIP

Cut Two on Fold of
Pink Rayon Faille

Place on Fold

Attach hook
and eye

Cut piece of fine pink nylon
net 2-1/2" x 36". Bind one
long edge with pink tape.
Gather other long edge to dash
line on half-slip.

Turn under 1/8" hem and top
stitch pink ric-rac over hem
stitches.

Add 1/4" Seam Allowance

**18" Miss Revlon
"Queen of Diamonds"**

**20" Cissy
by Mme. Alexander**

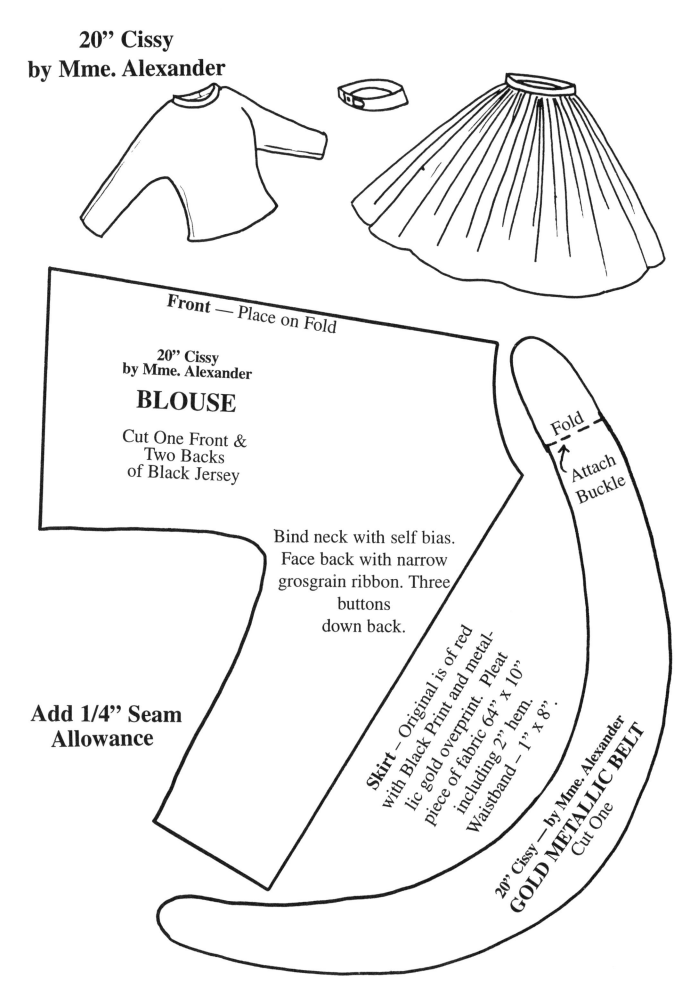

Front — Place on Fold

**20" Cissy
by Mme. Alexander**

BLOUSE

Cut One Front &
Two Backs
of Black Jersey

Bind neck with self bias.
Face back with narrow
grosgrain ribbon. Three
buttons
down back.

**Add 1/4" Seam
Allowance**

Fold

Attach
Buckle

Skirt – Original is of red
with Black Print and metallic gold overprint. Pleat
piece of fabric 64" x 10"
including 2" hem.
Waistband – 1" x 8".

**20" Cissy — by Mme. Alexander
GOLD METALLIC BELT**
Cut One

23" SWEET SUE GIRL PARTY DRESS

This dress, found on an old store stock doll, never played with, is of salmon-pink organdy with white flocked dots. Lower sleeves and under-bodice, which makes a dickey effect at front, are of white organdy with salmon-pink flocked dots.

Skirt is 10-1/2" by 54" long, including a 2-1/2" hem. Lace is sewn flat along hem line. Bows are black velvet ribbon, each with a rhinestone set on one tab.

Lower sleeves are 3" by 12", edged with lace and stitched with elastic thread 1/4" from lower edge, and gathered to lower edge of sleeve along other long edge.

Sash is a strip of plain white organdy measuring 3-3/4" by 45", with the tips angled and a very narrow hem all around.

To complete this outfit a big garden party hat may be made from the same two flock-dotted organdy fabrics, using the white for facing. Cut circles 14" in diameter, cut out circles for crown to fit your doll's head, edge with lace, tie with white organdy tie of same measurements as dress tie. This hat is not original to the doll, but would complement the outfit.

23" Sweet Sue Girl
by American Character

Add 1/4" Seam Allowance

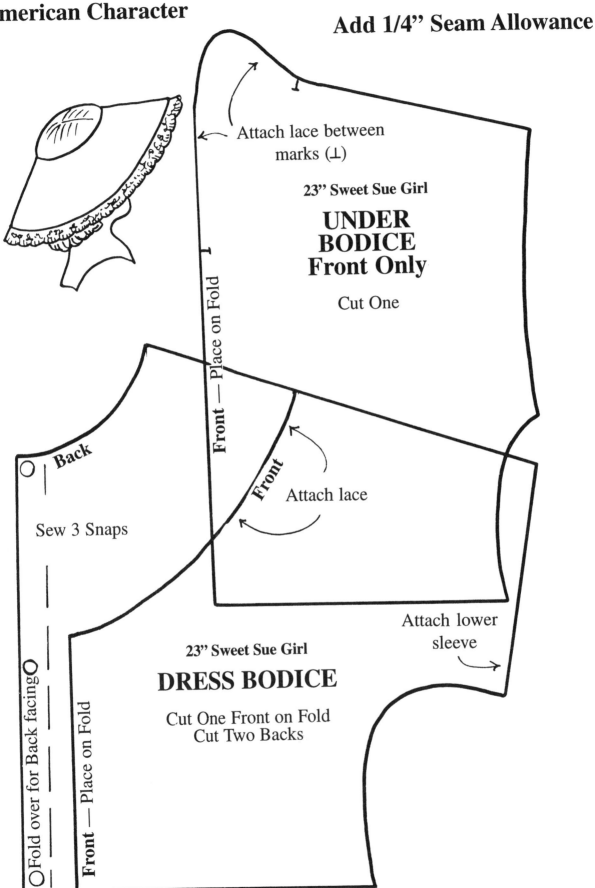

Attach lace between
marks (⊥)

23" Sweet Sue Girl

UNDER
BODICE
Front Only

Cut One

Front — Place on Fold

Back

Sew 3 Snaps

Front

Attach lace

Attach lower
sleeve

Fold over for Back facing○

Front — Place on Fold

23" Sweet Sue Girl

DRESS BODICE

Cut One Front on Fold
Cut Two Backs

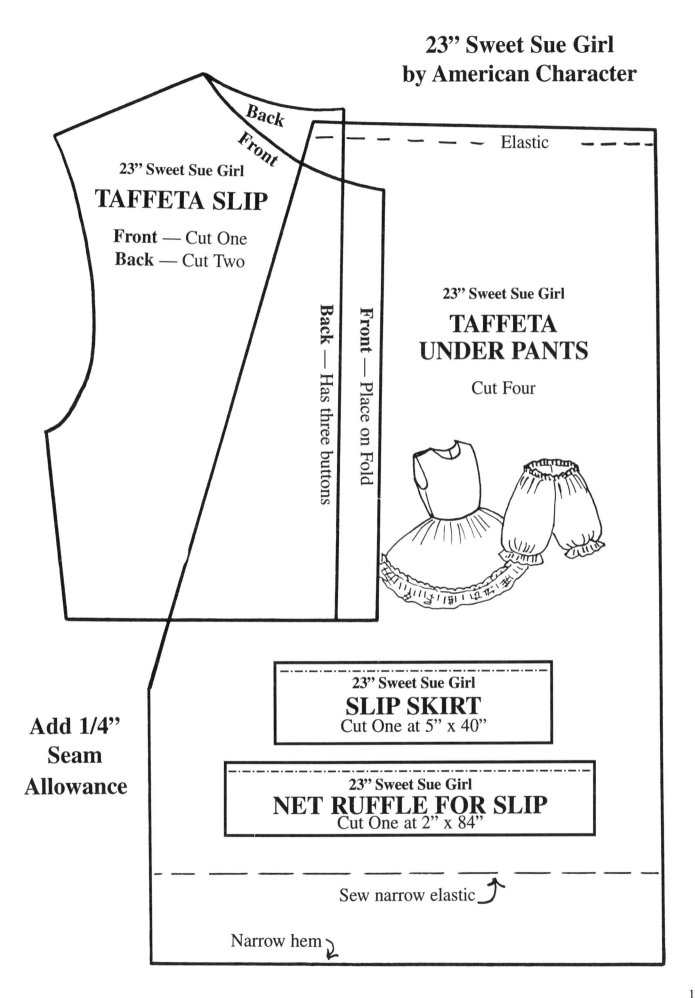

23" Sweet Sue Girl
by American Character

Back

Front

Elastic

23" Sweet Sue Girl

TAFFETA SLIP

Front — Cut One
Back — Cut Two

Back — Has three buttons

Front — Place on Fold

23" Sweet Sue Girl

TAFFETA
UNDER PANTS

Cut Four

Add 1/4"
Seam
Allowance

23" Sweet Sue Girl
SLIP SKIRT
Cut One at 5" x 40"

23" Sweet Sue Girl
NET RUFFLE FOR SLIP
Cut One at 2" x 84"

Sew narrow elastic

Narrow hem

21" Cowgirl Girl Doll
1950s

Decorative Stitching

21" Cowgirl Girl Doll
SHIRT BACK

Cut One

Place on Fold

Cut One after making pattern

Double and re-double
to make paper pattern

21" Cowgirl Girl Doll
HAT BRIM

HOLSTER

Place on Fold

21" Cowgirl Girl Doll
SLEEVE

Cut Two

21" Cowgirl Girl Doll
HAT

Cut One of Felt
Side of Crown

Place on Fold

Decorative Stitching

Add 1/4" Seam Allowance

21" Cowgirl Girl Doll
1950s

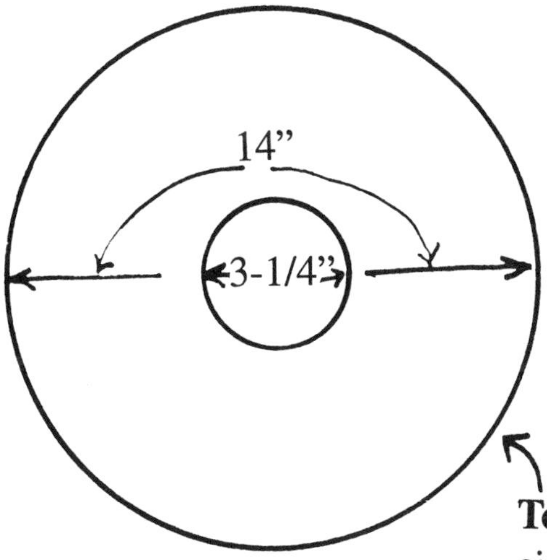

14"

3-1/4"

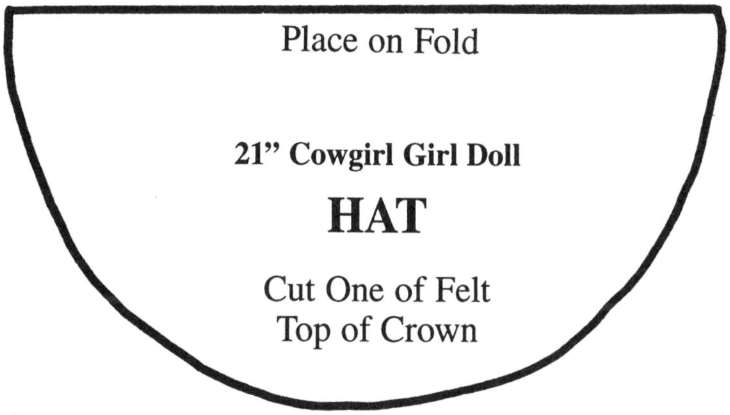

Place on Fold

21" Cowgirl Girl Doll

HAT

Cut One of Felt
Top of Crown

To make skirt: cut 14" dia. circle, cut 3-1/4" circle for waist. Add fringe around hem if desired.

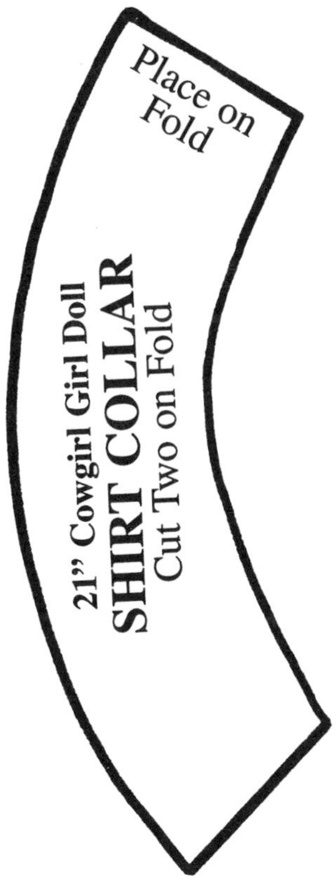

Place on Fold

21" Cowgirl Girl Doll
SHIRT COLLAR
Cut Two on Fold

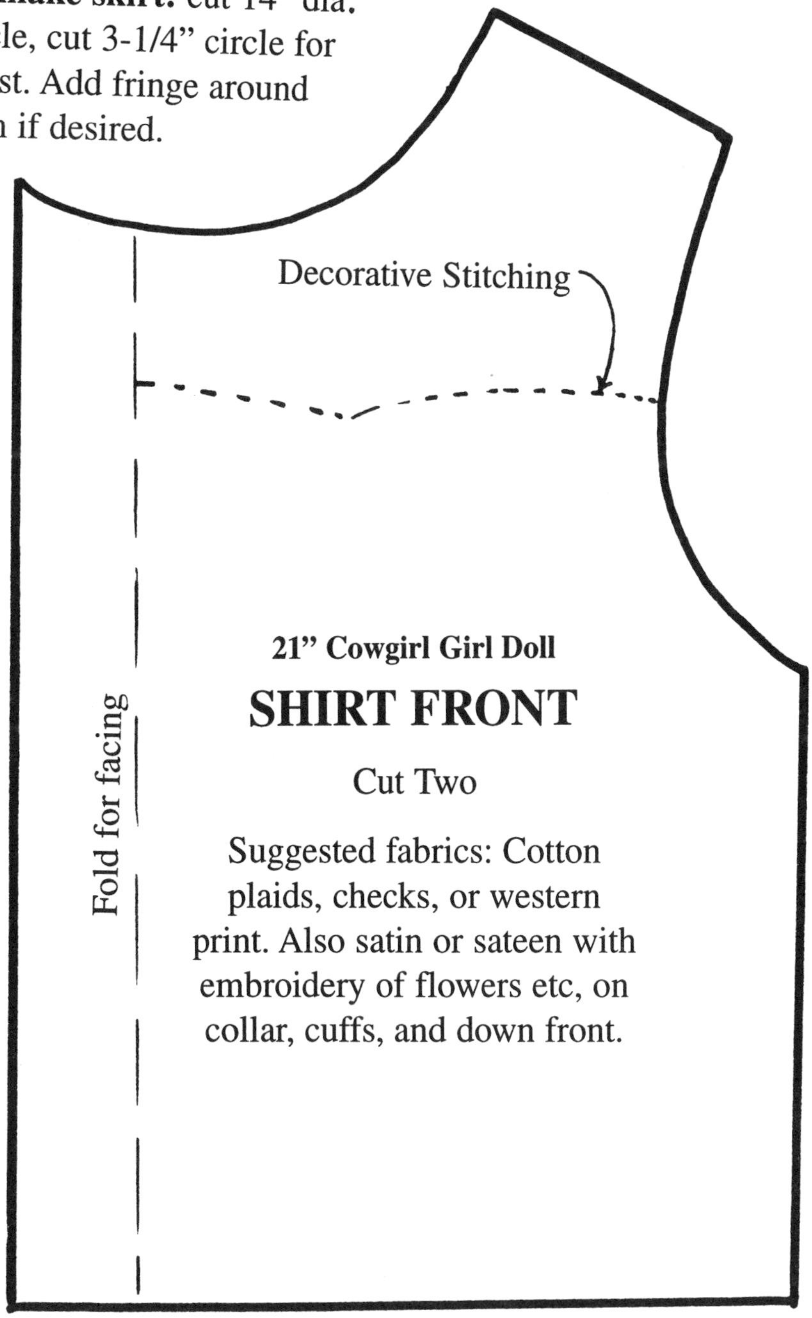

Decorative Stitching

Fold for facing

21" Cowgirl Girl Doll

SHIRT FRONT

Cut Two

Suggested fabrics: Cotton plaids, checks, or western print. Also satin or sateen with embroidery of flowers etc, on collar, cuffs, and down front.

Add 1/4" Seam Allowance

For Cowgirl boots see Chapter 6 Stockings and Shoes.

199

20" Sweet Sue Sophisticate
by American Character

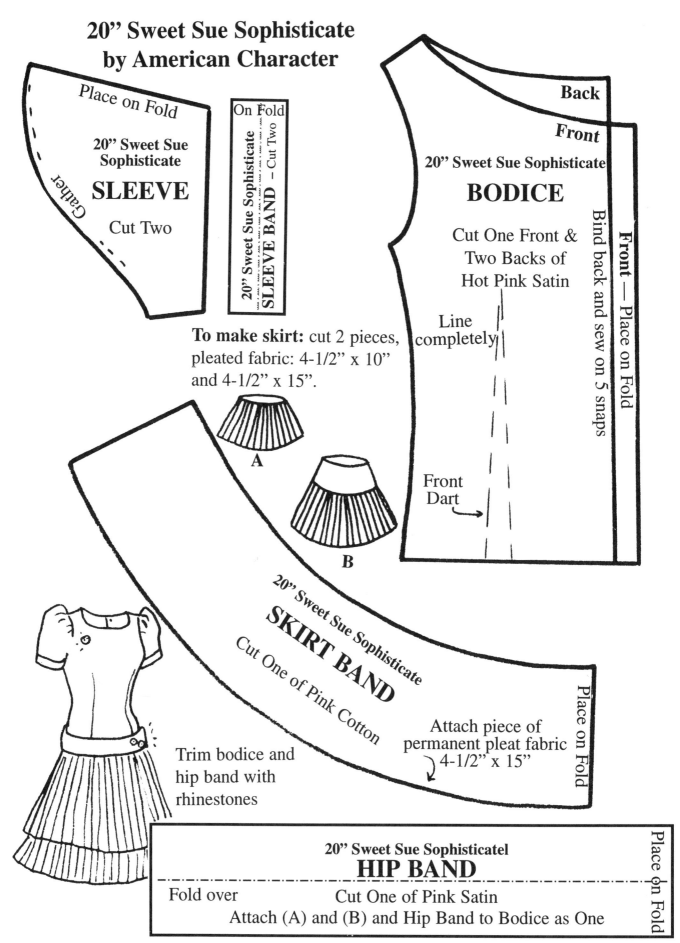

Place on Fold

20" Sweet Sue Sophisticate
SLEEVE

Cut Two

Gather

On Fold

20" Sweet Sue Sophisticate
SLEEVE BAND – Cut Two

Back

Front

20" Sweet Sue Sophisticate
BODICE

Cut One Front &
Two Backs of
Hot Pink Satin

Line
completely

Front — Place on Fold

Bind back and sew on 5 snaps

Front
Dart

To make skirt: cut 2 pieces, pleated fabric: 4-1/2" x 10" and 4-1/2" x 15".

A

B

20" Sweet Sue Sophisticate
SKIRT BAND

Cut One of Pink Cotton

Place on Fold

Attach piece of permanent pleat fabric 4-1/2" x 15"

Trim bodice and hip band with rhinestones

20" Sweet Sue Sophisticatel
HIP BAND

Fold over

Cut One of Pink Satin

Attach (A) and (B) and Hip Band to Bodice as One

Place on Fold

Add 1/4" Seam Allowance

**20" Sweet Sue Sophisticate &
Other 1950s Lady Dolls**

BRA
Cut Two
Lace-Bind   with Satin

**20" Sweet Sue Sophisticate &
Other 1950s Lady Dolls**

PANTY BRIEF

Cut One on Fold

Place on Fold

Leave open to here

Attach Lace

20" Sweet Sue Sophisticate
PETTICOAT WAISTBAND
Cut One at 1-1/2" x 8"

Gather

20" Sweet Sue Sophisticate
PETTICOAT SKIRT
Cut One at 6-1/2" x 34"
Attach 1/4" lace

Also use for skirt to cotton dress.

Bind with Self Bias

Sew 3 snaps at back
opening

Front — Place on Fold

**20" Sweet Sue Sophisticate &
20" Effanbee "Mother"**

DRESS BODICE

Cut One Front on Fold
& Two Backs from
Cotton Print

Print in dress matches
aqua of coat

Attach gathered skirt

201

20" Effanbee 1950s Mother & Child

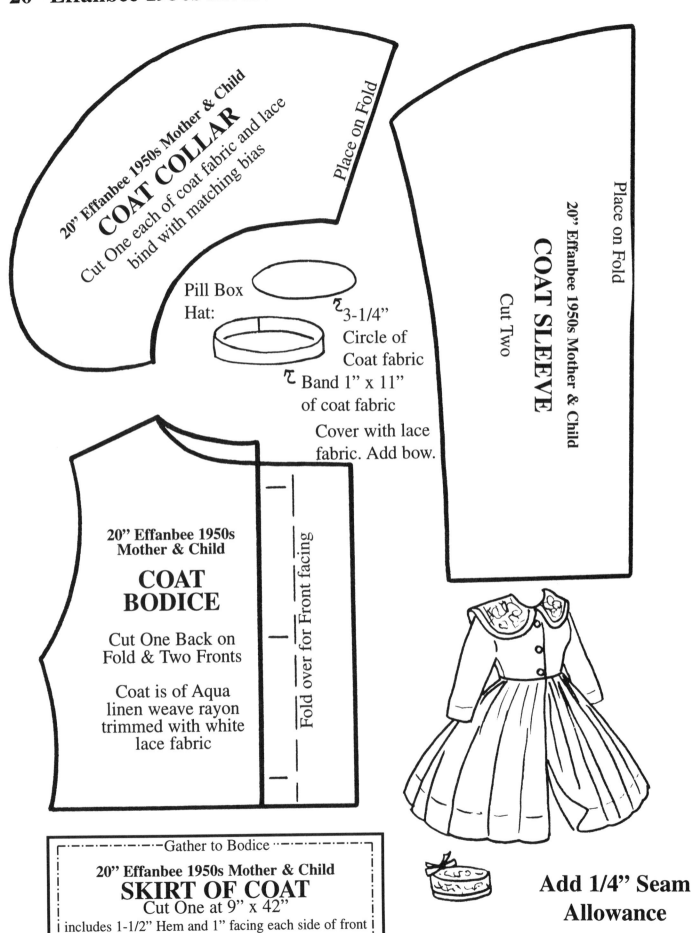

20" Effanbee 1950s Mother & Child
COAT COLLAR
Cut One each of coat fabric and lace
bind with matching bias

Place on Fold

Pill Box
Hat:
3-1/4"
Circle of
Coat fabric
Band 1" x 11"
of coat fabric
Cover with lace
fabric. Add bow.

Place on Fold

20" Effanbee 1950s Mother & Child
COAT SLEEVE

Cut Two

**20" Effanbee 1950s
Mother & Child**

**COAT
BODICE**

Cut One Back on
Fold & Two Fronts

Coat is of Aqua
linen weave rayon
trimmed with white
lace fabric

Fold over for Front facing

Gather to Bodice
20" Effanbee 1950s Mother & Child
SKIRT OF COAT
Cut One at 9" x 42"
includes 1-1/2" Hem and 1" facing each side of front

**Add 1/4" Seam
Allowance**

202

8" — 9-1/2" Dolls such as Muffie, Betsy McCall, Alexander-kins, Ginny (1950s Fashions)

8–9-1/2" Dolls (1950s Fashions)
DRESS BODICE
May open Front or Back

8-9-1/2" Dolls (1950s Fashions)
TWO COLLAR TREATMENTS
Cut Four Round
Cut Two on Fold for Squared
Fold

8–9-1/2" Dolls (1950s Fashions)
PETTICOAT
Cut one at 2" x 13"

8–9-1/2" Dolls (1950s Fashions)
TIE
Cut two at 1" x 8"

8–9-1/2" Dolls (1950s Fashions)
SKIRT
Cut one at 3-1/2" x 18"

Add 1/4" Seam Allowance for 9-1/2" Dolls

8" — 9-1/2" Dolls such as Ginny, Muffie, Betsy McCall, Alexander-kins (1950s Fashions)

Place on Fold

- - Machine stitch elastic thread - - -

8–9-1/2" Dolls
(1950s Fashions)
UNDER PANTS
Cut One on Fold

- - Gather - - -
8–9-1/2" Dolls
(1950s Fashions)
PEDAL PUSH-ERS, SHORTS & LONG PANTS
Cut Two
for shorts

Cutting line for shorts

Place on Fold

Place on Fold

8–9-1/2" Dolls
(1950s Fashions)
SKIRT
Cut One on fold for circular skirt. Cut Two on fold and gather at waist for extra full skirt.

Pedal Pushers cutting line

Back

Front

Cutting line for Short Skirt

8–9-1/2" Dolls
(1950s Fashions)
OVER BLOUSE
May Open Front or Back

Add 1/4" Seam Allowance for 9-1/2" Dolls

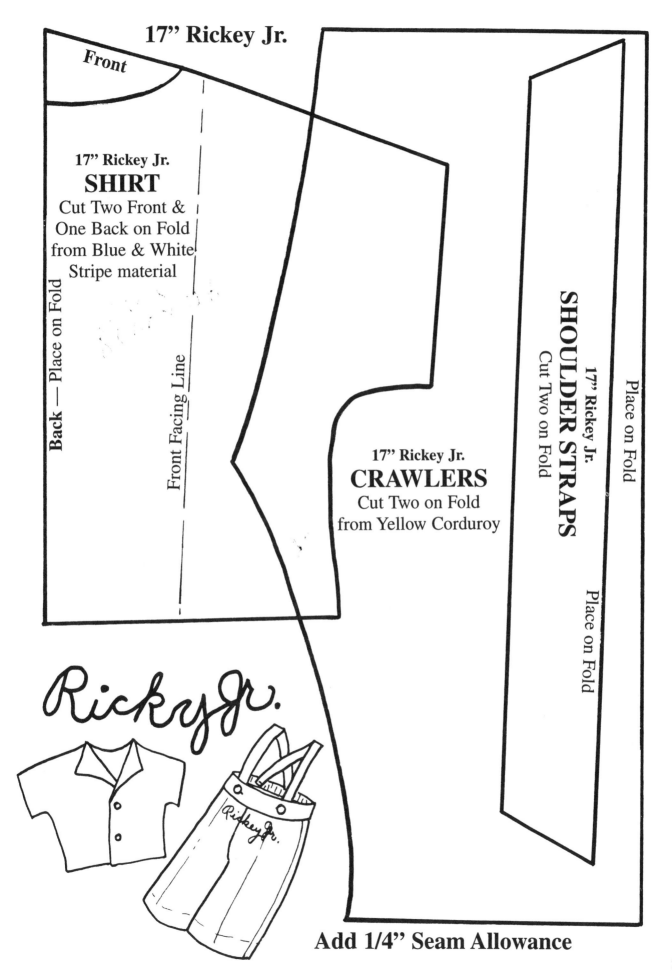

17" Rickey Jr.

Front

17" Rickey Jr.
SHIRT
Cut Two Front &
One Back on Fold
from Blue & White
Stripe material

Back — Place on Fold

Front Facing Line

17" Rickey Jr.
CRAWLERS
Cut Two on Fold
from Yellow Corduroy

17" Rickey Jr.
SHOULDER STRAPS
Cut Two on Fold

Place on Fold

Place on Fold

Ricky Jr.

Add 1/4" Seam Allowance

Chapter 13

THE 1960s

The 1960s saw a swing in fashion from the lady-like styles of the early decade to the kooky, kicky, swingy fads of the later years. Chanel suits with their box jackets and slim skirts, more or less classic sportswear, and slim, basic dinner dresses marked the early years. A return to the styles of other decades created a potpourri of fashion later in the period.

Granny dresses of calico, gingham, and even permanent press fabrics were a counterpoint to the mini dresses which were no longer than absolutely necessary. Every length in between was considered acceptable and sleeve treatments were just as varied. Juliet sleeves on blouses were popular, as well as leg-o-mutton, and the full bell sleeve, often finished off with a ruffle created by running elastic several inches above the hem. Skirts were short and straight or short and full. Lounge wear became important with the introduction of at-home clothes. These ranged from lounging pajamas to hostess coats and blouse and skirt separates.

Pantsuits became a symbol of women's emancipation from the traditional role to a widening circle of interest and activities. Few women failed to include at least one pantsuit or pantdress in their wardrobes. Comfort and utility were two of the factors which contributed to the popularity of this fashion.

Probably one of the most important changes in dress in many years occurred in this decade. New fabrics, new fibres, and more importantly, the advent of *permanent press* fabrics offered possibilities heretofore unknown. Many women, freed at last from the tyranny of the ironing board, were able to step into new roles as volunteer workers or even into careers. It is true that permanent press alone did not affect these changes; however, permanent press fabrics coupled with other technological advances in home appliances have wrought great changes in modern life.

The dolls of this decade were fashion's darlings. *Chatty Cathy*, The *Dr. Littlechap Family*, *BARBIE®* doll and her friends, *Penny Brite, Suzy Cute,* and *Coquette,* were all products of the early decade. These dolls not only had extensive wardrobes, but also were fully equipped with homes, automobiles, swimming pools, offices, sports equipment, and every imaginable accessory.

The dolls of the late years of the 1960s were led by *Beautiful Crissy,* from Ideal. *Crissy* had growing hair, a slender, pre-teen figure, and an up-to-the-minute wardrobe. She was later joined by several other dolls her size (17-1/2") and a smaller (15") equally stylish young lady named *Velvet.*

The reader may note the absence of patterns for *BARBIE®* doll and similar dolls. Patterns for this type doll have been marketed commercially almost since the introduction of the doll and it seemed advisable to use the space to better advantage. *Tammy* patterns may be adjusted slightly to fit *BARBIE®* doll and other teen-type dolls.

THE LITTLECHAP FAMILY
by Remco (1963)

DR JOHN'S BUSINESS SUIT

Dark brown suit, three button jacket with narrow lapels, slim tapered slacks, white classic shirt.

Accessories: Striped blue and brown slim tie, black shoes, black socks, pipe, and tobacco pouch.

DR. JOHNS TUXEDO

Black dress suit, satin lapels, and dress trousers with satin stripe. White sheer shirt with pleated front and pearl studs.

Accessories: Black bowtie, black satin pleated cummerbund, black socks, black shoes, black wallet, and white carnation.

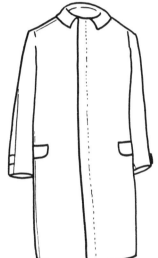

DR. JOHN'S ALL-WEATHER COAT

Natural twill coat for rain or shine lined in red, beige, and black cotton plaid.

Accessories: Brown hat, red scarf, doctor's bag containing tongue depressor, fountain pen, stethoscope, hypodermic needle, pill bottles, and doctor's mallet.

DR. JOHN'S WARDROBE

DR. JOHN'S GOLF OUTFIT

White wool cardigan sweater, black jersey polo shirt, red twill golf slacks.

Accessories: Plaid cap, two golf clubs, golf balls, golf trophy, black socks, black shoes.

DR. JOHN'S MEDICAL TUNIC AND SLACKS

White oxford cloth slacks and tunic with stand-up collar and side closing of regulation white metal snaps.

Accessories: White shoes, white socks, stethoscope, tongue depressor, fountain pen, wrist watch, and doctor's bag.

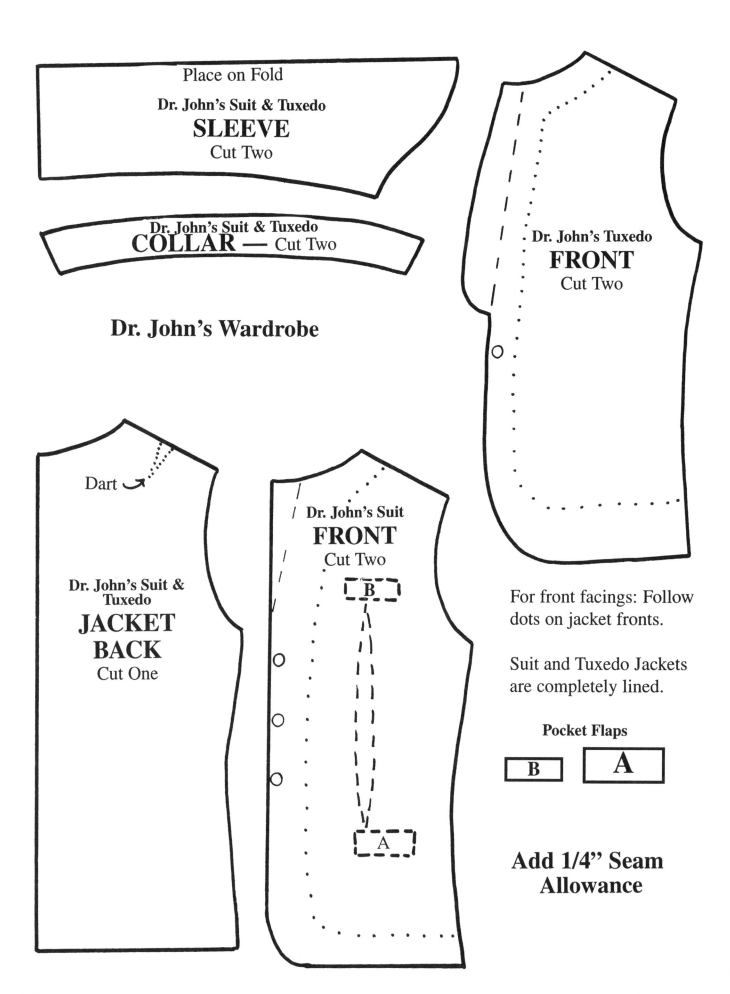

Place on Fold

Dr. John's Suit & Tuxedo
SLEEVE
Cut Two

Dr. John's Suit & Tuxedo
COLLAR — Cut Two

Dr. John's Wardrobe

Dr. John's Tuxedo
FRONT
Cut Two

Dart

Dr. John's Suit &
Tuxedo
JACKET
BACK
Cut One

Dr. John's Suit
FRONT
Cut Two

B

A

For front facings: Follow
dots on jacket fronts.

Suit and Tuxedo Jackets
are completely lined.

Pocket Flaps

B   A

Add 1/4" Seam
Allowance

Dr. John's Wardrobe

Slacks pattern may be used for medical uniform, golf slacks, suit pants, or pajamas. Heavy dotted line indicates crease for dress slacks: may be stitched in permanently by folding along crease and machine stitching with tiny stitches as close to fold edge as possible, after slacks are hemmed.

Medical jacket has back belt stitched down all around after back tucks are stitched and before being sewn to jacket front.

Tuck

Front

Back

Dr. John's Suit & Tuxedo
SLACKS
Cut Two Backs and Two Fronts

Fold

Dr. John's Suit & Tuxedo
SLACKS WAISTBAND
Cut One

Dr. John's Medical Jacket
LEFT FRONT
Cut One

Add 1/4" Seam Allowance

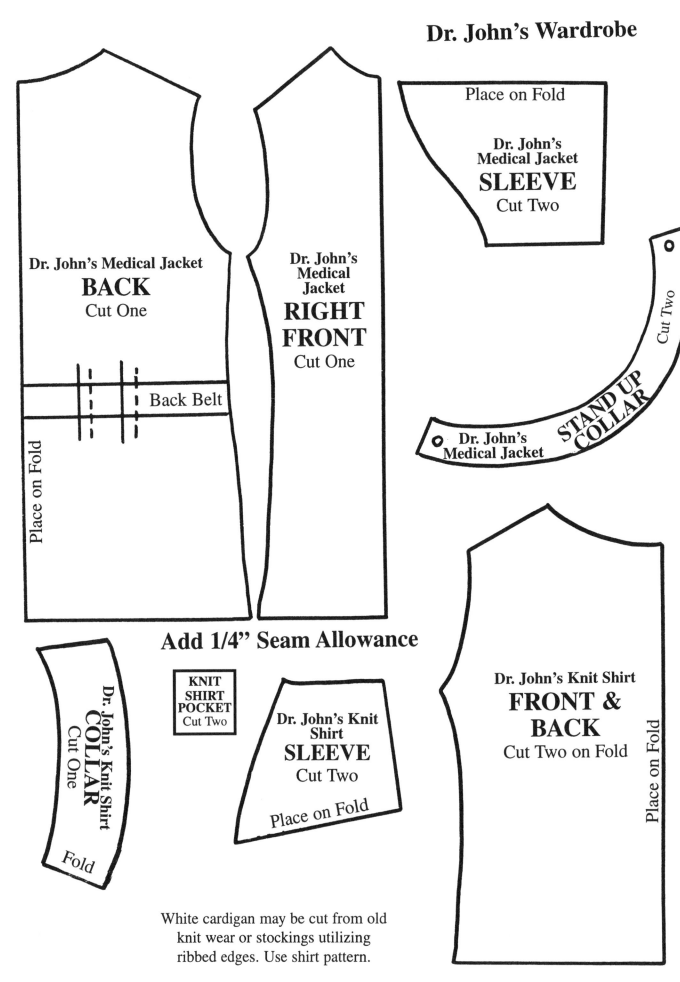

Dr. John's Wardrobe

Place on Fold

Dr. John's
Medical Jacket
SLEEVE
Cut Two

Cut Two

STAND UP COLLAR

Dr. John's
Medical Jacket

Dr. John's Medical Jacket
BACK
Cut One

Back Belt

Place on Fold

Dr. John's
Medical
Jacket
**RIGHT
FRONT**
Cut One

Add 1/4" Seam Allowance

Dr. John's Knit Shirt
COLLAR
Cut One

Fold

**KNIT
SHIRT
POCKET**
Cut Two

Dr. John's Knit
Shirt
SLEEVE
Cut Two

Place on Fold

Dr. John's Knit Shirt
**FRONT &
BACK**
Cut Two on Fold

Place on Fold

White cardigan may be cut from old
knit wear or stockings utilizing
ribbed edges. Use shirt pattern.

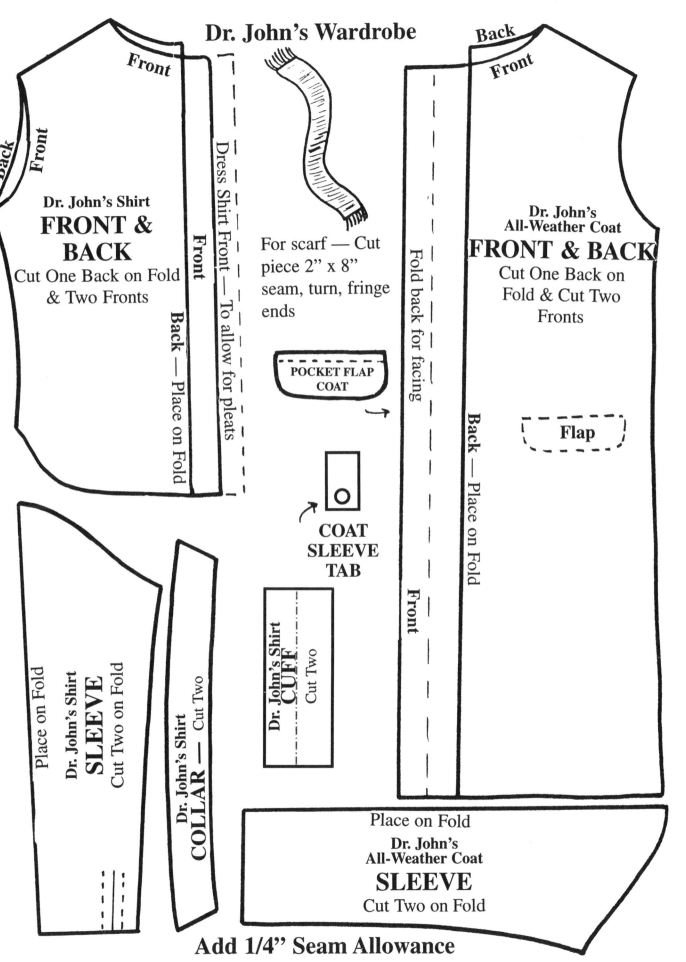

Dr. John's Wardrobe

Dr. John's Shirt
FRONT & BACK
Cut One Back on Fold
& Two Fronts

Front

Back

Front

Dress Shirt Front — To allow for pleats

Front

Back — Place on Fold

For scarf — Cut
piece 2" x 8"
seam, turn, fringe
ends

POCKET FLAP
COAT

COAT
SLEEVE
TAB

Back

Front

Dr. John's
All-Weather Coat
FRONT & BACK
Cut One Back on
Fold & Cut Two
Fronts

Fold back for facing

Flap

Back — Place on Fold

Front

Place on Fold

Dr. John's Shirt
SLEEVE
Cut Two on Fold

Dr. John's Shirt
COLLAR — Cut Two

Dr. John's Shirt
CUFF
Cut Two

Place on Fold

Dr. John's
All-Weather Coat
SLEEVE
Cut Two on Fold

Add 1/4" Seam Allowance

211

LISA'S WHITE TWO-PIECE DRESS

Completely lined two-piece dress with slim skirt and V-necked, long-sleeved overblouse belted in tawny beige suede with gold buckle.

Accessories: Tawny beige printed chiffon scarf, golden tan pumps, golden tan leatherette over-sized tote bag. Gold sunburst pin and gold button earrings. Beige gloves.

LISA'S FUR-TRIMMED SUEDE COAT

Slim line wrap around coat in tawny suede cloth. Trimmed in creamy beige fake fur with a sheared fur look, matching taffeta lining.

Accessories: Matching fake fur hat, golden tan pumps, large golden tan leatherette tote bag, beige gloves.

LISA'S THREE PIECE CHANEL SUIT

Straight, slim skirt and box jacket of brown crepe with blue binding, trim, and lining with matching sleeveless blue blouse.

Accessories: Brown fake alligator handbag, gold button earrings, beige gloves, shopping bag, shoes.

LISA'S LINGERIE

Black lace, bra, black tricot half-slip with lace trim and matching black lace-trimmed panties, nylon stockings.

LISA'S FORMAL EVENING ENSEMBLE

Sweeping full length coat of blue satin, lined in silver and blue patterned brocade. Standaway portrait neck-line, deep cuffs of white ermine-like fur, long slim blue satin evening skirt with fishtail hemline, fitted overblouse with scoop neckline and slim straps of blue and silver brocade.

Accessories: Silver slippers, silver clutch bag, drop earrings, hair ornament, beautiful necklace, opera length white nylon gloves.

LISA'S BASIC BLACK DRESS

Fully-lined black crepe dress, slim skirt, high-waisted effect accented with black velvet bow.

Accessories: Black clutch bag, pearl button earrings, opera length pearl necklace, black pumps, white nylon gloves, black velvet hairbow with net vail.

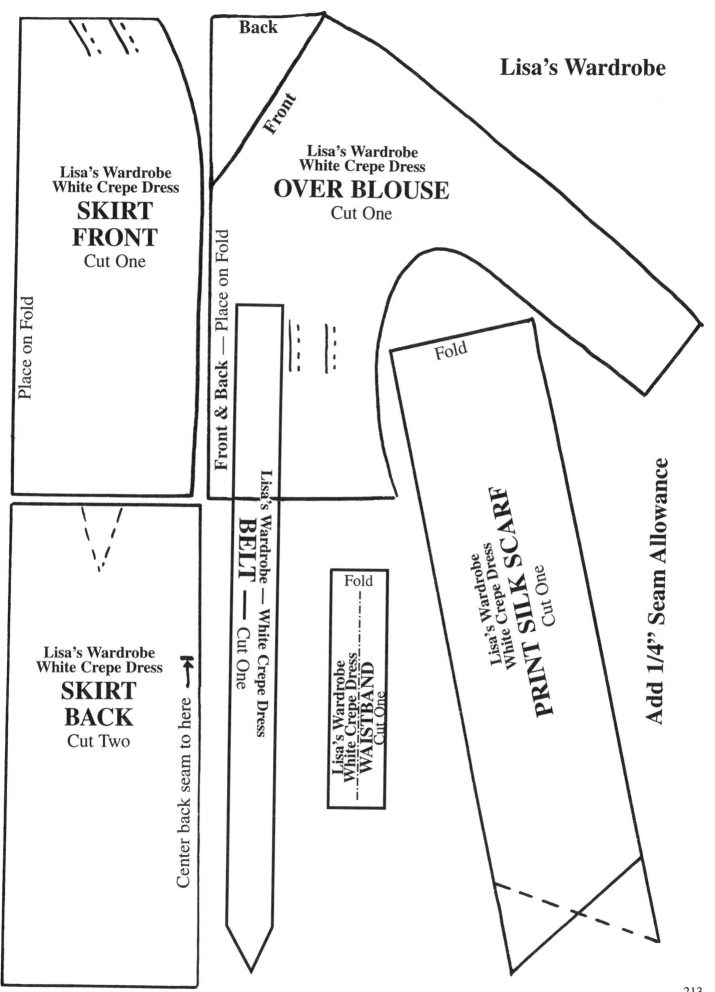

Back

Front

Lisa's Wardrobe

Lisa's Wardrobe
White Crepe Dress
OVER BLOUSE
Cut One

Lisa's Wardrobe
White Crepe Dress
**SKIRT
FRONT**
Cut One

Place on Fold

Front & Back — Place on Fold

Lisa's Wardrobe — White Crepe Dress
BELT — Cut One

Fold

Lisa's Wardrobe
White Crepe Dress
**SKIRT
BACK**
Cut Two

Center back seam to here

Fold

Lisa's Wardrobe
White Crepe Dress
WAISTBAND
Cut One

Lisa's Wardrobe
White Crepe Dress
PRINT SILK SCARF
Cut One

Add 1/4" Seam Allowance

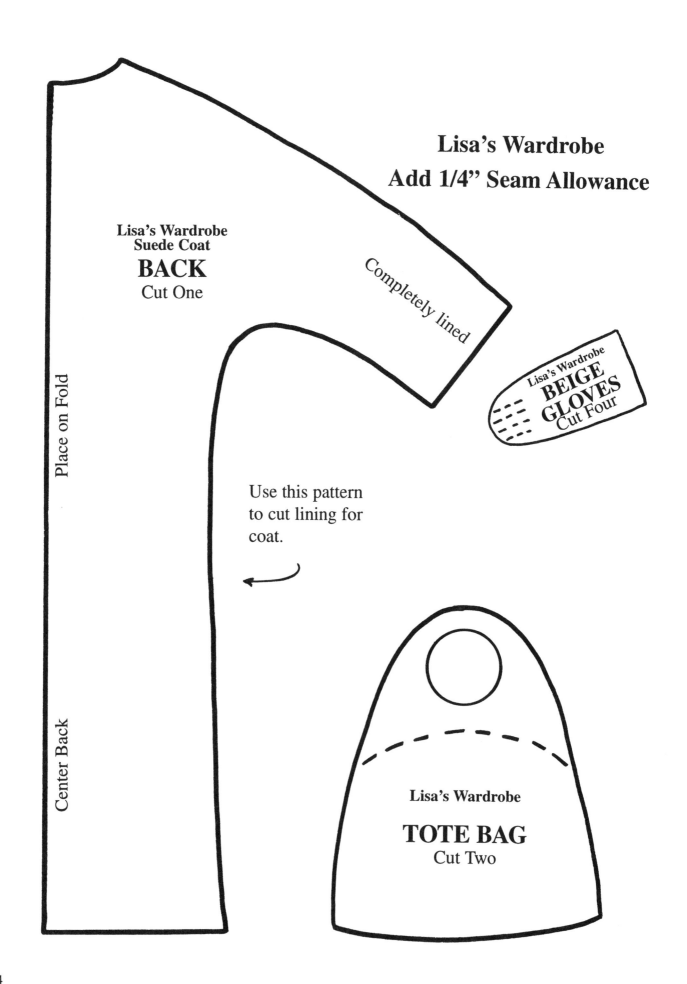

Lisa's Wardrobe
Add 1/4" Seam Allowance

Lisa's Wardrobe
Suede Coat
BACK
Cut One

Completely lined

Lisa's Wardrobe
BEIGE GLOVES
Cut Four

Use this pattern to cut lining for coat.

Place on Fold

Center Back

Lisa's Wardrobe

TOTE BAG
Cut Two

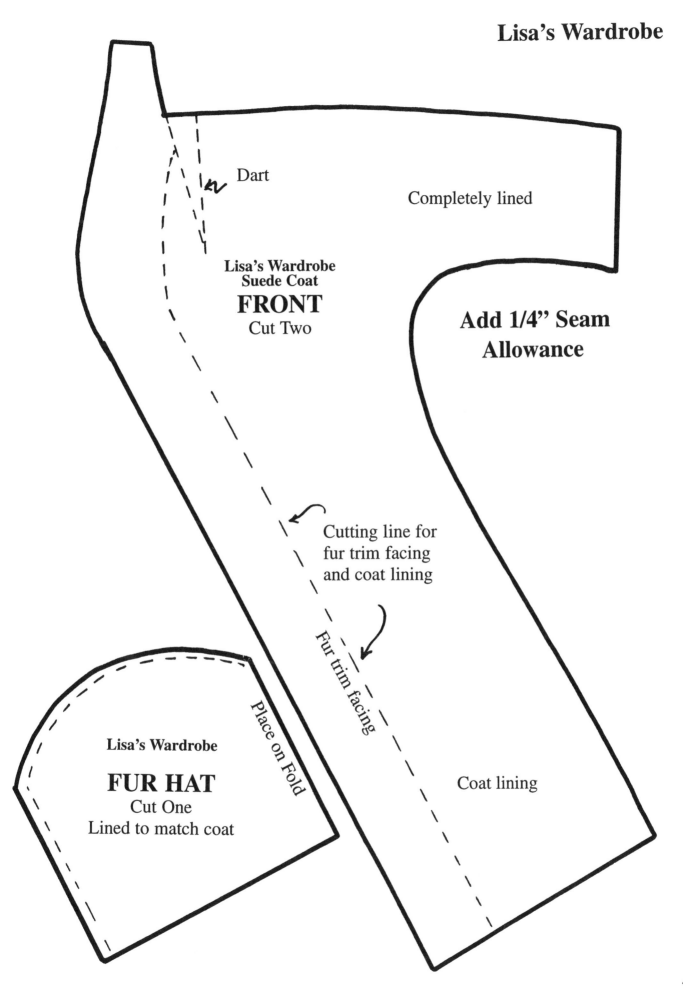

Dart

Completely lined

**Lisa's Wardrobe
Suede Coat**
FRONT
Cut Two

**Add 1/4" Seam
Allowance**

Cutting line for
fur trim facing
and coat lining

Fur trim facing

Coat lining

Lisa's Wardrobe

FUR HAT
Cut One
Lined to match coat

Place on Fold

Lisa's Wardrobe
Chanel Suit
SKIRT FRONT
Cut Two

Lisa's Wardrobe
Chanel Suit
SKIRT BACK
Cut Two

Back seam to here

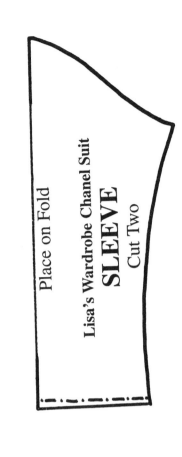

Place on Fold

Lisa's Wardrobe Chanel Suit
SLEEVE
Cut Two

Lisa's Wardrobe
WHITE GLOVES
Cut Four

Fold

Lisa's Wardrobe Chanel Suit
WAISTBAND
Cut One

Front

Back

Lisa's Wardrobe
Chanel Suit
JACKET FRONT & BACK
Cut Two Fronts &
One Back on Fold

Place on Fold

Front

Back

Lisa's Wardrobe
Chanel Suit
SLEEVELESS BLOUSE
Cut Two Backs &
One Front on Fold

- A -

Front — Place on Fold

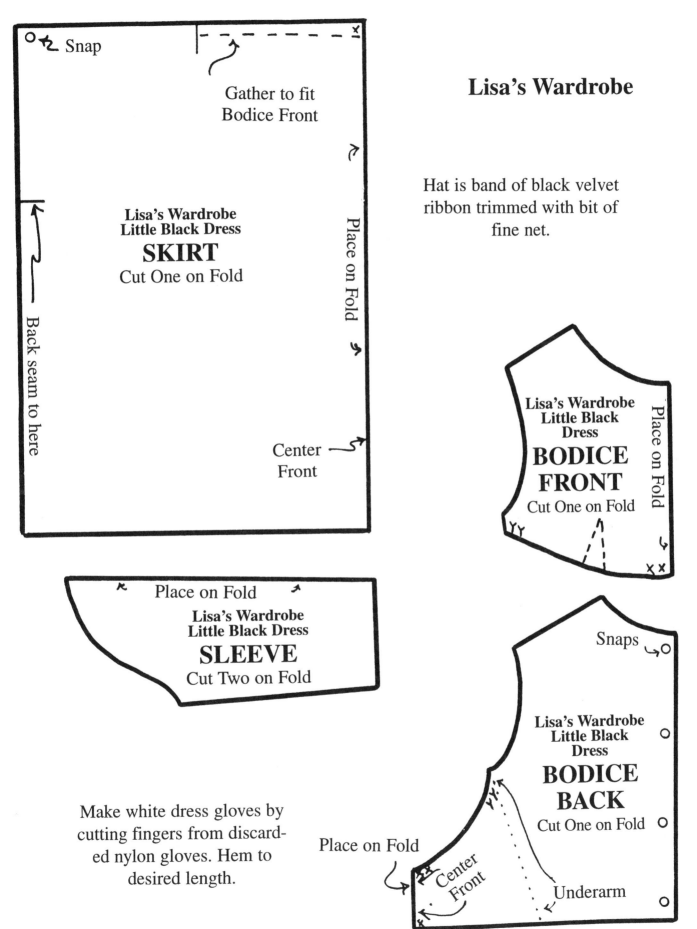

Snap

Gather to fit
Bodice Front

**Lisa's Wardrobe
Little Black Dress
SKIRT**
Cut One on Fold

Place on Fold

Back seam to here

Center
Front

Lisa's Wardrobe

Hat is band of black velvet
ribbon trimmed with bit of
fine net.

**Lisa's Wardrobe
Little Black
Dress
BODICE
FRONT**
Cut One on Fold

Place on Fold

Place on Fold

**Lisa's Wardrobe
Little Black Dress
SLEEVE**
Cut Two on Fold

Snaps

**Lisa's Wardrobe
Little Black
Dress
BODICE
BACK**
Cut One on Fold

Underarm

Place on Fold

Center
Front

Make white dress gloves by
cutting fingers from discarded nylon gloves. Hem to
desired length.

Add 1/4" Seam Allowance

217

Lisa's Wardrobe

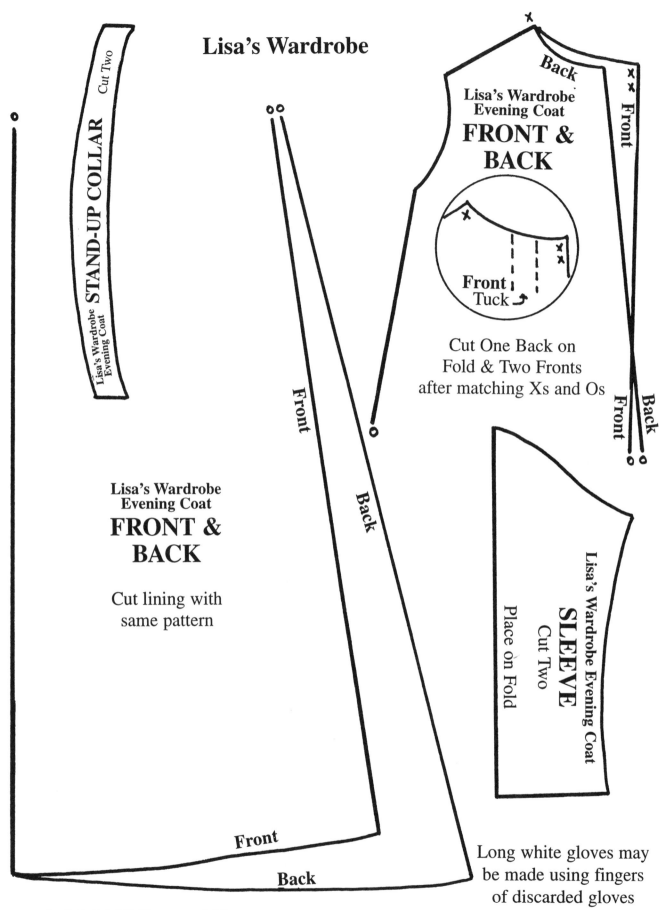

STAND-UP COLLAR
Lisa's Wardrobe Evening Coat
Cut Two

Lisa's Wardrobe Evening Coat
FRONT & BACK

Cut lining with same pattern

Front

Back

Front

Back

Lisa's Wardrobe Evening Coat
FRONT & BACK

Front Tuck

Cut One Back on Fold & Two Fronts after matching Xs and Os

Back

Front

Front

Back

Lisa's Wardrobe Evening Coat
SLEEVE
Cut Two
Place on Fold

Long white gloves may be made using fingers of discarded gloves

Add 1/4" Seam Allowance

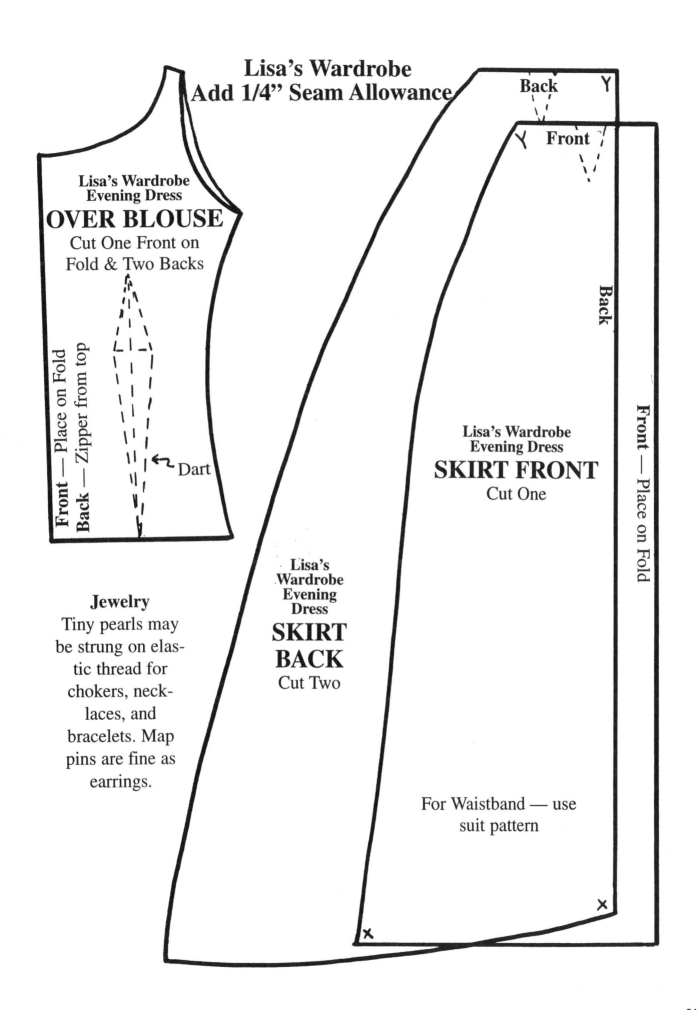

**Lisa's Wardrobe
Add 1/4" Seam Allowance**

Back

Front

Y

Y

**Lisa's Wardrobe
Evening Dress
OVER BLOUSE**
Cut One Front on
Fold & Two Backs

Back

**Front — Place on Fold
Back — Zipper from top**

Dart

**Lisa's Wardrobe
Evening Dress
SKIRT FRONT**
Cut One

Front — Place on Fold

Jewelry
Tiny pearls may
be strung on elas-
tic thread for
chokers, neck-
laces, and
bracelets. Map
pins are fine as
earrings.

**Lisa's
Wardrobe
Evening
Dress
SKIRT
BACK**
Cut Two

For Waistband — use
suit pattern

JUDY'S PARTY DRESS

Bright pink moire sleeveless dress with low, scooped neckline, bell-shaped skirt and large flat bow.

Accessories: Pink ballet slippers, gold clutch bag, pearl choker, pearl bracelet, pearl button earrings, white nylon shortie gloves.

JUDY'S SPORTSWEAR OUTFIT

Box-pleated, knee tickler skirt (made to be worn above knees) in cream, gray, gold and brown hounds-tooth check, gold suede jerkin, beige shirt with panel front.

Accessories: Deep red, tie-print triangle headscarf, brown loafers, gold knee socks, gold pin, black framed eyeglasses, and play script.

JUDY'S RED CHESTERFIELD COAT

Basketweave tweed, pimento red, semi-fitted coat with matching velvet notched collar and lapels, matching red taffeta lining.

Accessories: Leopard print velveteen pillbox hat, ascot, pouch handbag, golden hatpin, beige gloves, black pumps, paper shopping bag containing three colorful packages.

JUDY'S THREE-PIECE SUIT

Red waist-length matador jacket with flap pockets piped in navy, red lining, flared skirt, pencil-striped sleeveless shirt with pert bow.

Accessories: Navy pumps, white shortie nylon gloves, gold button earrings, red tote bag.

JUDY'S DANCE DRESS

Two-piece ensemble with yellow taffeta sleeveless, scooped neckline dance dress, belted in dainty floral embroidered French Ribbon, matching yellow velveteen waist-length jacket bound in same French ribbon.

Accessories: Gold ballet slippers, gold clutch bag, pearl choker, white nylon shortie gloves, hair corsage of a red rose on bobby pin in clear plastic flower box , green chiffon triangle headscarf.

JUDY'S LINGERIE

Pink lace bra, pink tricot half-slip with lace trim, and matching pink lace-trimmed panties, nylon stockings.

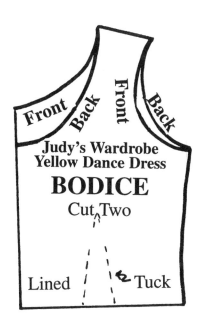

Judy's Wardrobe

Judy's Wardrobe
Yellow Dance Dress
BODICE
Cut Two

Front Back Front Back

Lined

Tuck

JUDY'S PINK PARTY DRESS

Use patterns for bodice and skirt of yellow DANCE DRESS, cutting only two panels of the skirt. Refer to sketches and description of PARTY DRESS. Add flat bow of dress material. Line dress completely with fine sheath lining.

Add 1/4" Seam Allowance

Judy's Wardrobe
Yellow Dance Dress Jacket
SLEEVE
Cut Four of Yellow Velveteen

Lined

Gather to fit
bodice

Judy's Wardrobe
Yellow Dance Dress
SKIRT
Cut Four

Lined

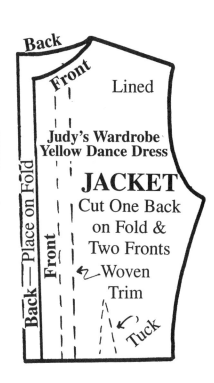

Back

Front

Lined

Back — Place on Fold

Front

Judy's Wardrobe
Yellow Dance Dress
JACKET
Cut One Back
on Fold &
Two Fronts

Woven
Trim

Tuck

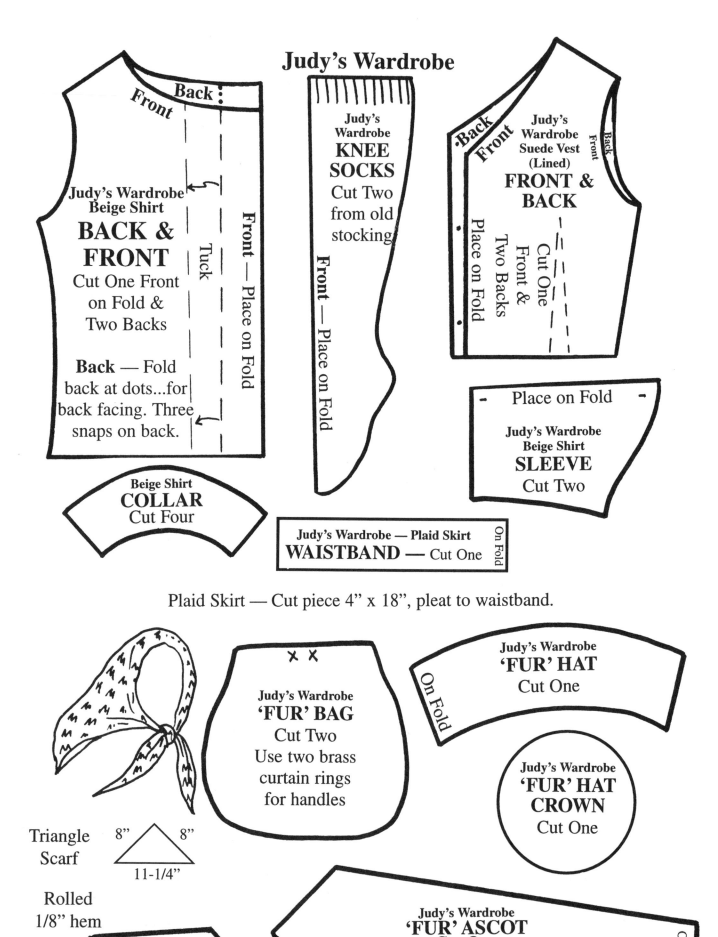

Judy's Wardrobe

Front **Back**

Judy's Wardrobe
Beige Shirt
BACK & FRONT
Cut One Front
on Fold &
Two Backs

Back — Fold
back at dots...for
back facing. Three
snaps on back.

Tuck

Front — Place on Fold

Judy's
Wardrobe
KNEE SOCKS
Cut Two
from old
stocking

Front — Place on Fold

Back **Front** Back

Judy's
Wardrobe
Suede Vest
(Lined)
FRONT & BACK
Cut One
Front &
Two Backs

Place on Fold

Place on Fold

Judy's Wardrobe
Beige Shirt
SLEEVE
Cut Two

Beige Shirt
COLLAR
Cut Four

Judy's Wardrobe — Plaid Skirt
WAISTBAND — Cut One — On Fold

Plaid Skirt — Cut piece 4" x 18", pleat to waistband.

X X
Judy's Wardrobe
'FUR' BAG
Cut Two
Use two brass
curtain rings
for handles

On Fold

Judy's Wardrobe
'FUR' HAT
Cut One

Judy's Wardrobe
'FUR' HAT CROWN
Cut One

Triangle
Scarf

8" 8"
11-1/4"

Rolled
1/8" hem

X Judy's Wardrobe O
X 'FUR' BAG TAB
Cut One
X

Snap

Judy's Wardrobe
'FUR' ASCOT
Cut One
Line accessories with coat lining

On Fold

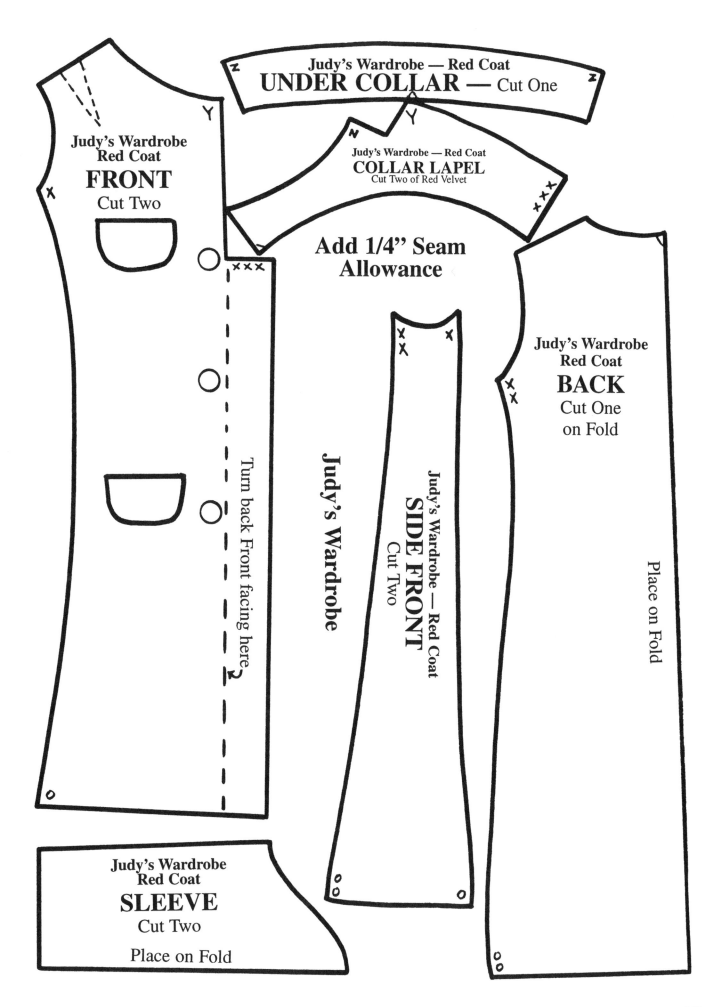

Judy's Wardrobe
Red Coat
FRONT
Cut Two

Judy's Wardrobe — Red Coat
UNDER COLLAR — Cut One

Judy's Wardrobe — Red Coat
COLLAR LAPEL
Cut Two of Red Velvet

Add 1/4" Seam Allowance

Judy's Wardrobe
Red Coat
BACK
Cut One
on Fold

Turn back Front facing here

Judy's Wardrobe

Judy's Wardrobe — Red Coat
SIDE FRONT
Cut Two

Place on Fold

Judy's Wardrobe
Red Coat
SLEEVE
Cut Two

Place on Fold

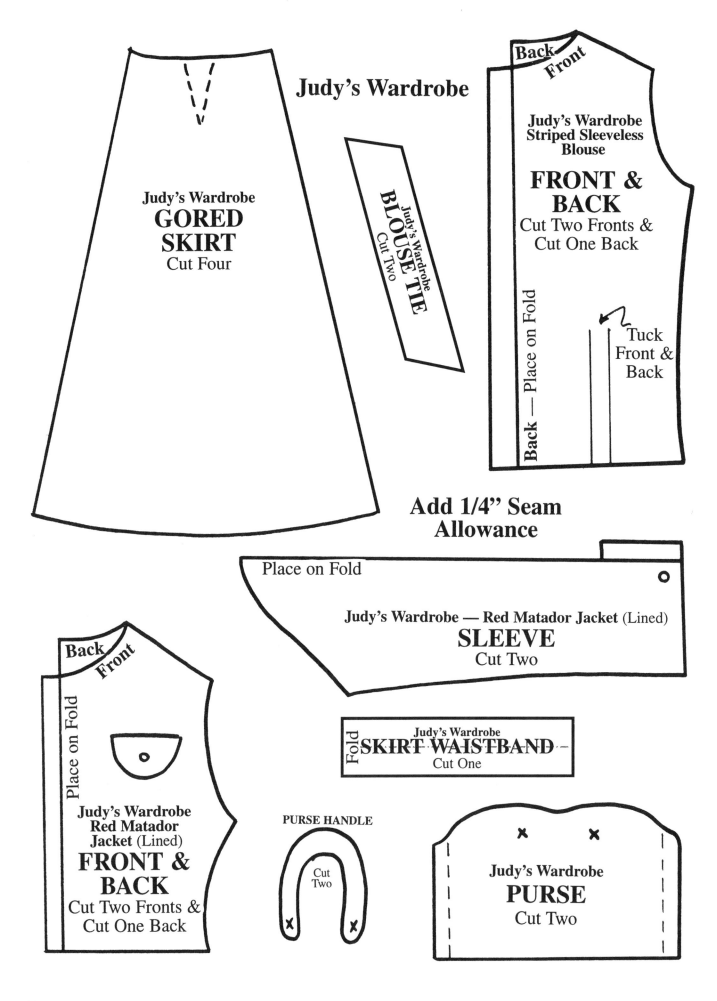

Judy's Wardrobe

Judy's Wardrobe
GORED SKIRT
Cut Four

Judy's Wardrobe
BLOUSE TIE
Cut Two

Judy's Wardrobe
Striped Sleeveless Blouse
FRONT & BACK
Cut Two Fronts &
Cut One Back

Back — Place on Fold

Tuck Front & Back

Add 1/4" Seam Allowance

Place on Fold

Judy's Wardrobe — Red Matador Jacket (Lined)
SLEEVE
Cut Two

Place on Fold

Judy's Wardrobe
Red Matador Jacket (Lined)
FRONT & BACK
Cut Two Fronts &
Cut One Back

Fold

Judy's Wardrobe
SKIRT WAISTBAND
Cut One

PURSE HANDLE

Cut Two

Judy's Wardrobe
PURSE
Cut Two

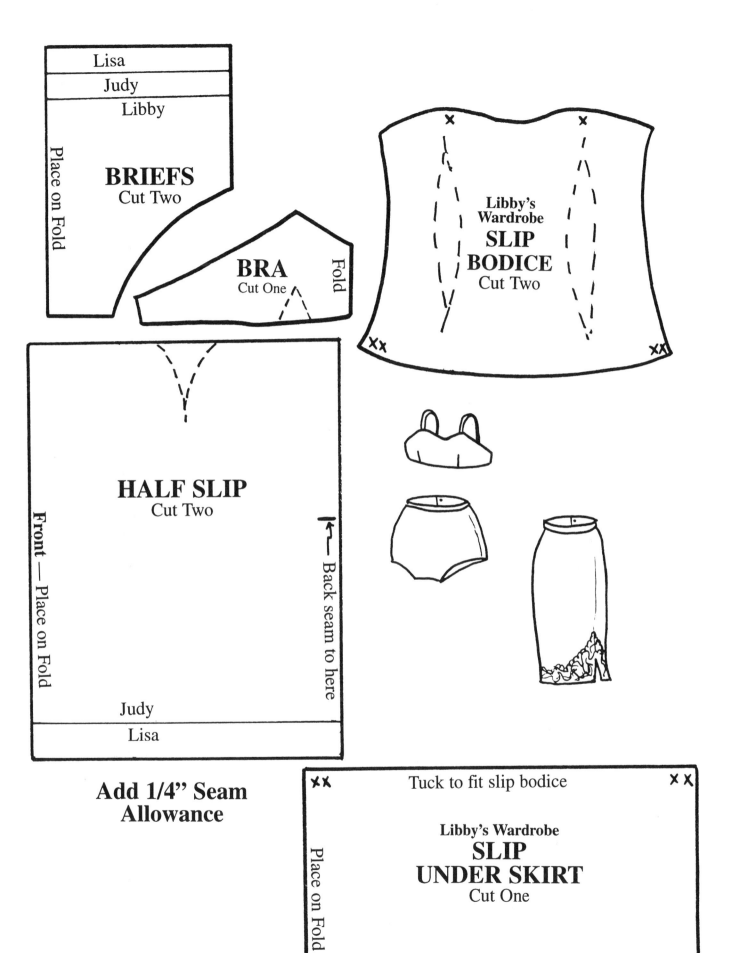

BRIEFS
Cut Two

Lisa
Judy
Libby

Place on Fold

BRA
Cut One

Fold

Libby's Wardrobe
SLIP BODICE
Cut Two

HALF SLIP
Cut Two

Front — Place on Fold

Back seam to here

Judy
Lisa

Add 1/4" Seam Allowance

Tuck to fit slip bodice

Libby's Wardrobe
SLIP UNDER SKIRT
Cut One

Place on Fold

225

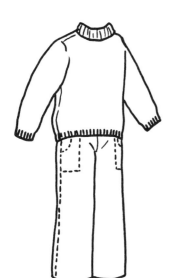

LIBBY'S LEVIS AND SWEATSHIRT

Blue denim Levis with fly front and white stitching, classic white sweatshirt.

Accessories: Red and white sneakers, comic book and YoYo, white socks.

LIBBY'S THREE-PIECE BLAZER OUTFIT

Brilliant blue blazer, buttoned in brass with heraldic crest, worn with bright red and blue plaid box-pleated skirt (skirt matches her coat), white tailored shirt blouse.

Accessories: Brown Pumps, bright blue knee socks, schoolbook with leatherette strap.

LIBBY'S PLAID REEFER COAT

Bright red and blue plaid, double-breasted coat with patch pockets and self belt.

Accessories: Red high boots, red knit scarf, red leatherette mittens, red leatherette schoolbag.

LIBBY'S LINGERIE

White tricot lace-trimmed panties, lace-trimmed white cotton slip with petticoat bottom of pleated nylon. A pink puppy came with this set.

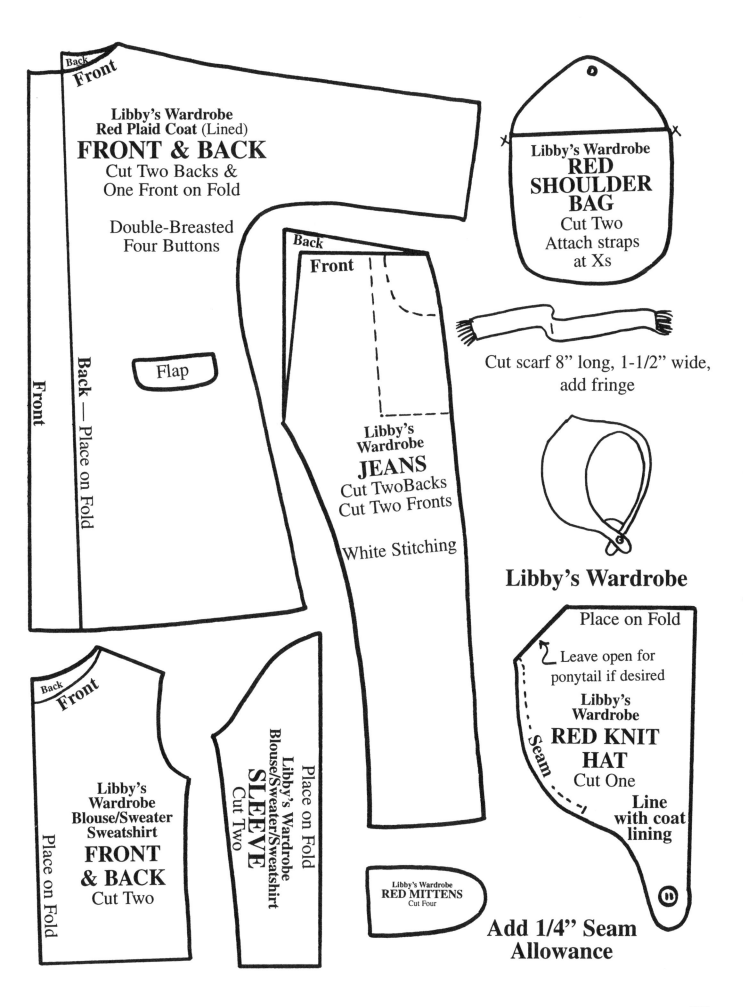

Back Front

Libby's Wardrobe
Red Plaid Coat (Lined)
FRONT & BACK
Cut Two Backs &
One Front on Fold

Double-Breasted
Four Buttons

Front

Back — Place on Fold

Flap

Back Front

Libby's
Wardrobe
JEANS
Cut TwoBacks
Cut Two Fronts

White Stitching

Place on Fold

Libby's
Wardrobe
Blouse/Sweater/Sweatshirt
SLEEVE
Cut Two

Libby's
Wardrobe
Blouse/Sweater
Sweatshirt
FRONT
& BACK
Cut Two

Place on Fold

Libby's Wardrobe
RED
SHOULDER
BAG
Cut Two
Attach straps
at Xs

Cut scarf 8" long, 1-1/2" wide,
add fringe

Libby's Wardrobe

Place on Fold

Leave open for
ponytail if desired

Libby's
Wardrobe
RED KNIT
HAT
Cut One

Seam

Line
with coat
lining

Libby's Wardrobe
RED MITTENS
Cut Four

Add 1/4" Seam
Allowance

227

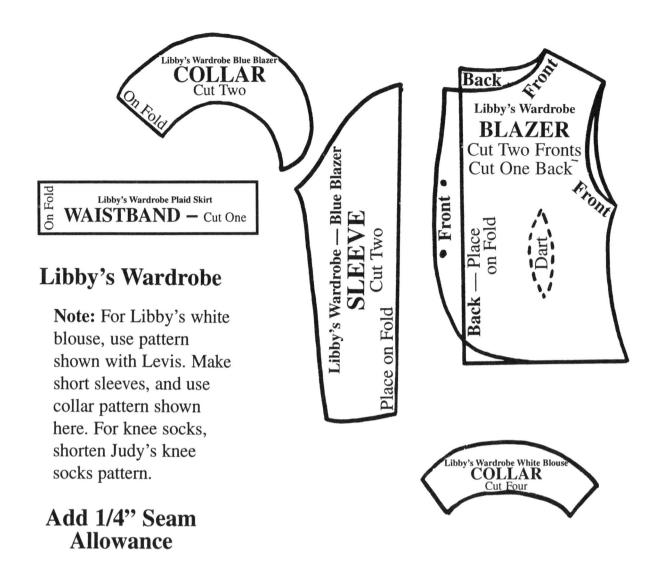

Libby's Wardrobe Blue Blazer
COLLAR
Cut Two

On Fold

Libby's Wardrobe Plaid Skirt
WAISTBAND — Cut One

On Fold

Libby's Wardrobe — Blue Blazer
SLEEVE
Cut Two

Place on Fold

Back Front

Libby's Wardrobe
BLAZER
Cut Two Fronts
Cut One Back

• Front •

Back — Place on Fold

Dart

Front

Libby's Wardrobe

Note: For Libby's white blouse, use pattern shown with Levis. Make short sleeves, and use collar pattern shown here. For knee socks, shorten Judy's knee socks pattern.

Add 1/4" Seam Allowance

Libby's Wardrobe White Blouse
COLLAR
Cut Four

Libby's Wardrobe

PLAID SKIRT

Cut One

Pleat evenly to Waistband

This plaid skirt matches
Libby's Plaid Coat

Place on Fold

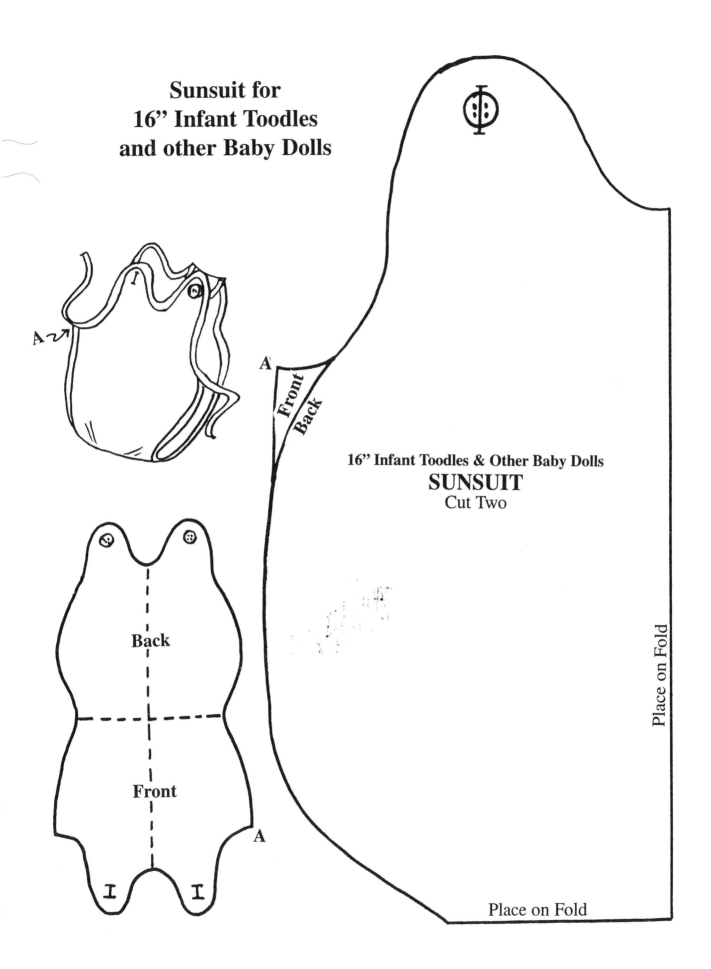

Sunsuit for
16" Infant Toodles
and other Baby Dolls

Front
Back

16" Infant Toodles & Other Baby Dolls
SUNSUIT
Cut Two

A

Back

Front

A

Place on Fold

Place on Fold

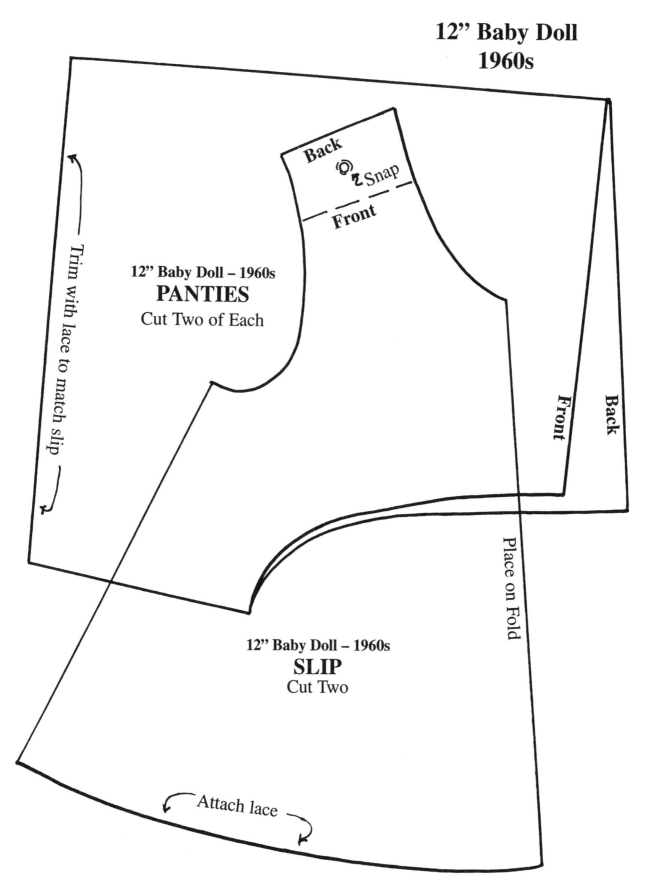

**12" Baby Doll
1960s**

Back

Snap

Front

Trim with lace to match slip

**12" Baby Doll – 1960s
PANTIES**
Cut Two of Each

Front

Back

Place on Fold

**12" Baby Doll – 1960s
SLIP**
Cut Two

Attach lace

1/4" Seam Allowed

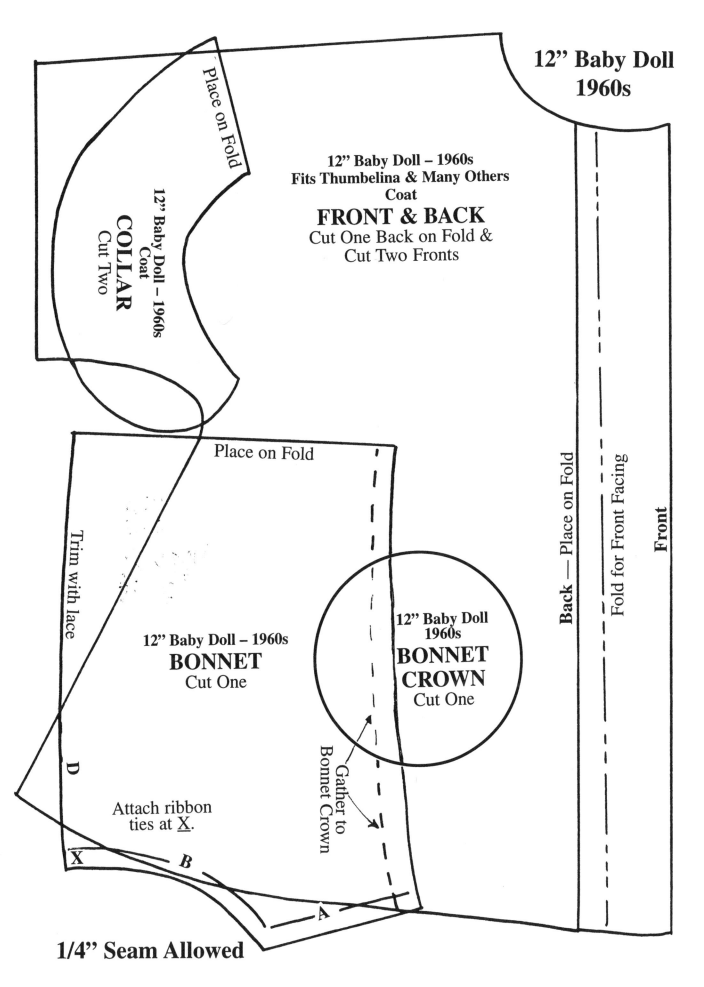

Place on Fold

12" Baby Doll
1960s

12" Baby Doll – 1960s
Coat
COLLAR
Cut Two

12" Baby Doll – 1960s
Fits Thumbelina & Many Others
Coat
FRONT & BACK
Cut One Back on Fold &
Cut Two Fronts

Back — Place on Fold

Fold for Front Facing

Front

Place on Fold

Trim with lace

12" Baby Doll – 1960s
BONNET
Cut One

12" Baby Doll
1960s
**BONNET
CROWN**
Cut One

Gather to
Bonnet Crown

D

Attach ribbon
ties at X.

X

B

A

1/4" Seam Allowed

12" Baby Doll — 1960s

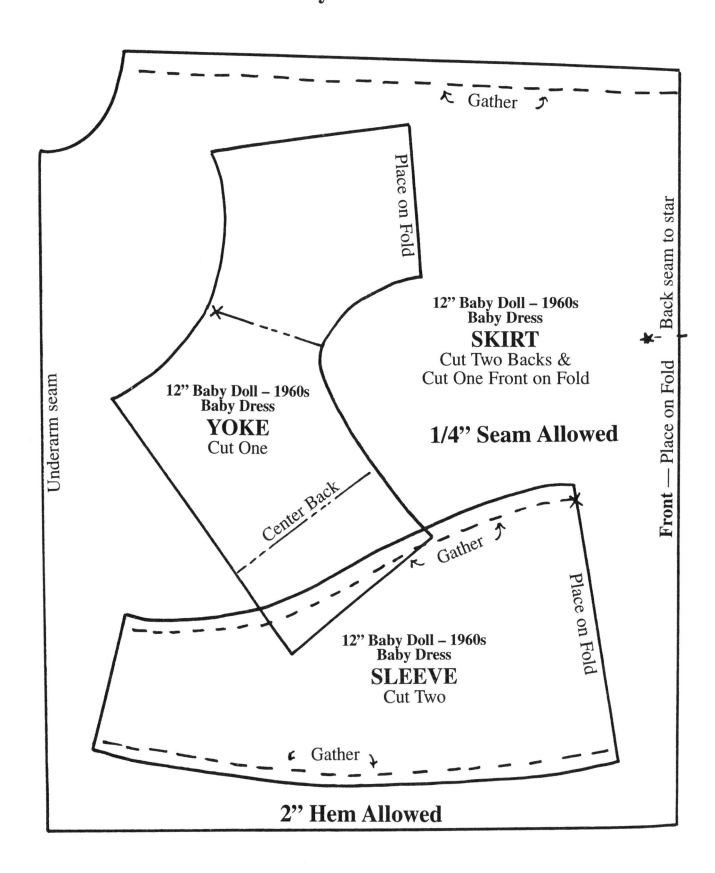

Gather

Place on Fold

**12" Baby Doll – 1960s
Baby Dress
SKIRT**
Cut Two Backs &
Cut One Front on Fold

1/4" Seam Allowed

Back seam to star

Underarm seam

**12" Baby Doll – 1960s
Baby Dress
YOKE**
Cut One

Center Back

Gather

Front — Place on Fold

Place on Fold

**12" Baby Doll – 1960s
Baby Dress
SLEEVE**
Cut Two

Gather

2" Hem Allowed

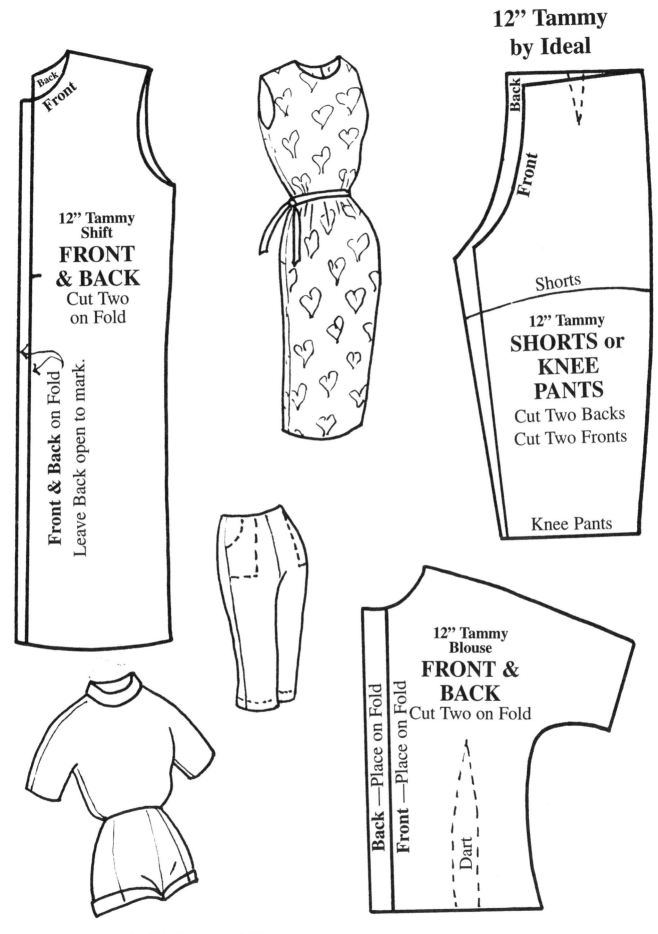

**12" Tammy
by Ideal**

**12" Tammy
Shift
FRONT
& BACK**
Cut Two
on Fold

Front & Back on Fold
Leave Back open to mark.

Back
Front

Back
Front

Shorts

**12" Tammy
SHORTS or
KNEE
PANTS**
Cut Two Backs
Cut Two Fronts

Knee Pants

**12" Tammy
Blouse
FRONT &
BACK**
Cut Two on Fold

Back —Place on Fold
Front —Place on Fold

Dart

Add 1/4" Seam Allowance

ALL -PURPOSE FASHION PATTERN FOR 20" CHATTY CATHY (BY MATTEL)

These patterns, with only slight adjustment, will fit Charmin' Chatty and Chatty Baby. See Chapter 3 "FITTING PATTERNS TO YOUR DOLL".

(A) May be used to design a coat, robe, nightgown, or pajama top. For coat, robe, and pajama top, place back on fold and extend front 3/4" to allow for overlap. For gown, place both front and back on fold and slit back for opening which is then bound or hemmed.

(B) Rounded collar may be used on dress, pajamas, or robe. Pointed collar is suitable for dress, robe, or coat.

(C) Short sleeve for dress, blouse, or nightgown.

(D) Long sleeve is suitable for coat, robe, dress, pajamas, or blouse.

(E) Bodice pattern gives choice of rounded or squared neckline and arm openings. Use for dress, sun top; lengthen slightly for overblouse. Cut a rectangle of fabric for skirt and gather or pleat to bodice for dress.

(F) Shorts, underpants, or knee pants may be produced with this pattern.

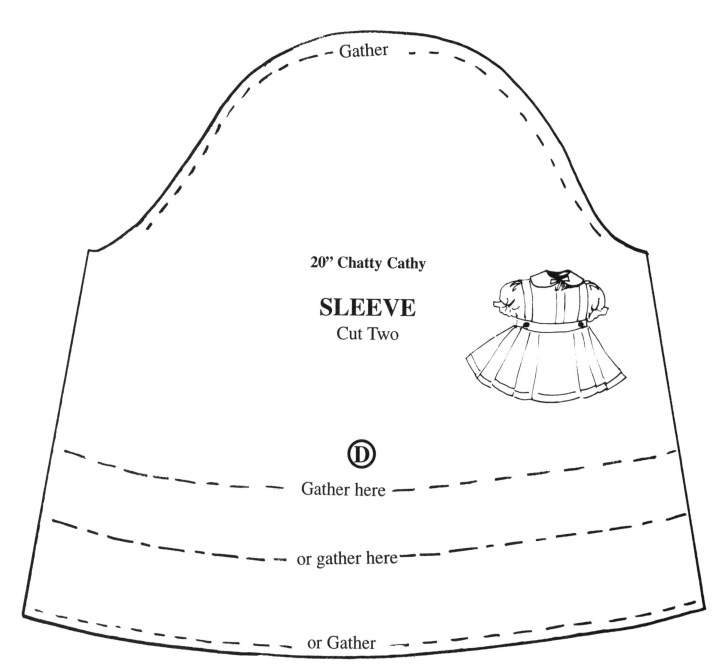

Gather

20" Chatty Cathy

SLEEVE
Cut Two

(D)

Gather here

or gather here

or Gather

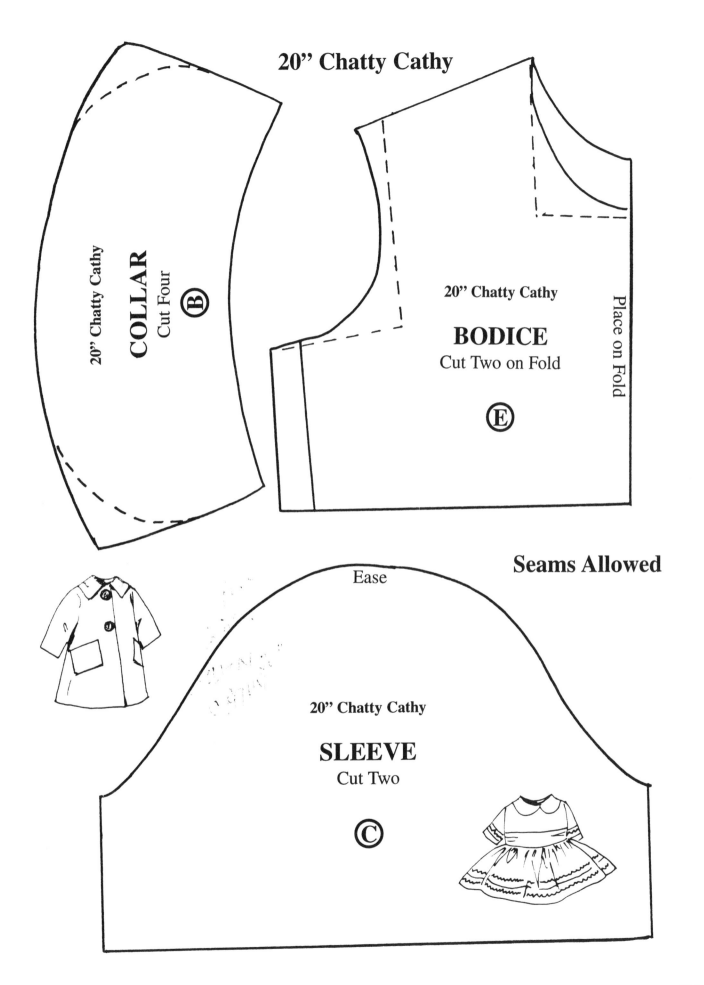

20" Chatty Cathy

20" Chatty Cathy

COLLAR

Cut Four

Ⓑ

20" Chatty Cathy

BODICE

Cut Two on Fold

Ⓔ

Place on Fold

Seams Allowed

Ease

20" Chatty Cathy

SLEEVE

Cut Two

Ⓒ

235

Place on Fold

Back

Front

20" Chatty Cathy
Robe/Dress/Coat etc.

FRONT & BACK
Cut Two on Fold
after matching Xs and Os

Ⓐ

Seams Allowed

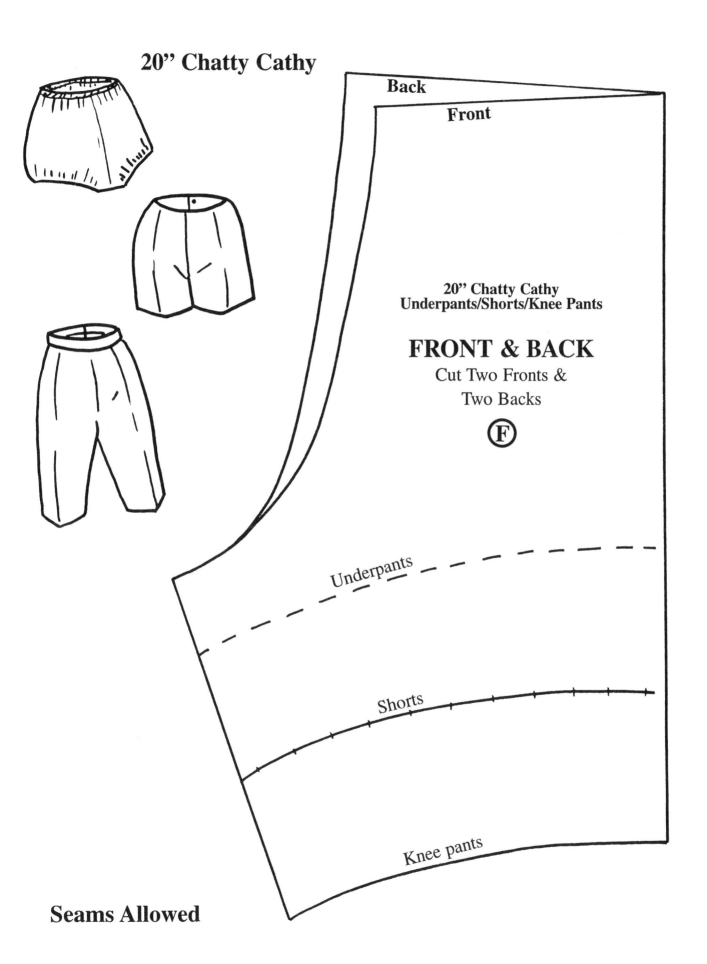

20" Chatty Cathy

Back

Front

**20" Chatty Cathy
Underpants/Shorts/Knee Pants**

FRONT & BACK
Cut Two Fronts &
Two Backs

(F)

Underpants

Shorts

Knee pants

Seams Allowed

9"-10" Dolls – Betsy McCall, Penny Brite, Skooter, Skipper 1960s Fashions

Add lace

9"-10" Dolls – Betsy McCall, Penny Brite, Skooter, Skipper

Place on Fold

DRESS FRONT
Cut One

*Cutting line for dress with flounce

Add lace

Black velvet, white lace, red flowers

Alternate style

9"-10" Dolls – Betsy McCall, Penny Brite, Skooter, Skipper

DRESS BACK
Cut Two
*Cutting line for dress with flounce

Fold for facing

See*

Add lace

Shoulder Straps 1/4" lace

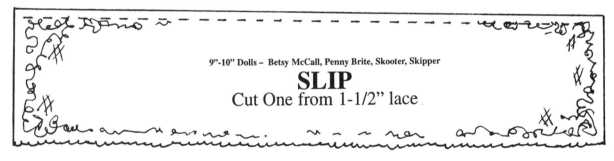

9"-10" Dolls – Betsy McCall, Penny Brite, Skooter, Skipper

SLIP BODICE
Cut One from 1/2" lace

9"-10" Dolls – Betsy McCall, Penny Brite, Skooter, Skipper

SLIP
Cut One from 1-1/2" lace

Also use panty pattern to make matching undies for dresses

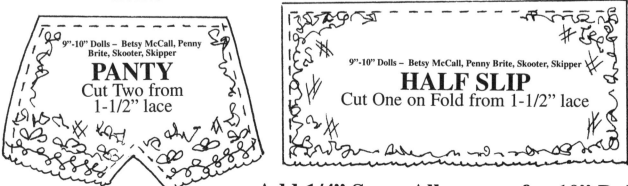

9"-10" Dolls – Betsy McCall, Penny Brite, Skooter, Skipper

PANTY
Cut Two from 1-1/2" lace

9"-10" Dolls – Betsy McCall, Penny Brite, Skooter, Skipper

HALF SLIP
Cut One on Fold from 1-1/2" lace

Add 1/4" Seam Allowance for 10" Dolls

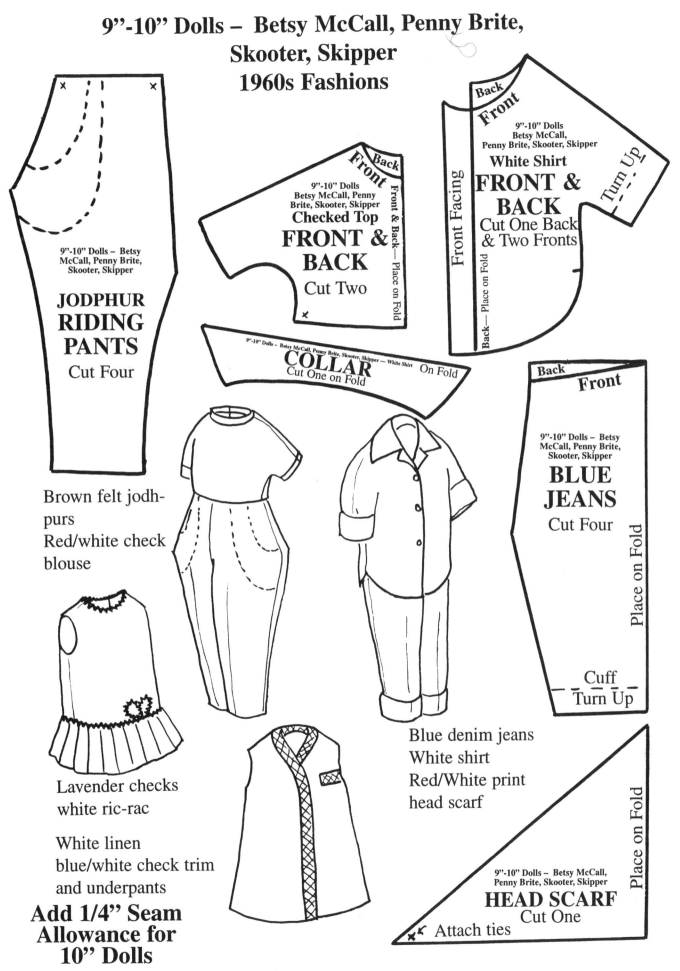

9"-10" Dolls – Betsy McCall, Penny Brite, Skooter, Skipper 1960s Fashions

9"-10" Dolls – Betsy McCall, Penny Brite, Skooter, Skipper

JODPHUR RIDING PANTS
Cut Four

9"-10" Dolls Betsy McCall, Penny Brite, Skooter, Skipper
Checked Top FRONT & BACK
Cut Two

Front & Back — Place on Fold

9"-10" Dolls Betsy McCall, Penny Brite, Skooter, Skipper
White Shirt FRONT & BACK
Cut One Back & Two Fronts

Front Facing

Back — Place on Fold

Turn Up

Back — Front

9"-10" Dolls – Betsy McCall, Penny Brite, Skooter, Skipper — White Shirt
COLLAR
Cut One on Fold — On Fold

9"-10" Dolls – Betsy McCall, Penny Brite, Skooter, Skipper
BLUE JEANS
Cut Four

Place on Fold

Cuff Turn Up

Brown felt jodh-purs
Red/white check blouse

Lavender checks white ric-rac

White linen blue/white check trim and underpants

Add 1/4" Seam Allowance for 10" Dolls

Blue denim jeans
White shirt
Red/White print head scarf

Place on Fold

9"-10" Dolls – Betsy McCall, Penny Brite, Skooter, Skipper
HEAD SCARF
Cut One

Attach ties

2457   **2457**   **2457**   **2457**   **2457**

These illustrations show patterns available for *Betsy McCall* and *Tiny Tears*. They are taken from a booklet packed with a *Betsy McCall* doll and are ca. 1960.

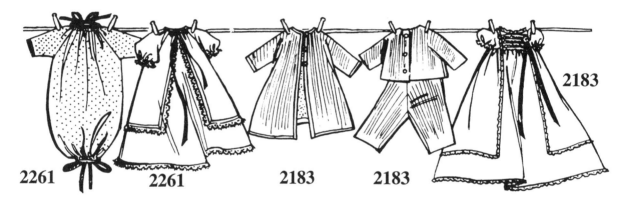

2261   **2261**   **2183**   **2183**   **2183**

Wardrobes for Betsy McCall dolls (sizes 8-1/2" and 30"); McCall's 2457.
Wardrobes for Tiny Tears dolls (sizes 11" to 20"); McCall's 2261, 2349, 2183, and 2412.
Wardrobes for Toodles Dolls (size 25"); McCall's 2349 and 2412. Wardrobes for Toodles Dolls (size 30"); McCall's 2412.

ALL OF THE ABOVE LISTED DOLLS ARE PRODUCTS OF THE...

AMERICAN DOLL & TOY CORP.

2349   **2349**   **2349**   **2412**   **2412**

7" - 8" Babies — Suzy Cute, Baby Cheerful Tearful, etc.

Back **Front**

7"-8" Babies
Suzy Cute, Baby
Cheerful Tearful, etc.

NIGHTGOWN
Cut One Front &
Two Backs

Front — Place on Fold

Attach lace

Fold over for Back facing

7"-8" Babies – Suzy Cute, Baby
Cheerful Tearful, etc.

Diaper Suit
TOP
Cut One or Cut One
each of contrasting
material

Place on Fold

7"-8" Babies – Suzy Cute,
Baby Cheerful Tearful, etc.

Dress
YOKE
Cut One

Fold

7"-8" Babies – Suzy
Cute, Baby Cheerful
Tearful, etc.

Bonnet
CROWN
Cut One

7"-8" Babies – Suzy Cute,
Baby Cheerful Tearful, etc.

Bonnet
BRIM
Cut One

On Fold

Gather to yoke

Gather

Front — Place on Fold

Fold over for Back facing

7"-8" Babies – Suzy Cute, Baby
Cheerful Tearful, etc.

DRESS
Cut One

**Add 1/4"
Seam
Allowance
for
8" Dolls**

Add hem

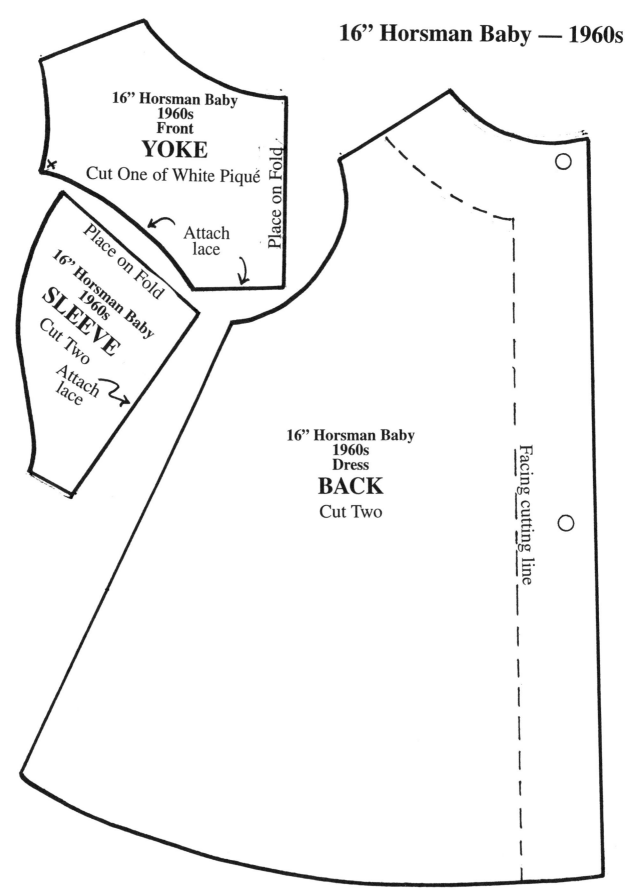

16" Horsman Baby — 1960s

16" Horsman Baby
1960s
Front
YOKE
Cut One of White Piqué

Place on Fold

Attach
lace

Place on Fold

16" Horsman Baby
1960s
SLEEVE
Cut Two
Attach
lace

16" Horsman Baby
1960s
Dress
BACK
Cut Two

Facing cutting line

Add 1/4" Seam Allowance

16" Horsman Baby — 1960s

Original dress is red cotton with white piqué yoke and white lace.

On Fold.

16" Horsman Baby
1960s
FRONT FACING
Cut One

Place on Fold.

Gather to fit lower edge of yoke

16" Horsman Baby
1960s
Dress
FRONT
Cut One on Fold
after matching Xs and Os

Add 1/4" Seam Allowance

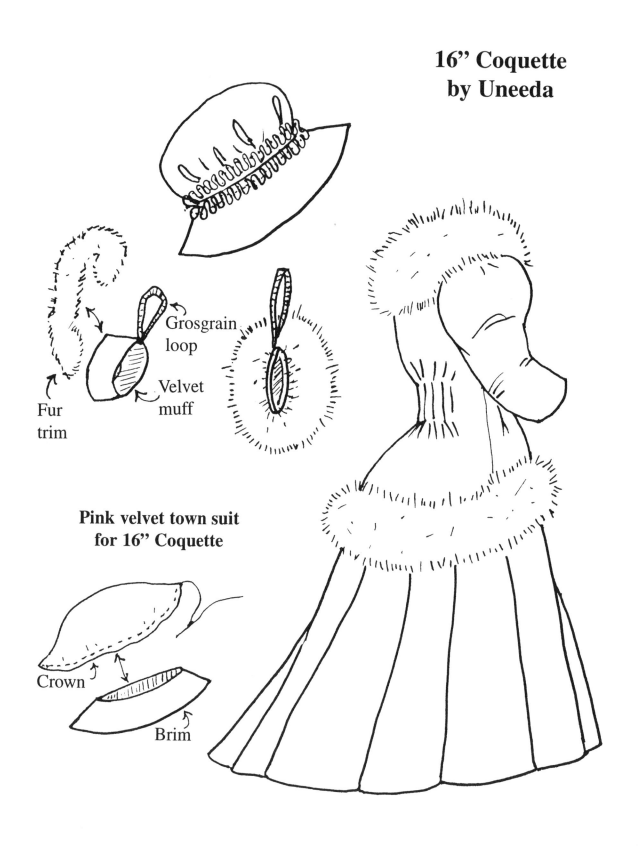

16" Coquette
by Uneeda

Grosgrain loop

Velvet muff

Fur trim

Pink velvet town suit for 16" Coquette

Crown

Brim

For Hat — Brim is a 6-1/4" circle with a 3-1/2" circle cut out to fit crown. Crown is an 8" circle, one each of velvet and lining, gathered as one and sewn to brim. Brim is velvet both sides, may have interlining for additional stiffness. Trim with lace or rutching.

16" Coquette

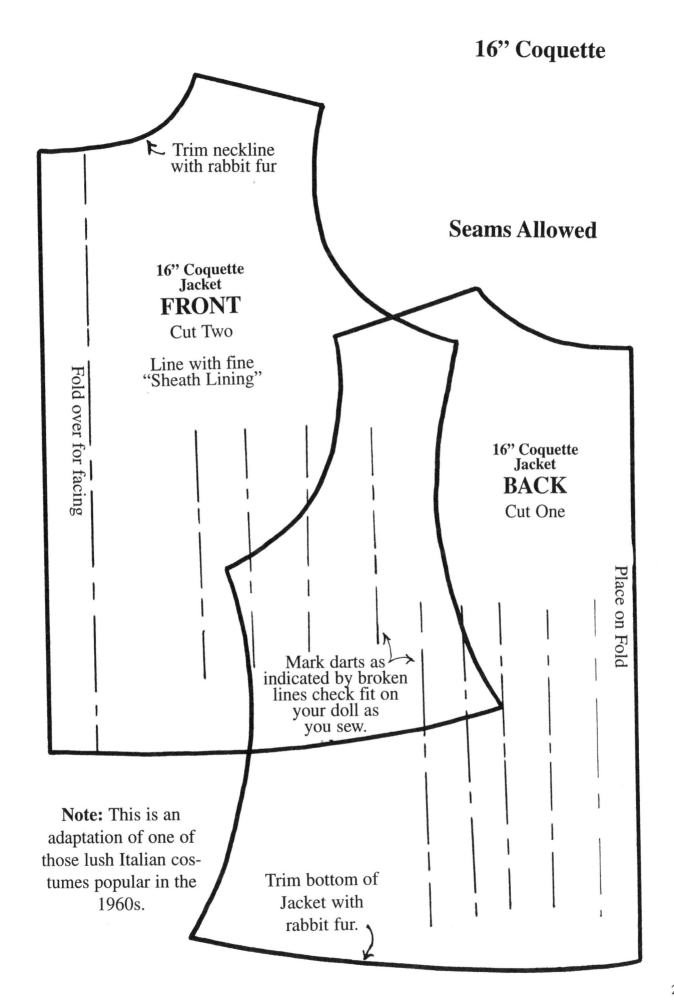

Seams Allowed

Trim neckline with rabbit fur

16" Coquette Jacket FRONT
Cut Two

Line with fine "Sheath Lining"

Fold over for facing

16" Coquette Jacket BACK
Cut One

Place on Fold

Mark darts as indicated by broken lines check fit on your doll as you sew.

Note: This is an adaptation of one of those lush Italian costumes popular in the 1960s.

Trim bottom of Jacket with rabbit fur.

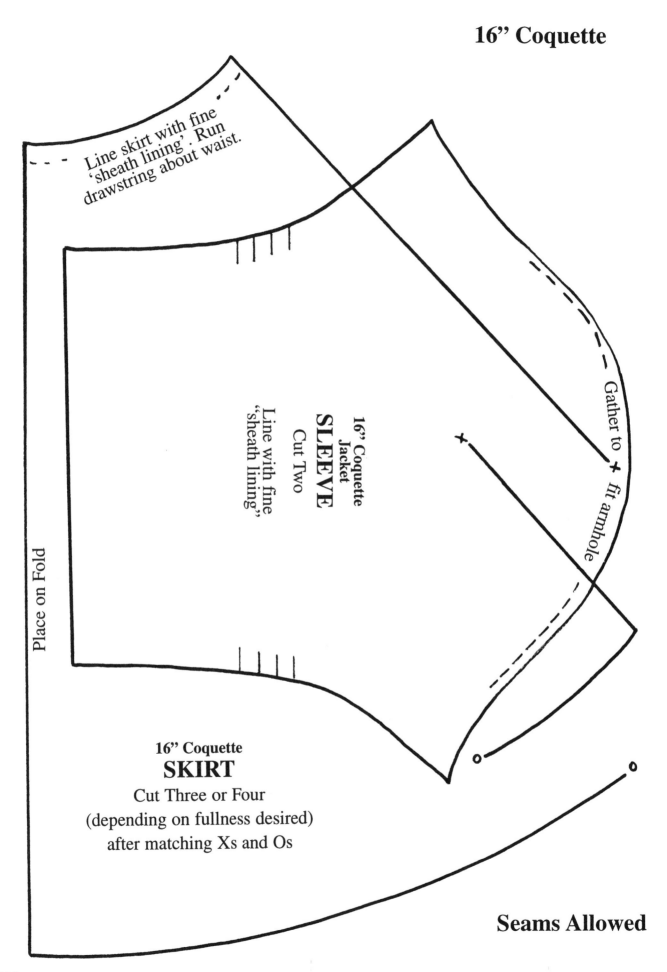

16" Coquette

Line skirt with fine 'sheath lining'. Run drawstring about waist.

Gather to   fit armhole

Place on Fold

Line with fine "sheath lining"

16" Coquette Jacket
SLEEVE
Cut Two

16" Coquette
SKIRT
Cut Three or Four
(depending on fullness desired)
after matching Xs and Os

Seams Allowed

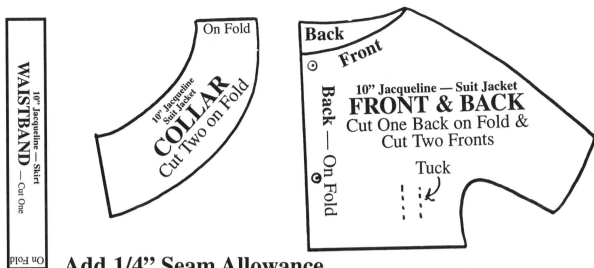

On Fold

WAISTBAND
10" Jacqueline — Suit Jacket
WAISTBAND — Skirt
Cut One

On Fold

10" Jacqueline
Suit Jacket
COLLAR
Cut Two on Fold

Back

Front

Back — On Fold

10" Jacqueline — Suit Jacket
FRONT & BACK
Cut One Back on Fold &
Cut Two Fronts

Tuck

Add 1/4" Seam Allowance

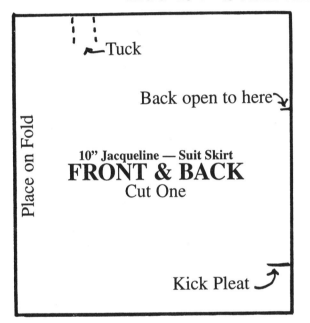

←Tuck

Back open to here ↘

10" Jacqueline — Suit Skirt
FRONT & BACK
Cut One

Place on Fold

Kick Pleat ↗

Suit is of very fine, soft blue wool.
Hat is of same material.

10" Jacqueline
Hat
CROWN
Cut One

1/4" Seam Allowed
Line hat with
Buchram or
Pellon

10" Jacqueline
by Mme. Alexander

Completely line skirt, attach waistband, then overlap back to form tiny
kick pleat. Jacket has snaps with
buttons sewn on for effect only.

10" Jacqueline
HAT
Cut One

On Fold

14" Caroline
by Mme. Alexander

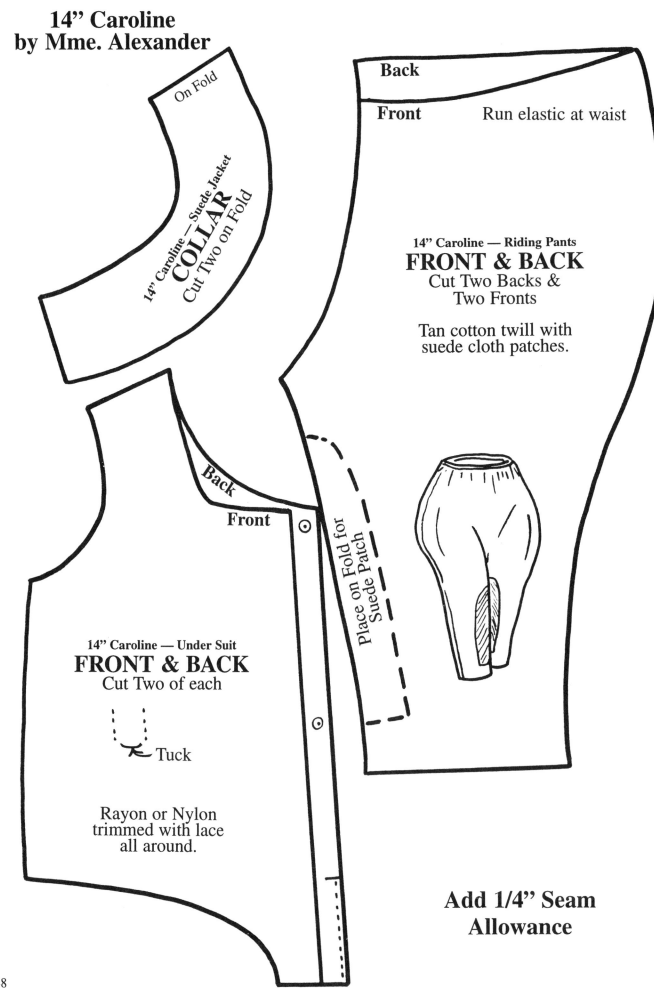

On Fold

14" Caroline—Suede Jacket
COLLAR
Cut Two on Fold

Back

Front   Run elastic at waist

14" Caroline — Riding Pants
FRONT & BACK
Cut Two Backs &
Two Fronts

Tan cotton twill with
suede cloth patches.

Back

Front

Place on Fold for Suede Patch

14" Caroline — Under Suit
FRONT & BACK
Cut Two of each

Tuck

Rayon or Nylon
trimmed with lace
all around.

Add 1/4" Seam
Allowance

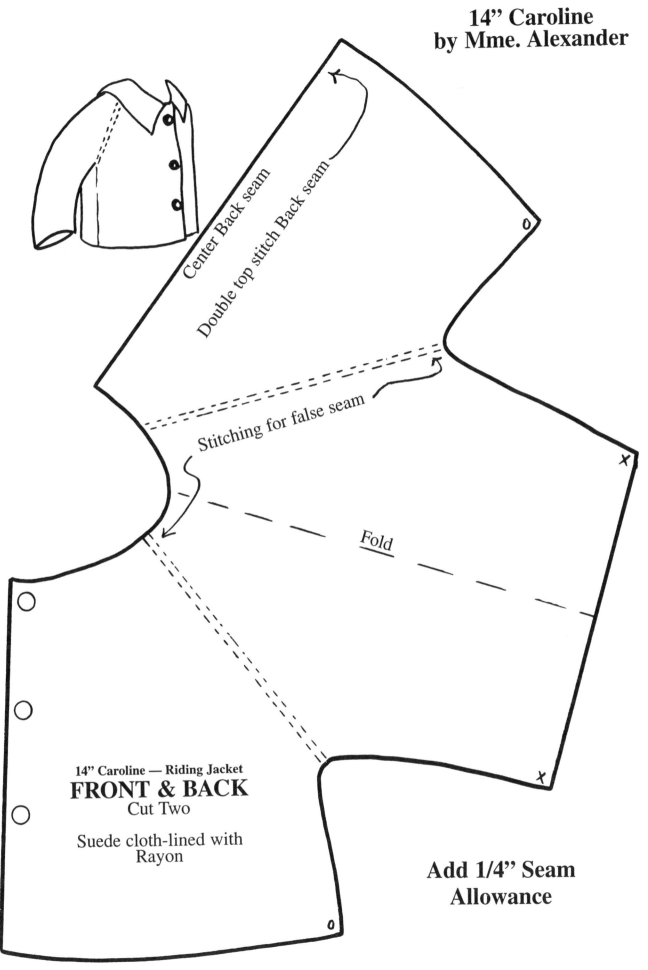

14" Caroline
by Mme. Alexander

Center Back seam

Double top stitch Back seam

Stitching for false seam

Fold

14" Caroline — Riding Jacket
FRONT & BACK
Cut Two

Suede cloth-lined with
Rayon

**Add 1/4" Seam
Allowance**

17-1/2" "BEAUTIFUL CRISSY BY IDEAL

These patterns also fit *Tressy, Dianna Ross,* and *Kerry.* To adjust for *Velvet, Cricket,* and *Mia,* see Chapter 3 "FITTING PATTERNS TO YOUR DOLL".

ALL PURPOSE PATTERNS FOR CRISSY

These all-purpose patterns give the versatility needed to represent the potpourri styling of the late 1960s and early 1970s.

PIECE A — Follow pattern lines carefully to discover 1) an Empire waistline, 2) a bodice for a natural waistline dress, 3) a bodice for a low or dropped-waist dress, a tuck-in blouse, or long vest, 4) an overblouse, 5) a tunic top or mini-dress, 6) dress, or 7) extend pattern to midi (mid-calf) or maxi (ankle length).

A choice of two necklines is given with the alternative or a jumper neckline. Use jumper neckline for a "hippy" vest of simulated leather and add fringe for a swingy look.

Skirts for above dresses are simply rectangles cut to desired length, allowing for amount of fullness desired, and gathered or pleated to bodice of your choice thus a skirt for the dropped-waist dress would require a rectangle 3-1/4" by 18", gathered along one long side.

PIECE B — This Pattern gives a choice of straight or flared (Bell) pants. Opening may be placed front, side, or back.

PIECE C — Three sleeve choices are available: 1) sleeve with some fullness gathered to cuff E which may be trimmed with lace or braid; 2) straight sleeve suitable for knit blouse, pantsuit jacket, or coat; and 3) full sleeve in which the fullness is held by narrow elastic in a casing along lower edge.

PIECES D AND F — Two choices of collars: D) standup collar for dresses, knit blouses, or tunic; and F) for coat, jacket, blouse, or dress.

PIECE G — Briefs or underpants: cut to match dress or cut from tricot, cotton, or other suitable fabric.

In trimming fashions for these up-to-date lasses, use imagination and whatever is at hand. The fashions of the late 1960s and early 1970s featured everything from old fashioned lace and tatted edgings to permanent press ruffles and orlon yarns. Strings of beads, bangle bracelets, rings on every finger, and headbands were all important additions to the "in" look.

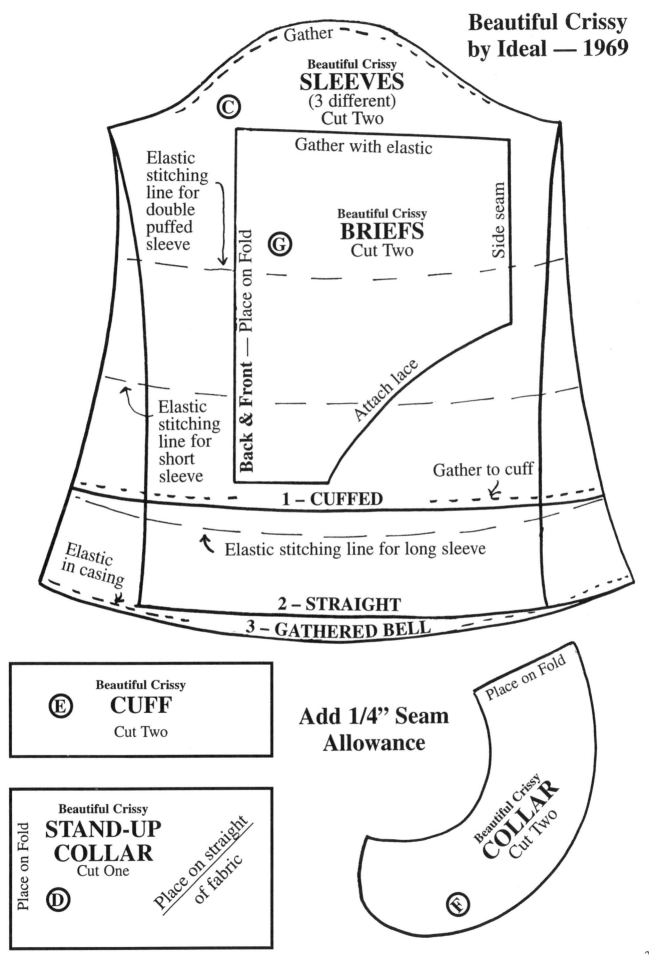

Beautiful Crissy
by Ideal — 1969

Gather

Beautiful Crissy
SLEEVES
(3 different)
Cut Two

©

Elastic stitching line for double puffed sleeve

Gather with elastic

Back & Front — Place on Fold

Beautiful Crissy
BRIEFS
Cut Two

Side seam

G

Elastic stitching line for short sleeve

Attach lace

Gather to cuff

1 – CUFFED

Elastic stitching line for long sleeve

Elastic in casing

2 – STRAIGHT

3 – GATHERED BELL

Beautiful Crissy
CUFF
Cut Two

Ⓔ

Add 1/4" Seam Allowance

Place on Fold

Place on Fold

Beautiful Crissy
COLLAR
Cut Two

Place on Fold

Beautiful Crissy
STAND-UP COLLAR
Cut One

Place on straight of fabric

Ⓓ

Ⓕ

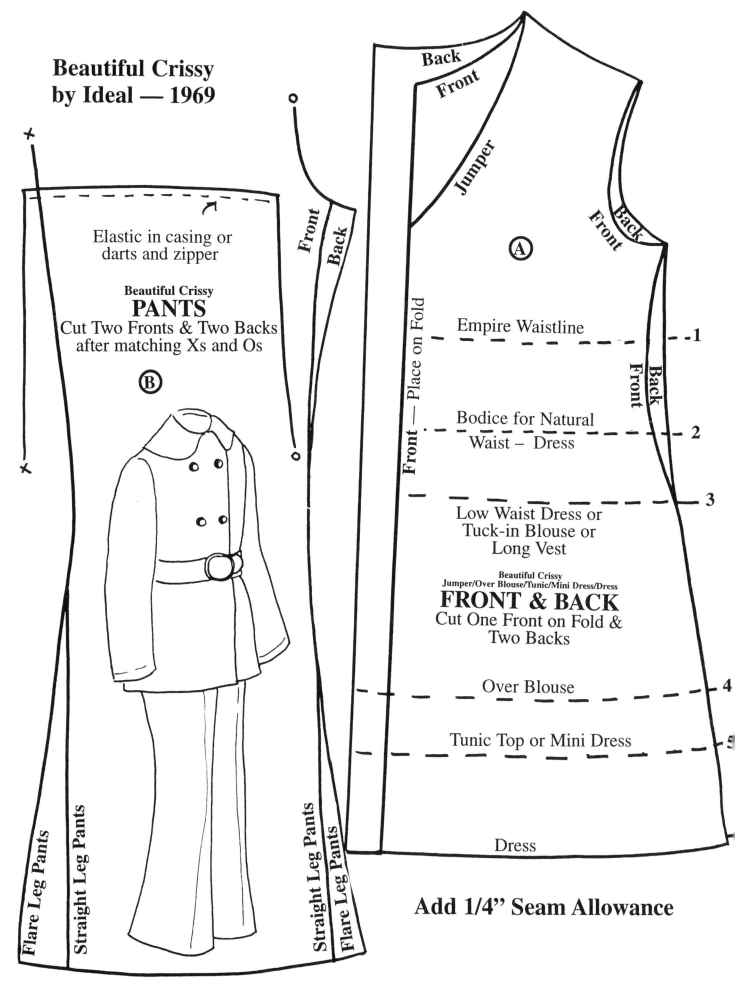

**Beautiful Crissy
by Ideal — 1969**

Elastic in casing or
darts and zipper

**Beautiful Crissy
PANTS**
Cut Two Fronts & Two Backs
after matching Xs and Os

B

Front

Back

Flare Leg Pants

Straight Leg Pants

Straight Leg Pants

Flare Leg Pants

Back

Front

Jumper

Back

Front

A

Front — Place on Fold

Back

Front

Empire Waistline — 1

Bodice for Natural
Waist – Dress — 2

Low Waist Dress or
Tuck-in Blouse or
Long Vest — 3

**Beautiful Crissy
Jumper/Over Blouse/Tunic/Mini Dress/Dress
FRONT & BACK**
Cut One Front on Fold &
Two Backs

Over Blouse — 4

Tunic Top or Mini Dress — 5

Dress

Add 1/4" Seam Allowance

Yoke Line
(A)

Yoke Line
(B)

**18" Giggles
by Ideal**

253

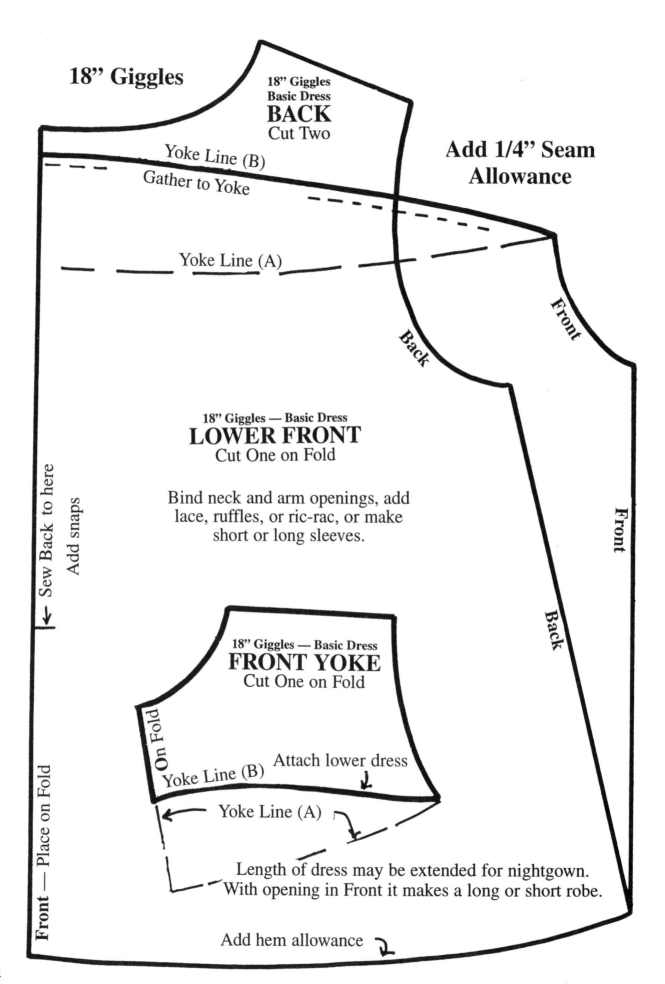

18" Giggles

18" Giggles
Basic Dress
BACK
Cut Two

Add 1/4" Seam Allowance

Yoke Line (B)

Gather to Yoke

Yoke Line (A)

Front

Back

Front

Back

Sew Back to here

Add snaps

18" Giggles — Basic Dress
LOWER FRONT
Cut One on Fold

Bind neck and arm openings, add lace, ruffles, or ric-rac, or make short or long sleeves.

18" Giggles — Basic Dress
FRONT YOKE
Cut One on Fold

On Fold

Yoke Line (B)

Attach lower dress

Yoke Line (A)

Length of dress may be extended for nightgown. With opening in Front it makes a long or short robe.

Front — Place on Fold

Add hem allowance

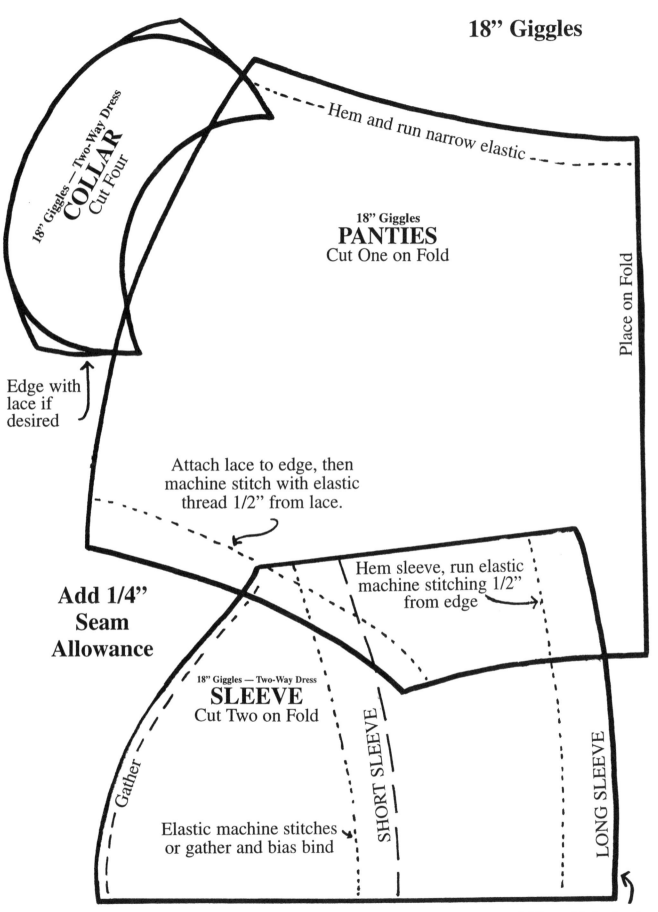

18" Giggles

18" Giggles — Two-Way Dress
COLLAR
Cut Four

Hem and run narrow elastic

18" Giggles
PANTIES
Cut One on Fold

Place on Fold

Edge with lace if desired

Attach lace to edge, then machine stitch with elastic thread 1/2" from lace.

Add 1/4" Seam Allowance

Hem sleeve, run elastic machine stitching 1/2" from edge

18" Giggles — Two-Way Dress
SLEEVE
Cut Two on Fold

Gather

SHORT SLEEVE

LONG SLEEVE

Elastic machine stitches or gather and bias bind

add lace if desired

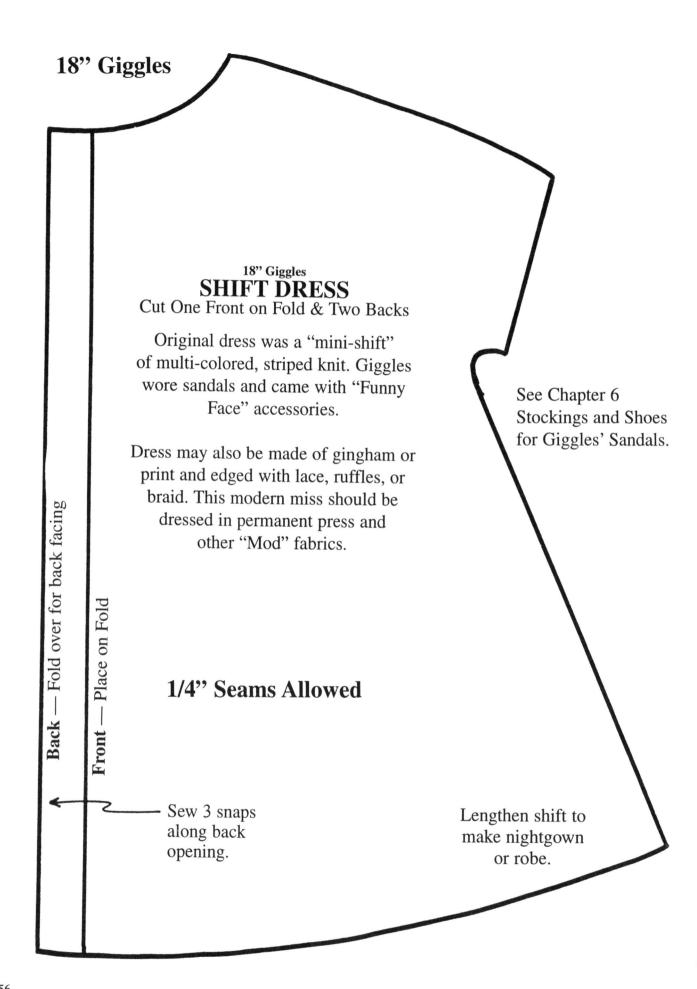

18" Giggles
SHIFT DRESS
Cut One Front on Fold & Two Backs

Original dress was a "mini-shift" of multi-colored, striped knit. Giggles wore sandals and came with "Funny Face" accessories.

Dress may also be made of gingham or print and edged with lace, ruffles, or braid. This modern miss should be dressed in permanent press and other "Mod" fabrics.

See Chapter 6 Stockings and Shoes for Giggles' Sandals.

Back — Fold over for back facing

Front — Place on Fold

1/4" Seams Allowed

Sew 3 snaps along back opening.

Lengthen shift to make nightgown or robe.

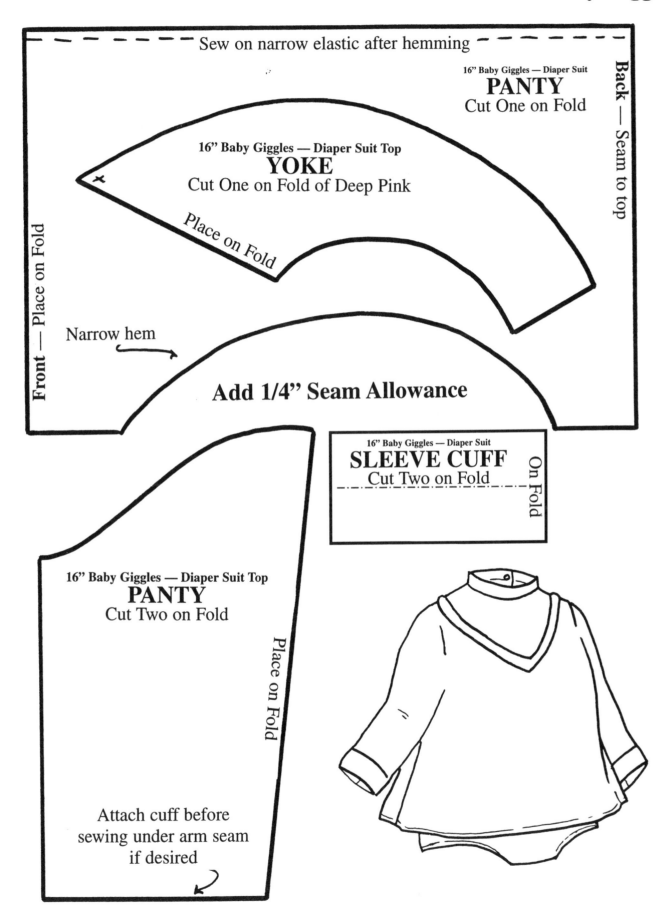

Sew on narrow elastic after hemming

16" Baby Giggles — Diaper Suit
PANTY
Cut One on Fold

Back — Seam to top

16" Baby Giggles — Diaper Suit Top
YOKE
Cut One on Fold of Deep Pink

Place on Fold

Front — Place on Fold

Narrow hem

Add 1/4" Seam Allowance

16" Baby Giggles — Diaper Suit
SLEEVE CUFF
Cut Two on Fold

On Fold

16" Baby Giggles — Diaper Suit Top
PANTY
Cut Two on Fold

Place on Fold

Attach cuff before
sewing under arm seam
if desired

16" Baby Giggles

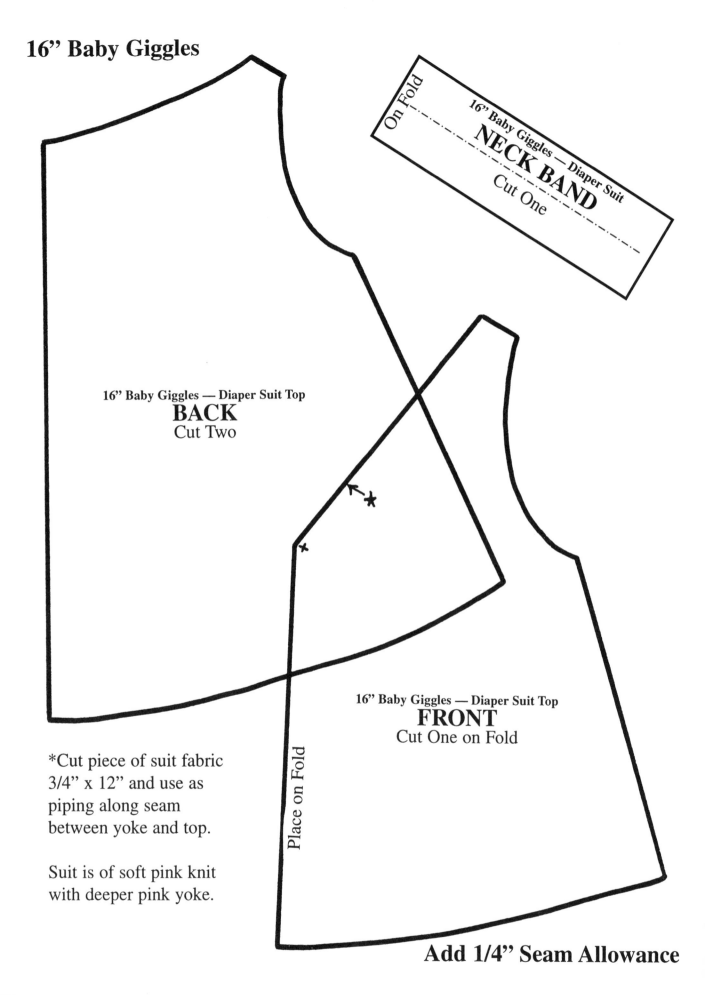

16" Baby Giggles — Diaper Suit
NECK BAND
Cut One

On Fold

16" Baby Giggles — Diaper Suit Top
BACK
Cut Two

16" Baby Giggles — Diaper Suit Top
FRONT
Cut One on Fold

Place on Fold

*Cut piece of suit fabric 3/4" x 12" and use as piping along seam between yoke and top.

Suit is of soft pink knit with deeper pink yoke.

Add 1/4" Seam Allowance

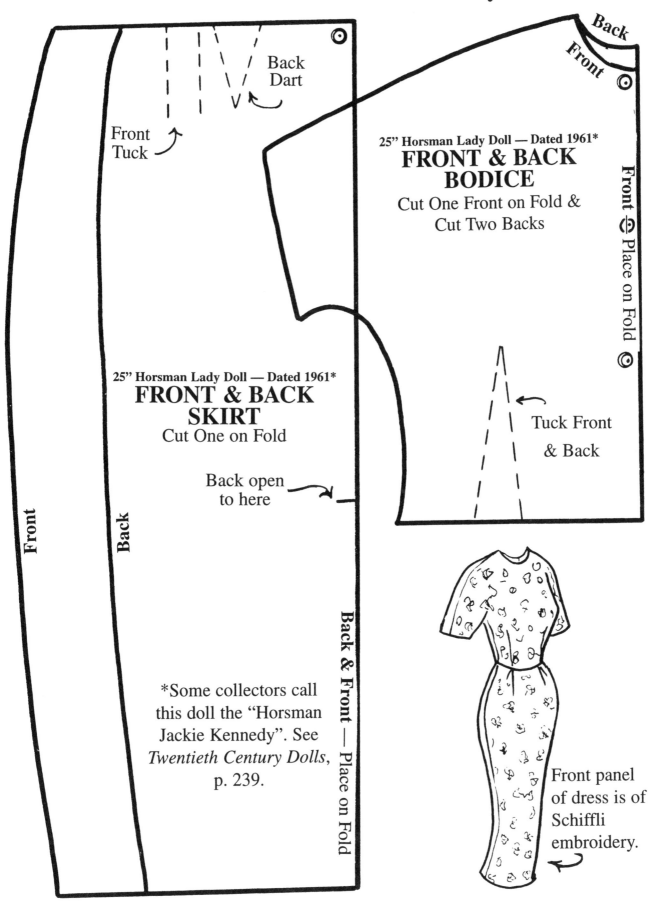

Back Dart

Front Tuck

25" Horsman Lady Doll — Dated 1961*
FRONT & BACK BODICE
Cut One Front on Fold &
Cut Two Backs

Back

Front

Front • Place on Fold •

Tuck Front & Back

25" Horsman Lady Doll — Dated 1961*
FRONT & BACK SKIRT
Cut One on Fold

Back open to here

Front

Back

Back & Front — Place on Fold

*Some collectors call this doll the "Horsman Jackie Kennedy". See *Twentieth Century Dolls*, p. 239.

Front panel of dress is of Schiffli embroidery.

Add 1/4" Seam Allowance

Chapter 14

ENTERING THE 1970S

What can be said of the fashions of the 1970s that hasn't been said about those of other decades? Someone has noted there is nothing new under the sun and this is certainly true in the world of fashion where trends come full circle upon themselves. Thus we see the 1940s reflected in kick-pleated skirts and long sweaters of the 1970s. The Sloppy Joe sweaters, tennis skirts, and short shorts of the 1940s have become the knit tops, skooter skirts, and hot pants of the 1970s.

The diversity of early 1970s fashions is striking; bareness and near-nudity co-exist with cover-up, almost Victorian styles. The rule seems to be all or nothing at all. Added to this mainstream of style, or quite aside from it are the fashions generated by the sub-culture, the world of hippies and drop-outs, which have profoundly influenced the dress of young people. The floppy hats, fringed leather vests, moccasins, bell-bottom trousers, and put-together styles of this element have influenced even the more sedate styles of the French designers.

Fashion might best be described as a whirling tornado, dancing through the decades, picking up the elements of design here and depositing them there as it continues to whirl along, never at any given moment the same as it was a moment ago.

— JGA, 1972

Since the above was written, the world has changed dramatically. New technology has given us personal computers, desktop copiers, telephone capability beyond belief, and cyberspace. Hundreds of innovations have changed our lives immeasurably.

One thing, however, remains a constant: Our basic need for food, water, shelter, and protective clothing. Being humans, we have never been satisfied with merely covering our bodies. Instead we have created a world of fashion ranging from necessity to indulgence. In the past 25 years, our search for something different has led designers to create a range of garments which include nearly every vagary, conceit, and nuance of the fashions of the last several hundred years.

In addition, lifestyle changes, new fabrics and expanded technologies have influenced design. Automatic washing machines and clothes dryers efficiently clean mountains of laundry. Permanent press and the "wrinkled look" have made ironing largely unnecessary. Shopping has become the new recreation and our closets overflow with ever larger wardrobes. The styles worn by our dolls and the accessories created for them reflect these changes.

All of which makes it ever more important that we take steps to preserve the original clothing and accoutrements of our old dolls as well as authentic information concerning their design and construction. Perhaps the reprinting of this work and its forthcoming sequel are evidence of the enthusiasm of doll collectors who are attempting to achieve those goals.

JGA

15 July 1996

ILLUSTRATIONS SOURCES

Butler Bros., New York,
Catalog, 1933, p. 128

Delineator, The, New York,
March, 1918, p. 52
February, 1919, pp. 53, 54

Designer, The, New York,
November, 1915

Home Arts Needlecraft, Augusta, Maine,
April, 1936, p. 129
September, 1936, p. 138;
September, 1937, pp. 129, 130, 136, 140,
150, 151;
September, 1938, p. 131
September, 1939, p. 131
January, 1940, pp. 17, 156, 157.

Ladies Home Journal, The, Philadelphia,
December 1904, pp. 29, 30, 34, 38, 40,
41, 43, 45
March, 1911, p. 48.

McCall's Magazine, New York,
September, 1925, pp. 113, 120
September, 1943, pp. 158, 159

McCall's Needlework and Decorative Arts, New York,
Winter, 1930-1931, pp. 16, 17, 102, 103, 127

Modern Priscilla, Boston,
March, 1920, pp. 11, 12
October, 1934, pp. 117, 121

Needlecraft Magazine, Augusta, Maine,
August, 1924, p. 78
February, 1925, p. 126

Pictorial Review, New York,
December, 1910, pp. 26-28, 30-32
October, 1913, pp. 16, 17, 49, 54, 57, 91, 112
October, 1914, p. 17

Pictorial Review Fashion Book, Spring, 1923, p. 79.

Schoenhut Catalog, 1915,
pp. 68-70.

Woman's Home Companion, Springfield, Ohio,
October, 1915, pp. 15, 16, 264
January, 1916, pp. 50, 51

ABOUT THE AUTHOR

Johana Gast Anderton began writing and drawing at an early age. As a first-grader, she sent poems and drawings to the children's page of the *Kansas City Journal Post*. Johana's first efforts for collectors was a pioneer work on what is commonly known today as "Depression Glass." Before going out of print, *The Glass Rainbow, the Story of Depression Glass* went through eight printings and is now considered a collector's item in itself. The author is well-known in the doll and paper doll worlds for her *Twentieth Century Dolls* series of reference books, hundreds of magazine and newspaper articles, and dozens of black-and-white and full-color paper doll sets published in collector magazines and as convention souvenirs.

She is a founding member of the Original Paper Doll Artists Guild (OPDAG), a member of the executive board of the Modern Doll Convention (MDC), a member-at-large of the United Federation of Doll Clubs (UFDC), and a charter member of the Sun, Sand, and Sea Paper Doll Collectors Club of Florida. She has created souvenir paper dolls for MDC since 1984, with the exception of 1986 and acted as MDC Souvenir Book editor for several years. Her specially commissioned full color paper dolls have been given as souvenirs for UFDC regional conferences across the county. She is also a doll designer; her pattern book, *Sewing the Last Christmas Doll*, first in a series, is now in its fourth

Photograph by Sandra Vanderpool

printing. Also in the works is a series of dolls she hopes to have produced by a mold company. In her spare time she works on a book of fairy tales for children and two novels she hopes to publish "some day".

Her activities have included teaching oil painting, instructing YWCA craft classes, personal appearances on television, radio, and at antique and doll shows and conventions throughout the country. Her experience in planning and directing conventions has made her, she says, much more appreciative of such functions. She also teaches occasional workshops and does some lecturing, an activity that is necessarily limited by her full schedule.

In 1972 she founded her own publishing company, Athena, and produced books on a variety of subjects in the collectibles field written by well-known authors. Of interest to doll collectors are *The American Doll Artist, Vol. II* by Helen Bullard; *Dressing Dolls in Nineteenth Century Fashions* by Albina Bailey, *Much Ado About Dolls* by R. Lane Herron, and the *Collectors Art Series* paper dolls and coloring books. The Athena books were sold to American Broadcasting Company in 1976 and were subsequently published by Wallace-Homestead Book Company and Chilton Books.

After a thirteen-year sojourn in Florida, Johana and husband Harold (Andy) returned "home" to Kansas City in 1995 where she has a more spacious studio. There she plans to complete a large number of unfinished paper dolls, articles, doll designs, and books. The first project will be finalizing her book, "Sewing for Twentieth Century Dolls, Vol. 2" for Hobby House Press.

Other books by the Author:

The Glass Rainbow, The Story of Depression Glass
Twentieth Century Dolls, From Bisque to Vinyl
More Twentieth Century Dolls, From Bisque to Vinyl
Sewing The Last Christmas Doll, Story, Paper Doll, and Patterns
The Collectors Encyclopedia of Cloth Dolls (From Rag Doll to Art Object)
Johana's Dolls, A Reprint of Her Columns and Articles
Edited: *Favorite Recipes From OPDAG; a Collection of Recipes and Paper Dolls*
Coming Next Year: *Sewing for 20th Century Dolls, Volume 2*